Grid Computing

Simon C. Lin · Eric Yen
Editors

Grid Computing

International Symposium on Grid Computing
(ISGC 2007)

 Springer

Editors
Simon C. Lin
Academia Sinica
Taipei, Taiwan
simon.lin@twgrid.org

Eric Yen
Academia Sinica
Taipei, Taiwan
Eric.Yen@twgrid.org

ISBN: 978-1-4419-4613-3   e-ISBN: 978-0-387-78417-5

Printed on acid-free paper

springer.com

Preface

ISGC (International Symposium on Grid Computing) is one of the most important annual events in Asia that brings together scientists and engineers worldwide to exchange ideas, to present on challenges, solutions and future development in the field of Grid Computing. The objective of this Symposium is to facilitate the information exchange as well as to explore the global collaboration and interoperation among various Grid projects.

ISGC 2007 was held at Academia Sinica, Taipei, Taiwan from 26 to 29 March 2007 and participated by around 200 people from 22 countries. In order to bridge the Asia Pacific and the world, the Symposium consists of invited talks and demonstrations from leading international projects in Grid operation, Grid Middleware and e-Science applications. Lectures also highlight related national Grid projects from Asia Pacific countries.

To promote the awareness of the global Grid operation and collaboration between Asia Pacific region and the world, the Symposium offers an excellent opportunity to learn from the latest achievements from Europe, America and Asia. The major topics of ISGC 2007 are concentrated on Global Grid Projects, Grid Projects in Asia Pacific, High Energy Physics Applications, Biomedical Applications, e-Science Applications, Humanities & Social Sciences Applications, Operation & Management, Grid Middleware, Interoperation, Grid Security, Networking as well as Industry Track. By sharing experiences from a variety of Grid systems, this Symposium provides the potential Grid developers and users with invaluable insights for developing Grid technology and application.

In this book, a comprehensive report towards Grid Activities in Asia Pacific has prepared and abstracted from invited talks in different fields across Asia countries. Besides, various e-Science applications including High Energy Physics, Biomedical and Life Sciences have been discussed with practical approaches. As to the state-of-the-art Grid technology, Grid Middleware and Interoperability are addressed with the relevance of current and emerging standards to facilitate a grid with global reach. Furthermore, the topic of Grid Operations and Management cover the recent advances in managing the large scale grid infrastructures.

By means of publishing ISGC 2007 Proceedings, we would like to take this opportunity to express our gratitude to all the participants, program committee members, as well as corporate sponsors. They made this event a great success. Last but not the least, we hope that by publishing this symposium materials, not only could this event be better documented, but also could serve as a professional reference for Grid Computing and its applications, especially in Asia Pacific.

Contents

Program Committee

Ian Bird,
CERN
Switzerland

Kors Bos,
NIKHEF
Netherlands

Fabrizio Gagliardi,
Microsoft
Italy

Robert Jones (Chair),
EGEE
Switzerland

Setsuya Kawabata,
KEK
Japan

Yannick Legre,
Healthgrid
France

Simon C. Lin,
ASGC
Taiwan

Klaus-Peter Mickel,
FZK
Germany

Reagan Moore,
SDSC
USA

John O'Callaghan,
Australian Partnership for Advanced Computing
Australia

Ruth Pordes,
Fermi National Accelerator Laboratory
USA

Peter Rice,
European Bioinformatics Institute
UK

Leslie Robertson,
CERN
Switzerland

Hiroshi Sakamoto,
University of Tokyo
Japan

Takashi Sasaki,
KEK
Japan

Jennifer M. Schopf,
MCS, Argonne National Laboratory
USA
JISC, National eScience Centre
UK

Pansak Siriruchatapong,
NECTEC
Thailand

Contributors

Julia Andreeva
European Organization for Nuclear Research CERN G06910, CH-1211 Geneva 23, Switzerland, Julia.Andreeva@cern.ch

B. Asvija
Centre for Development of Advanced Computing (C-DAC), Bangalore, India, asvijab@cdacb.ernet.in

R. Breu
Forschungszentrum Jülich GmbH, Germany, r.breu@fz-juelich.de

Kihyeon Cho
e-Science Applications Research Team, Korea Institute of Science and Technology Information (KISTI), Daejeon, 305-806, Korea, cho@kisti.re.kr

L. Clementi
CINECA, Italy, l.clementi@cineca.it

Jeremy Coles
GridPP Production Manager, Science & Technology Facilities Council, RAL, Chilton, Oxfordshire OX11 0QX and Senior Research Associate, University of Cambridge, Cavendish Laboratory, JJ Thomson Avenue, Cambridge CB3 0HE, UK, J.Coles@rl.ac.uk

Xiaolei Ding
College of Computer Science and Technology, Jilin University, China, weixh@jlu.edu.cn, pp.jordan@email.jlu.edu.cn, gjs0064114@126.com, dxlxiaolei@163.com

Andrea Domenici
DIIEIT, University of Pisa, v. Diotisalvi 2, I-56122 Pisa, Italy, Andrea.Domenici@iet.unipi.it

Flavia Donno
CERN, European Organization for Nuclear Research, Switzerland Andrea DOMENICI, DIIEIT, University of Pisa, Italy, Flavia.Donno@cern.ch

Giuseppe Evangelista
Department of Biology, University Roma Tre, 00146 Rome, Italy,
giuseppe_evangelista@yahoo.it

Jürgen Falkner
Fraunhofer Institute for Industrial Engineering, Nobelstr. 12, 70569 Stuttgart,
Germany, juergen.falkner@iao.fraunhofer.de

Thomas Fieseler
Jülich Supercomputing Centre, Forschungszentrum Jülich GmbH, 52425 Julich,
Germany, t.fieseler@fz-juelich.de

Jishan Gao
College of Computer Science and Technology, Jilin University, China,
weixh@jlu.edu.cn, pp.jordan@email.jlu.edu.cn, gjs0064114@126.com,
dxlxiaolei@163.com

Benjamin Gaidioz
European Organization for Nuclear Research CERN G06910, CH-1211 Geneva 23,
Switzerland, Benjamin.Gaidioz@cern.ch

Gabriele Garzoglio
Fermi National Accelerator Laboratory Pine st. And Kirk Rd. 60510 Batavia, IL,
USA, garzogli, tlevshin, parag, timm@fnal.gov

A. Giesler
Forschungszentrum Jlich GmbH, Germany, a.giesler@fz-juelich.de

Wolfgang Gürich
Jülich Supercomputing Centre, Forschungszentrum Jülich GmbH, 52425 Jülich,
Germany, w.guerich@fz-juelich.de

Rajesh Kalmady
Bhabha Atomic Research Centre, India, rajesh@barc.gov.in

Tanya Levshina
Fermi National Accelerator Laboratory Pine st. And Kirk Rd. 60510 Batavia, IL,
USA, garzogli, tlevshin, parag, timm@fnal.gov

Simon C. Lin
Academia Sinica Grid Computing Centre (ASGC), Taiwan, sclin@twgrid.org

Pier Luigi Luisi
Department of Biology, University Roma Tre, 00146 Rome, Italy, luisi@mat.ethz.ch

Yuan Luo
College of Computer Science and Technology, Jilin University, China,
weixh@jlu.edu.cn, pp.jordan@email.jlu.edu.cn, gjs0064114@126.com,
dxlxiaolei@163.com

R. Menday
Jülich Supercomputing Centre, Forschungszentrum Jülich GmbH, 52425 Jülich, Germany, r.menday@fz-juelich.de

Parag Mhashilkar
Fermi National Accelerator Laboratory Pine st. And Kirk Rd. 60510 Batavia, IL, USA, garzogli, tlevshin, parag, timm@fnal.gov

Giovanni Minervini
Department of Biology, University Roma Tre, 00146 Rome, Italy, gminervini@uniroma3.it

Mohanram N
Centre for Development of Advanced Computing (C-DAC), Bangalore, India, mohan@cdacb.ernet.in

Ralph Niederberger
Research Center Jülich, Germany, r.niederberger@fz-juelich.de

Fabio Polticelli
Department of Biology, University Roma Tre, 00146 Rome, Italy, polticel@uniroma3.it

Sijin Qian
Peking University, Beijing, China, sijin.qian@cern.ch

M. Rambadt
Forschungszentrum Jülich GmbH, Germany, m.rambadt,r.breu,t.fieseler,a.giesler, w.guerich,r.menday,a.streit@fz-juelich.de

Prahlada Rao
Centre for Development of Advanced Computing (C-DAC), Bangalore, India, prahladab@cdacb.ernet.in

J. Reetz
Rechenzentrum Garching (RZG) of the Max Planck Society and the IPP, Germany, johannes.reetz@rzg.mpg.de

Otto Rienhoff
Department of Medical Informatics, Georg-August-University Goettingen Robert-Koch-Str. 40, 37075 Gttingen, Germany, haegar@med.uni-goettingen.de

Giuseppe La Rocca
INFN Catania, 95123 Catania, Italy
Department of Biology, University Roma Tre, 00146 Rome, Italy, giuseppe.larocca@ct.infn.it

K.V. Shamjith
Centre for Development of Advanced Computing (C-DAC), Bangalore, India, shamjithkv@cdacb.ernet.in

Ian Stokes-Ress
SBGrid, Harvard Medical School, SGM-105, 250 Longwood Ave., Boston MA
02115, USA, ijstokes@crystal.harvard.edu

Henry Sukumar
Centre for Development of Advanced Computing (C-DAC), Bangalore, India,
henrys@cdacb.ernet.in

R. Sridharan
Centre for Development of Advanced Computing (C-DAC), Bangalore, India,
rsridharan@cdacb.ernet.in

A. Streit
Jülich Supercomputing Centre, Forschungszentrum Jülich GmbH, 52425 Jülich,
Germany, a.streit@fz-juelich.de

Steve Timm
Fermi National Accelerator Laboratory Pine st. And Kirk Rd. 60510 Batavia, IL,
USA, garzogli, tlevshin, parag, timm@fnal.gov

Min Tsai
Academia Sinica Grid Computing Centre (ASGC), Taiwan,
min17502@gate.sinica.edu.tw

Xiaohui Wei
College of Computer Science and Technology, Jilin University, China,
weixh@jlu.edu.cn, pp.jordan@email.jlu.edu.cn, gjs0064114@126.com,
dxlxiaolei@163.com

Anette Weisbecker
Fraunhofer Institute for Industrial Engineering, Nobelstr. 12, 70569 Stuttgart,
Germany, anette.weisbecker@iao.fraunhofer.de

Eric Yen
MIS Department, National Cheng-Chih University, Eric.Yen@twgrid.org

Part I
Grid Activities in Asia Pacific

Asia Federation Report International Symposium on Grid Computing 2007

Min Tsai and Simon C. Lin

1 Introduction

The focus of this report is to provide a summary of developments in Asia-Pacific region from the International Symposium on Grid Computing 2007. This document contains four sections. The first section provides a status update of EGEE activities in the region. This is followed by ideas for further extending EGEE III into Asia-Pacific. The third section contains a short description of networking, Grid and EGEE involvement for each country. The last section is the meeting minutes from the Asia Federation meeting at ISGC 2007.

2 EGEE

- **Applications**

    Asia-Pacific resource centers used 200 KSI2K years of computing resource this year compared to 41 KSI2K years in the previous year. Last year the main user communities were LHC experiments and Biomed VOs. This year, two new VO, Belle and TWGrid, have made significant use of EGEE infrastructure in Asia-Pacific.

    Significant achievement has also been made with the drug discovery against Avian Flu using an equivalent of 137 years of computing resources. Many of Asian resource centers provided support for Biomed including University of Melbourne, Global Operational Grid Singapore, Pakistan Atomic Energy Commission and ASGC. This work allowed scientist from Taiwan and Asia to collaborate with European laboratories to achieve important scientific results.

- **Operations**

    EGEE and ASGC have established the Asia-Pacific Regional Operations Center APROC since April of 2005. The mission of APROC is to provide operations support in the regional to facilitate the expansion of the Grid and

M. Tsai (✉)
e-mail: min17502@gate.sinica.edu.tw

S.C. Lin, E. Yen (eds.), *Grid Computing*,
© Springer Science+Business Media, LLC 2009

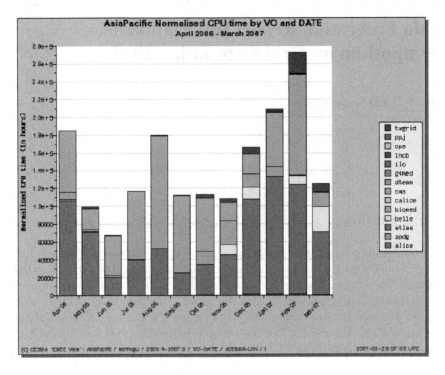

maximize the availability of Grid services that are available. APROC provides deployment, operation, regional CA and contributes to global operations support for EGEE.

The number of sites in the region has grown to be one of the largest in EGEE with 20 production EGEE sites spread over 8 countries (Australia, Hong-Kong, India, Japan, Tokyo, Korea, Pakistan and Taiwan). This past year alone, 9 resource centers have been certified and more recently HKU (Hong-Kong) and KISTI (Korea) have joined. There are also additional 3 institutions that are currently in the certification process (ASTI Philippines, KONKUK Korea and MAS IPT Mongolia).

Service availability for the region has improved from 60–70% to 70–80% availability range. Most failures were related to Data Management tests.

These tests were found to be sensitive to the availability and performance of Information System components. Many of performance issues have been addressed by hardware upgrades and middleware improvements. One of the most important root causes of many failures is poor network performance and availability. Many problems were found to be related to congestion in both the WAN and LAN levels. This year APROC has deployed regional monitoring using Nagios to further improve time to recovery of Grid service failures.

3 EGEE III Asia-Pacific

The following section proposes some ideas on the direction and activities for EGEE III in Asia-Pacific Region.

The overall objective of EGEE Asia-Pacific (EAP) region will be to promote collaboration in E-Science and scientific research between Europe and Asia and within Asia itself. The results should be evaluated by the quality of number of collaborations established based on the extended EGEE infrastructure. To efficiently achieve results EAP should leverage the existing application communities and infrastructure established by EGEE.

Developing regional communities that can gain real benefits from the infrastructure will create sustainability.

In addition EAP should directly benefit from the EGEE middleware development and integration effort. This will help reduce effort needed for interoperations related work. Interoperations will be too resource intensive of a task in Asia-Pacific, since many countries have integrated their own middleware stack that is always in constantly changing.

- **Application**

    In the first phase, EAP will select well established application communities and extend these communities to Asia-Pacific partners and researchers. The number of the communities should be limited at first and should be of interest to the regional research community. Training and support for these communities should be provided both by the application community and EAP partners.

    The second phase, EAP can then consider developing two regional collaborations lead by different EAP partners. EAP will work closely with the regional collaboration to meet their needs.

- **Operations**

    EAP should extend operations technology and experience to partner countries. Operations in Asia-Pacific are currently centralized at APROC in Taiwan. However, it is possible to create a federated Regional Operations Center where tasks are distributed among EAP partners that can specialize in facets of operations.

    By the time EGEE III begins, most countries should have established an EGEE resource center. EAP can then determine which partners have sufficient resources and help willing partners establish a national EGEE operation center. These centers will be responsible operations support for domestic resource centers.

    For countries without a domestic Certification Authority (CA) that is approved by IGTF, APROC can continue to provide CA services. However, EAP should work with APGridPMA to assist partners to establish domestic CA to serve their local communities.

- **Training**

    Training in EAP will require EGEE to provide "training trainer" courses that will assist the region further develop its training capability and capacity. Specialized training targeted at select application communities and resource center administrators will also be required.

- **Networking**

    Networking in Asia-Pacific may be outside of the scope of EGEE, however it has large impact of Grid development in the region. There are a number of issues currently existing in this region:

    o Relatively low bandwidth interconnecting countries in Asia-Pacific and to Europe.
    o Disparate network projects do not transparently exchange routing with each other
    o Usage-based charges for regional and international networks still exist and are discouraging collaboration over the Internet.

Asia-Pacific network projects need to work together to develop high speed backbone and improve coverage in this region. An idea would be to merge Asia-Pacific network projects to take advantage of each one's strengths without duplicating effort. Effort should also be placed to address usage-based network charges and create an environment that will promote researchers and NRENs to use these networks.

4 Representative Summaries

Summary and overview of countries that were present during ISGC 2007 Slides can be obtained from: http://event.twgrid.org/isgc2007/program.htm#ISGC

(1) Australia

- Representative: **Marco La Rosa**, University of Melbourne
- NREN Status:

    AARNet owns and operates a resilient and redundant multi-Gbps network across Australia. Diagrams of both international and domestic connectivity are shown in the diagrams below.
- National Grid Initiative and Grid Activities Status:

    Australia government has established the Australian Partnership for Advanced Computing (APAC) to lead the development of an Australia-wide advanced computing infrastructure supported by coordinated programs in research, education and technology diffusion.

    The APAC partnership was established in June 2000 and now has 8 partners. APAC's computing resources combines 25 supercomputers with over 25,000 CPUs and 3PB of storage.

    Middleware provided by APAC is based on VDT 1.6.1a (Globus 4.03 and GridFTP) and Prima Auth Module 0.5. Portal also is available based on Tomcat 5.5.20, Ant 1.6.5, Gridsphere 2.2.7 and Gridportlets 1.3.2. APAC has used Xen virtualization technology to enable multiple Grid interfaces to each site through a single Grid gateway server. APAC has also developed GRIX java based application to greatly simplify user's CA and authentication tasks.

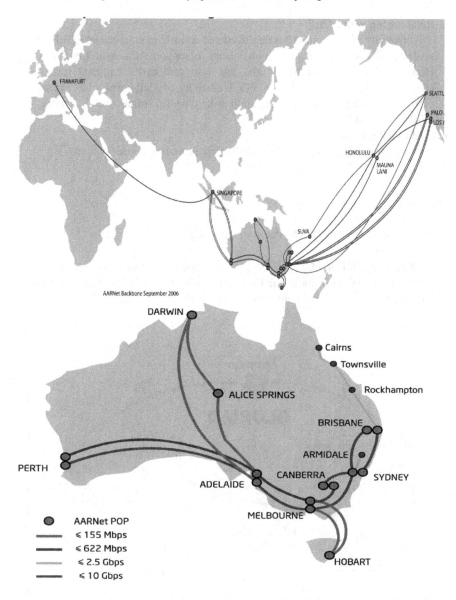

- APAC has also been working with the following application communities:

    o Geoscience
    o Earth Systems Science
    o High Energy Physics
    o Bioinformatics
    o Chemistry
    o Astronomy

- Relationship with EGEE:
    University of Melbourne has deployed and actively maintained an EGEE/LCG site since 2006. Their main focus has been to support Atlas as a Tier 2 center. However, University of Melbourne has also provided significant resources support for the biomed and belle VO. University of Melbourne's has extensive experience with gLite middleware and has held a Grid Administrator tutorial for KEK in late 2005.
- Additional Information:
    http://www.apan.net/meetings/manila2007/presentations/routing/2.ppt

(2) China

- Representative: **Sijin QIAN**, Peking University
- NREN Status:
    Both CERNET and CSTNET deploy and operate domestic and international connectivity in China. Backbone links range from 2.5 to 10G connections. China has multiple international connections via APAN and TIEN2.

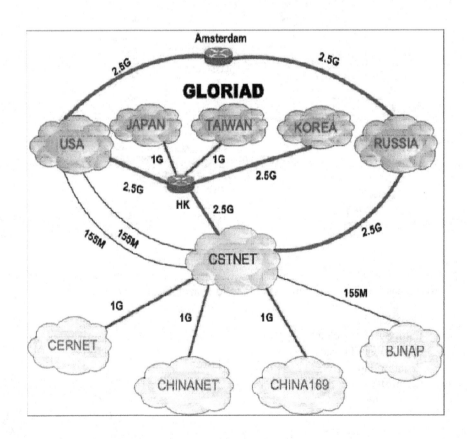

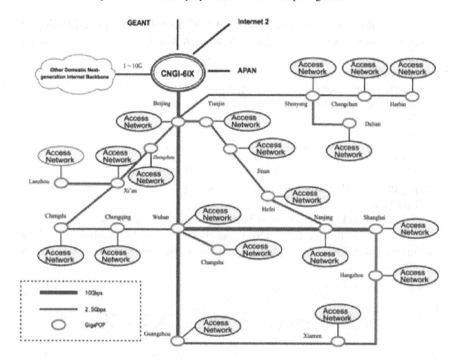

- National Grid Initiative and Grid Activities Status:

    ChinaGrid is a national Grid project started in 2003. The project has 22 partners from universities across China.

    ChinaGrid has produced middleware that follows WSRF and OSGA and features a container based on a Globus Toolkit 4 Core.
- Representative Grid application in ChinaGrid are:

    o Image processing
    o Bioinformatics
    o E-Learning
    o Computational Fluid Dynamics
    o Large scale information processing

- Relationship with EGEE:

    EUChinaGrid initiative has allowed EGEE to establish close ties with China. EUChinaGrid is a 2 year 1.3 million Euro project starting January 2006. The project consists of 10 partners, 4 of which are from China. EUChinaGrid focuses on providing interoperability between EGEE and CNGRID, dissemination of Grid technology and strengthening scientific collaboration between Europe and China.
- Key application areas of EUChinaGrid includes:

    o High Energy Physics
    o Astrophysics
    o Bioinformatics

In additional to EUChinaGrid, IHEP and CNIC have deployed LCG/EGEE production resource centers to enable collaboration with CMS, Atlas, Biomed and other experiments.

- Additional Information:
  http://www.edu.cn/cernet_1377/index.shtml
  http://www.cstnet.net.cn/

(3) India

- Representative: **P. S. Dhekne**, BARC
- NREN Status:
  ERNET's backbone consists of both terrestrial and satellite with 14 Points of Presence across the country. ERNET has also been able to establish a 45 Mbps connection to GEANT with plans to upgrade to 622 Mbps in 2007 and 1 Gbps in 2008.

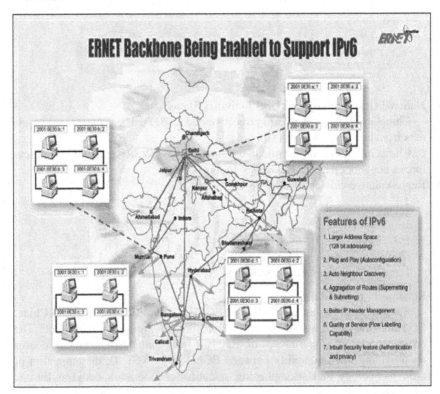

- National Grid Initiative and Grid Activities Status:
  Department of Information Technology (DIT), Govt. of India, has funded C-DAC (Centre for Development of Advanced Computing) to deploy nationwide computational Grid named GARUDA.

GARUDA connects 45 institutes in 17 cities across India over 10/100 Mbps network.

GARUDA middleware is based on GT2 while research will be performed on GT4 based middleware. Data management in GARUDA is based on Storage Resource Broker SRB.

- GARUDA will focus on the following application communities:

  o Computer Aided Engineering
  o Earth Sciences
  o High Energy Physics/Astro Physics
  o Life Sciences
  o Material Sciences/Nano Technology

- Relationship with EGEE:

  India has close relationship with EGEE via an associate project EUIndiaGrid which has a budget of 1.2 million EUR for a period of 2 years starting from Oct 2006. EUIndiaGrid is composed of 5 European and 9 Indian partners.
- Key application areas of EUIndiaGrid includes:

  o High Energy Physics
  o Material Science
  o Bioinformatics
  o Earth and Atmospheric Science

  In additional to EUInidiaGrid, TIFR and VECC have deployed Tier-2 LCG/EGEE resource centers to enable collaboration with CMS and Alice experiments.
- Additional Information:

  BARC has a history of strong collaboration with CERN involving the development of computing fabric management tools, monitoring application and problem tracking systems. Many of these contributions are directly used within the EGEE project.
  http://www.ernet.in/index.htm
  http://www.euindiagrid.org/
  http://www.garudaindia.in/index.asp

(4) Japan

- Representative: **Hiroshi SAKAMOTO**, University of Tokyo
                  Takashi SASAKI, KEK
- NREN Status:

  Super SINET is Japan's research and education network with a backbone consisting of 10G connections. Japan is also directly connected to many of Asian's NRENs through the APAN network.
- National Grid Initiative and Grid Activities Status:

  NAREGI, Japan's National Research Grid Initiative, was created in 2003 by the Ministry of Education, Culture, Sports, Science and Technology (MEXT).

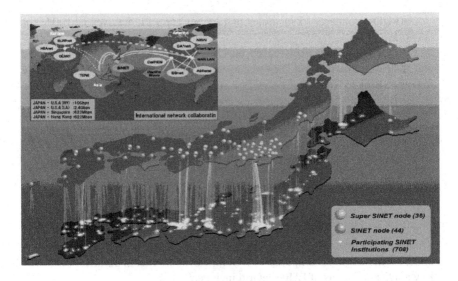

NEREGI has developed Grid middleware for super-computers and computational clusters to support Japan's Cyber Science Infrastructure (CSI).

NAREGI initially developed middleware components based on UNICORE and has more recently released middleware based on OGSA specification in May 2006.

NAREGI has a strong focus in both bio and nano-technology applications.

- Relationship with EGEE:

Japan and in particular University of Tokyo has a long history of working with European Data Grid (EDG) and was one of the earliest sites to join the LCG/EGEE production Grid in support of the Atlas HEP experiment. University of Tokyo has also provided local training to Japanese Institutes for gLite User Interface installation and the usage of gLite and Atlas experiment software.

KEK has also joined the EGEE infrastructure and have brought in new VOs such as Belle and Asia Pacific Data Grid. Support for other HEP and life science communities are also provided by KEK resource center in EGEE. KEK is also planning for expanded deployment of gLite with 5 collaborating institutes within Japan. KEK is also plans to hold EGEE system administration training in Japanese later this year.

NAREGI project has also been working closely with EGEE on making interoperable.

- Additional Information:
http://www.naregi.org/index_e.html

(5) Korea

- Representative: **Kihyeon CHO**, KISTI
- NREN Status:

KREONET (Korea Research Environment Open NETwork) is a national R&D network, run by KISTI (Korea Institute of Science and Technology Information) and supported by Korea government, in particular MOST (Ministry of Science and Technology) since 1988. For science and technology information exchange and supercomputing related collaboration, KREONET provides high-performance network services for Korean research and development community. KREONET has 15 regional network centers. It is also important to note that KREONET is connected to GLORIAD a ring network with 10G connecting Korea to Hong-Kong and the United States. KISTI is directly peered to CERN via 10Gbps network. KREONET's domestic connectivity to high energy physics Institutes and GLORIAD are shown below:

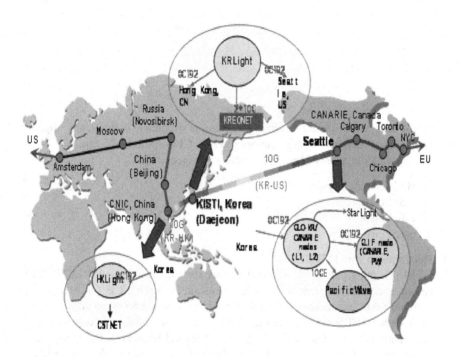

- National Grid Initiative and Grid Activities Status:

    Korea, in particular KISTI, has been carrying out two national Grid projects. One is K*Grid project supported by MIC (Ministry of Information and Communication) and the other is national e-Science project supported by MOST (Ministry Of Science and Technology). K*Grid project is focusing on building nation-wide Grid infrastructure. K*Grid project includes construction of Grid infrastructure, research and development of Grid middleware and scientific and business Grid applications. National e-Science project is a spin-off project from K*Grid project and is more focusing on scientific Grid application, especially on

Network for HEP

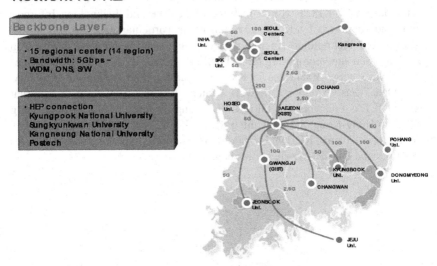

establishing world-class e-Science environment which will dramatically improve research productivity for high-energy physics, CFD and BT/NT, .etc.

- Key application areas of National e-Science project include:

  o High Energy Physics
  o Geo Sciences
  o Life Sciences
  o e-Engineering

- Relationship with EGEE

  KISTI and Kyungpook National University have established WLCG/EGEE resource centers to provide computing resources for ALICE (as Tier-2 center) and CMS experiment, respectively. There is also interest to support other VOs such as CDF and Biomed at KISTI. KISTI in collaboration with CKSC (Chonnam National University, Kangnung National University and Sejong University) are unfunded partners in the EGEE-II project and is also interested in middleware re-engineering as well as infrastructure operation to gain experiences about advanced Grid middleware technologies.

- Additional Information:
  http://www.gridcenter.or.kr
  http://www.escience.or.kr
  http://www.kreonet.net
  http://www.gloriad-kr.org

- Questionnaire Response:
  From: **Soonwook Hwang**, KISTI

1. What are the most important issues and road blocks to your National Grid and e-Science development?

Lack of funding is one of the biggest barriers to our National e-Science development. Compared to the budget for e-Science in UK, U.S. and Japan, the budget for the e-Science project in Korea, which started in 2005 as a three-year project, is too small to be able to be regarded as a national effort. I suspect that most of e-science projects in Asia-Pacific are suffering from the budget problem.

2. What do you feel EGEE can help do to effectively promote collaboration in e-Science within Asia-Pacific and with Europe?

As far as I know, the EGEE partners in Asia-Pacific region take part in the EGEE as an unfunded partner. I think it would be really helpful for the Asia-Pacific partners (AP partners) to be allowed to get funded from European Commission. If it is not allowed for each individual AP partners to get financial support, it could be an idea that the AP partners are allowed to form an Asia-Pacific federation and the federation is allowed to join EGEE III as a funded federation so that each individual AP partner can be supported from the AP federation. I expect this kind of AP federation to help promote collaboration in e-Science not only within Asia-Pacific but also with Europe.

3. What application areas are the strongest in your country and is actively seeking to collaboration with others? Are there other application areas that you feel would benefit from the Grid?

HEP is the strongest area in Korea, including ALICE, CDF (KISTI) and CMS (KNU). We are actively seeking to collaboration with CNRS/IN2P3 under the umbrella of LIA creation in e-Science areas such as bioinformatics.

4. Are you willing to join EGEE III and contribute to the project?

Yes, we are wiling to join EGEE III as a contracting partner like we did in EGEE II. In fact, we are hoping that we will be able to get more actively involved in EGEE activities.

5. Which areas are you most interested in contributing to? Dissemination, Training, Operation or Engineering? Please detail specific ideas you may have.

Like we did in EGEE II, we are going to continue to work on Grid Operation in EGEE III in collaboration with ASGC which acts as Asia-Pacific Regional Operation Center. We would like to participate in Engineering in EGEE III such as the development of applications in such areas as biomedical, geosciences on top of a service grid infrastructure that EGEE provides. We would like to work on the development of service testing framework in the context of EGEE, as well.

6. What benefits do you wish to obtain from your involvement in EGEE?

In addition to physical resources sharing, we will be able to gain experiences in the EGEE middleware and Grid operation through our involvement in EGEE and it is expected to facilitate joint R&D activities between Korea and Europe based on EGEE infrastructure.

(6) Malaysia

- Representative: **Suhaimi Napis**, Universiti Putra Malaysia, MYREN
- NREN Status:

MYREN was launched in 2005 connecting 12 of the largest public universities in Malaysia, with bandwidths ranging from 2Mbps to 8Mbps. International connectivity is available via TIEN2 through a 45 Mbps connection.

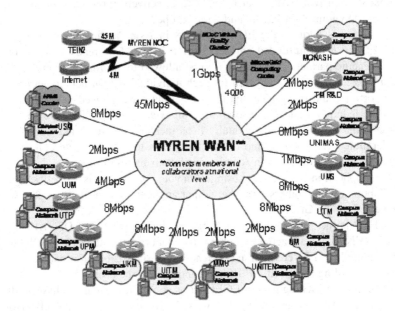

MYREN Network Topology (as of Aug 2006)

- National Grid Initiative and Grid Activities Status:
  The National Grid Computing Initiative (NGCI) is Malaysia's national Grid project lead by the Ministry of Science and Technology, Innovation (MOSTI).
- The application domain areas in NGCI include the following:

  - Scientific and engineering applications
  - Humanities, Social Science and Find Arts
  - E-Learning
  - Life Sciences

- Relationship with EGEE:
  The Universiti Putra Malaysia has expressed interest in establishing an EGEE resource center.
- Additional Information:
  http://nucleus.mygridusbio.net.my/ganglia/
- Questionnaire Response:
  From: **Jing-Yuan Luke**, Grid Computing Lab, MIMOS

1. What are the most important issues and road blocks to your National Grid or e-Science development?

Human Factor and Funding. Generally we had a situation where there is a huge gap between the researchers in the grid computing area and the eventual users/industries that would adopt the grid. This situation may have cause funding of grid projects difficult as the government may want to see tangible outcomes of researches being conducted in the grid computing area.

2. What do you feel EGEE can help do to effectively promote collaboration in e-Science within Asia-Pacific and with Europe?

An EGEE road-show in Malaysia to educate and create awareness to both researchers in grid and the users/industries how these 2 seemingly different "world" can help each others through better research and integration of grid technologies in day-to-day activities.

Of course it does not hurt if EGEE would able to inject some amount of seeding to fund grid researches that would have real users and outcome at the end of the project.

3. What application areas are the strongest in your country and is actively seeking to collaborate with others? Are there other application areas that you feel would benefit from the Grid?

From government perspective, Malaysia currently is putting lots of efforts in enhancing herself in biotechnology and revitalizing the agriculture sector. Not to mention to create new values from the manufacturing sector and ICT sector. Thus though we may not have the strongest applications in the above areas but the nation is no doubt want to excel in these areas.

4. Are you willing to join EGEE III and contribute to the project?
DEFINITELY YES.

5. Which areas are you most interested in contributing to? Dissemination, Training, Operations or Engineering? Please detail specific ideas you may have.

Operations and Engineering: Currently within our lab we are looking into areas of national grid testbed, middleware and grid portal. The goal is to first make grid as friendly as possible to the average citizens. The ultimate goal however is to innovate a possible grid economic/business model that eventual a lot of Grid Service Providers (GSP) can be set up to serve the nation as well as overseas users with a variety of applications and services.

6. What benefits do you wish to obtain from your involvement in EGEE?

Technical expertise and knowledge in middleware. Policies. Engineering of the Grid. Architecting the Grid.

(7) New Zealand

- Representative: **Orlon Petterson**, University of Cantebury
- NREN Status:

Kiwi Advanced Research and Education Network connects 9 research institutions, 8 university and the national library. The domestic backbone is based on 10G network. International connectivity is via a 622 Mbps connection to the US and 133 Mbps connection to Australia

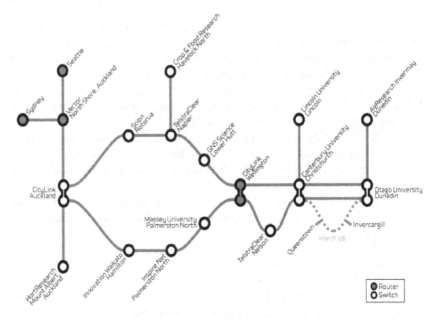

- National Grid Initiative and Grid Activities Status:

  BeSTGRID is a two year project staring 2006 that is focused on how to make eResearch work, to create a fully-functional eResearch ecosystem for New Zealand. BeSTGRID aims to build three core components: Collaboration, Data and Computational Grid.

- Relationship with EGEE:

  University of Canterbury has deployed a gLite testbed with the assistance of Marco La Rosa from the University of Melbourne. To support the CMS user community in New Zealand, there are plans to deploy a production EGEE resource center to establish a CMS Tier-2 site.

- Additional Information:

  http://www.bestgrid.org/

(8) Philippinies

- Representative: **Rhia Trogo**, De La Salle University-Manila
- NREN Status:

  Philippine Research and Government Information Network links academic, research and government institutions in the Philippines.

- National Grid Initiative and Grid Activities Status:

  The Philippine e-Science Grid Program is actively seeking to build a national Grid infrastructure, train people in relevant technologies and collaborate with the international Grid community.

  Application areas that are higher priority are Bioinformatics (Agricultural and Medical) and Disaster Mitigation.

- Relationship with EGEE:
    APROC is currently working with Advanced Science and Technology Institute in deploying an EGEE Resource center.
- Additional Information:
    http://www.asti.dost.gov.ph/

(9) Singapore

- Representative: **Hing-Yan LEE**, National Grid Office
- NREN Status:
    Singapore Advanced Research and Education Network (SingAREN) connects universities, research centers and similar non-profit institutes. Network connectivity for SingAREN is show below.
- National Grid Initiative and Grid Activities Status:

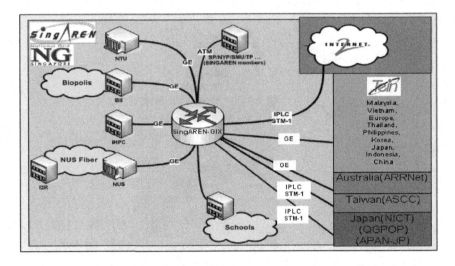

The National Grid in Singapore started in November 2003 providing nearly 1000 CPU with some 15 Grid-enabled applications from the R&D community. The project is now in it's second phase and is co-funded by the two research councils of the A*STAR – Science & Engineering Research Council and Biomedical Research Council, the Defence Science & Technology Agency (DSTA), the Infocomm Development Authority (IDA) of Singapore, NUS and NTU.

National Grid employs a LSF-meta Scheduler to provide seamless access to distributed resources within the National Grid. The LSF-meta Scheduler is able to interface with local resource schedulers such as Sun's N1GE, LSF and PBS Pro.

Phase 2 of the National Grid focuses on promoting the adoption of Grid by industry and business users. Application areas of interest for the project include:

○ digital media,
○ collaborative manufacturing
○ engineering services
○ education

• Relationship with EGEE:
 The National Grid Office has deployed and operated an EGEE production site for more than 2 years. Singapore has contributed significant resources to both the EGEE HEP and biomed VOs during this period.
• Additional Information:
 http://www.ngp.org.sg/index.html
 http://www.singaren.net.sg/

(10) Taiwan

• Representative: **Simon C. Lin**, Academia Sinica Grid Computing Center (ASGC)

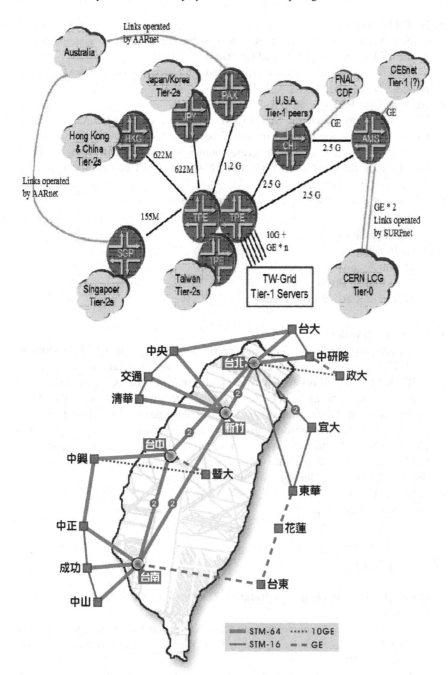

- NREN Status:
  ASNet extends Taiwan's international network connectivity to Asia-Pacific at speeds of 155–622Mbps, US and Europe at 2.5 Gbps.
  TWAREN operates domestic research and education network. TWAREN also provides connectivity to the US of 1.2 Gbps.
- National Grid Initiative and Grid Activities Status:
  TWGrid lead by Academia Sinica Grid Computing Center (ASGC) funded by the National Science Council include 7 partner institutes operating 8 resource centers. TWGrid has adopted the gLite middleware and is directly integrated into the EGEE production Grid. TWGrid also hosts an LCG Tier-1 center supporting Tier-2 centers in the region.
- TWGrid is involved with the following applications areas:

    – Bioinformatics
    – Earth Science
    – Digital Archive
    – High Energy Physics
    – Humanities and Social Science

- Relationship with EGEE:
  Taiwan has participated as one of the earliest resource center in LCG production Grid. The resource center is located at Academia Sinica and serves as a regional LHC Tier-1 center. This later led to the involvement into the EGEE Phase I, where Taiwan began operating as an EGEE Regional Operation Center in April of 2004. Taiwan has helped the region to grow to one of the largest region in EGEE. Taiwan has also participated in Wisdom project and has played a key role in the Avian Flu Data Challenge. Continuing in EGEE phase II, ASGC participates as a partner in NA2, NA3, NA4 and SA1. Since 2004 Taiwan has provided 7 tutorials domestically and 3 in Asia Pacific (Beijing, Mumbai and Manila).
- Additional Information:
  http://www.twgrid.org/

(11) Thailand

- Representative: **Dr. Tiranee Achalakul**, Thai National Grid Center
- NREN Status:
  In 2006 the inter-university network UNINET and Thai research network ThaiSARN are combined together to form the Thai Research and Education Network ThaiREN.
  UNINET connects over 130 research and education institutes in Thailand. The network provides the service speed of 155 Mbps to 2.5 Gbps in Bangkok and 34–155 Mbps elsewhere.
- National Grid Initiative and Grid Activities Status:

The Thai National Grid Project is a national project under Software Industry Promotion Agency, Ministry of Information and Communication Technology. The project is operated by the Thai National Grid Center. The project has 14 member institutes and collaborates with industry and international partners such as PRAGMA, AIST and SDSC.

- ThaiGrid will has the following 5 initial focus areas:

  o Life Science

    – Drug Design

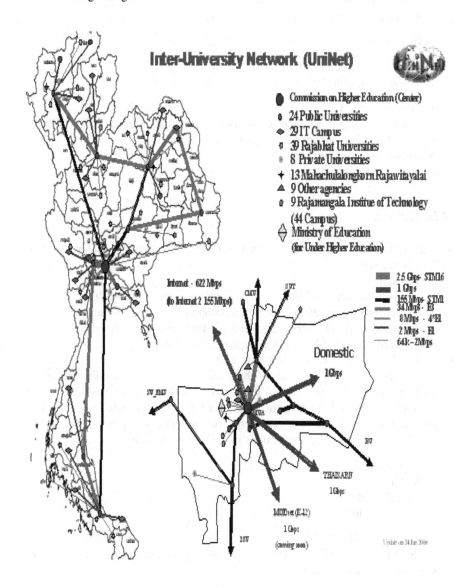

  o Computational Science and Engineering

     – Geoinformatics, CFD

  o Digital media

     – Rendering

  o Enterprise computing

     – WS/SOA Enterprise computing application
     – Industrial Simulation and Modeling
     – Financial analysis

  o Education

     – E-learning, collaborative environment
     – Grid education

- Relationship with EGEE:
     National Electronics and Computer Technology Center NECTEC has expressed interest in working with gLite middleware.
- Additional Information:
  http://iir.ngi.nectec.or.th/internet/map/firstpage.html

(12) Vietnam

- Representative: **Tran Van Lang, Do Van Long**, HCM City Institute of Information Technology
- NREN Status:
     Vietnam Research and Education Network (VinaREN) consist of a backbone that connects 5 major network operation centers in Vietnam. There are also plans to extend this network to connect over 50 institutions. International connectivity is also available through TIEN2 through a 45Mbps link.
- National Grid Initiative and Grid Activities Status:
     VNGrid Project is financed by the Ministry of Science and Technology of Vietnam and is a two year project that will end in Oct 2008 with a budge of 160 thousand USD. The project aims to build a Grid infrastructure to connect five institutes in Vietnam and achieve interoperation with other Grid systems.
     VNGrid aims to build applications in the following areas

  o Bioinframatics
  o Meterology
  o Virtual Reality
  o Cryptography

- Relationship with EGEE:
     HCM City Institute of Information Technology has expressed interest in working with gLite middleware.

o Additional Information:
   http://www.tein2.net/upload/pdf/TEIN2-VN-VinaREN-APEC2006dante.pdf
   http://www.vinaren.vn/english
o Collaborative environments

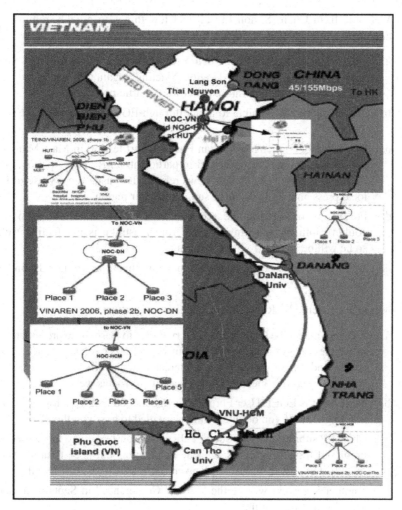

5 Asia Federation Meeting Minutes ISGC 2007

- **Time/Date**: 12 : 30 ~ 14 : 00, Thursday, 29 March 2007
- **Chair**: Simon Lin
- **Members**: (In last name's alphabetic order)
  Giuseppe Andronico (EUChinaGrid, Italy), Robert Jones (EGEE, Switzerland),
  Wing-Keung Kwan (Hong Kong SAR), Ying-Yen Lee (NGO, Singapore),
  Do Van Long (Vietnam), Alberto Masoni (EUIndiaGrid, Italy), Suhaimi Napis

(Malaysia), Orlon Petterson (New Zealand), Hiroshi Sakamoto (Japan), Suriya U-Ruekolan (Thailand), Min Tsai (ASGC, Taiwan), Eric Yen (ASGC, Taiwan)
- **Secretaries**: Vicky Huang, Jennifer Su (ASGC, Taiwan)
- **Meeting Note**:

  o Welcome from Chair, Simon Lin all and few things to quickly remind all attendees:

    a. Next event of **EGEE User Forum** (Manchester, UK) in May this year may run another "Asia Federation Meeting" again. We welcome and encourage all Asia federation countries to participate.

    b. Travel support is possible to apply through EGEE, but need to act very quickly.

    c. The 2nd data challenge of Avian Flu will start testing in May. Many of the Asia countries are interested in participating. By participation, you could have a joint or separate news release. It is usually very useful for local press and also gets more support in your region.

    d. For the record, Philippine representative has to leave early, so she couldn't join this meeting. Marco from Australia is not feeling well, so he will be absent from this meeting.

    e. Apart from usual Asia Federation meeting, this time we have EUIndia-Grid and EUChinaGrid to join us.

  o Message delivered by Robert Jones (EGEE)

    a. It is very nice to be here again and very useful to learn these presentations in all these sessions. For EGEE project and other related projects, we understand what exactly you are interested in and what you do. And, it is for sure that this meeting is also benefit for you as well.

    b. Next event is EGEE User Forum. It is understood that it's a long way for you to go, but if you do, we will be very glad to host you there.

    c. The CFP submission was due in Feb, so we can't take any more presentations. If travel funding is needed, we can help but need to apply very quickly. Otherwise, it will be also very difficult to get visa as well.

    d. Another big event will be the "Project Conference" in September. You are all welcome to join.

    e. ISGC is an event in promoting Grid activities in Asia and and the work we are doing on a global basis. What do you countries have specific point of view that you would like to raise about how the event is organized?

    f. One thing will be good in the future is that we should have poster and demo sessions during ISGC 2008.

    g. Countries in Asia can be included as an official partner in EGEE III. EGEE cannot fund manpower in countries outside of Europe, but can provide support for travel, visits to Europe or collaboration. EGEE III starts spring 2008.

h.   In EGEE III, we will try to recognize this event at the key Asian events where EGEE will participate.

o Brief thoughts from each country

a.   Mr. Wing-Keung Kwan (Hong Kong SAR)

- Hong Kong is part of China now, but it has a special position that allows us to do things that China cannot do. For example Hong Kong has been selected to establish a State Key Laboratory of Emerging Infectious Diseases to do SARs and other emerging infectious diseases analysis. Hong-Kong can better communicate with the international community.
- We are receiving many students from China. One interesting research is on the Nuclear Power Plant leakage simulation. There may be some plans to share this data using the Grid.
- Currently there are only two staff handling the HPC and Grid Computing services in Computer Centre, Hong Kong University. Because of the help of Simon (ASGC) and also APROC people, we now step into the Grid environment, that more sharable grid resources (data + computing power) is available. Some academic and research users in the Physics Dept. have also approached the Computer Centre enquiring for accessing the Grid resources.
- At the moment, they will keep on promoting the Grid computing literacy in the University, with more users to be exposed to the international Grid computing activities, but it is difficult for HKU to contribute non-trivial Grid resources at the moment

b.   Hiroshi Sakamoto (Japan)

- Activities in NAREGI. NAREGI has produced a beta version of its middleware and will also release a production version near the end of this year. (Min provides)
- Japanese institutes and especially KEK will review and evaluate NAREGI to see if it is suitable for their production requirements. (Min provides)
- KEK and RIKEN are also in discussion to on plans to establish a LHC Tier-1 center in Japan. This will probably take 2–3 years to implement and could possibly include ASGC to create a federated Tier-1. (Min provides)
- ALICE experiment starts to have some Japanese to join.

c.   Orlon Petterson (New Zealand)

- New Zealand will work more closely with APAC on Grid. We are also involved in Human Interactive Technology. University of Canterbury has its own HIT lab.
- Will collaborate with Australia on LHC Tier-2 Center.

- New Zealand has competitive research environment so many groups work independently.
- Will bring the message back that the international global infrastructure is here in Asia already also in happening in Southeast Asia. It should not only in HEP, but also great potential for eScience and other collaborated sciences.

d. Suhaimi Napis (Malaysia)

- We are still interested in Biodiversity and e-Culture (Cultural Heritage.)
- We know the infrastructure is there, but we need implement.
- ASGC's biodiversity people will talk to Suhaimi for further collaboration.

e. Ying-Yen Lee (NGO, Singapore)

- Have involved in EGEE for nearly 2 years now, so they have a good idea what it is now.
- NGO has found the biggest challenge is getting the users directly involved with Grid Computing. We need users to speak on our behalf so we can get our hardware refreshed.
- Singapore is not into HEP, but in bio-medicine (bio-medical). We do have such community in Singapore. Traveling to Geneva or other European countries for conference is that the typical event our users are willing to travel to. The events they travel to are more focused events.
- Singapore is involved in Avian Flu.

f. Suriya U-Ruekolan (NECTEC, Thailand)

- NECTEC has started to collaborate with PRAGMA project. EGEE project is new for NECTEC.
- They will keep in contact with Min Tsai (ASGC) if there are problems about EGEE Middleware test bed.

g. Do Van Long (Vietnam)

- Vietnam is fairly new country to Grid Computing, but do our best to develop our system by connecting to other projects, even only with few PCs.
- VietGrid project has very limited budget now. But, after attending ISGC 2007, they will try to promote more about developing gLite and encourage more collaboration.
- They would like to attend EGEE User Forum, is EGEE can sponsor 2 members of us to the event.

h. Alberto Masoni (EUIndiaGrid, Italy)

- In preparation for the new call, we need to think about the most effective solution for Asia Grids initiatives. It will be important to show to the European Commission that we are working together between different projects on this effort.

   – The idea is to put both projects in networking activity to work Grid projects in Asia and collaborate & coordination.

i.   Giuseppe Andronico (EUChinaGrid, Italy)

   – EUChinaGrid has specific activity to promote Grid in Asia and would like to work with Taiwan on this. Have developed a team that can speak in Chinese and English to provide training. Has discussed with EUIndiaGrid about 3 year proposal project to help maintain sustainable Grid infrastructure in Asia.

j.   Min Tsai (ASGC, Taiwan)

   – I will have a talk in the next session which provides an update on EGEE Asia Pacific Regional Operation Center status.

   – There are three institutes are currently started the certification process. They are located in the Philippine, Korea and Mongolia.

   – We also worked with Malaysia to set up a registration authority.

o Ending remarks from Simon Lin

   – "A journey of Thousand miles must start from a single step." We are now starting this single step. We keep on getting/promoting Asia countries to get registered and certified. We do actually spread the infrastructure & gLite. Collaboration is more important than technology, particular in the beginning. Collaboration would be a good framework. Collaboration starts from the bottom up. We are doing this bottom up job and then to hope to all of us together. There must be a single enterable infrastructure. We are certainly looking for all the possibilities, of course. And, thanks to Bob's support and all speakers and participants from all over the world to make a great program of ISGC 2007.

e-Infrastructure for Taiwan and International Collaboration

Eric Yen and Simon C. Lin

Abstract Academia Sinica Grid Computing Center (ASGC) is one of leading high performance computing and communication centers in Taiwan, which provides advanced services for Grid Computing from 2002, to support research by e-Science, on data intensive sciences and applications requiring cross-disciplinary large-scale distributed collaboration. Start from 2005, Asia Pacific Regional Operation Center is operated by ASGC and supporting 21 sites in 8 countries. More Asia countries are joining global e-Science community with vigorous potential. ASGC is working on the wider user community and evolving toward sustainable e-Infrastructure together with Asia partners, as the e-Science gateway between Asia and the world.

1 Introduction

"e-Science is about global collaboration in key areas of science and the next generation of infrastructure that will enable it."[1] Realization of this evolution lies on the push of progress of information and communication technology and the pull of e-Science applications.

Around five years ago, we first began to realize that grid middleware and toolkits alone are insufficient to achieve the vision of grid computing. For success, we must focus on deployment, taking advantage of user needs — such as the needs of the high energy physics community and the Large Hadron Collider (LHC) — to drive a production infrastructure.

On 4 October 2002, the Grid Deployment Board of the Worldwide LHC Computing Grid held their first meeting in Milano, Italy. The meeting was chaired by Mirco Mazzucato and included 26 participants as well as WLCG project leader Les Robertson, computing coordinators from the four LHC experiments, and numerous country representatives.

At this inaugural meeting, this group discussed the goal of providing a common production infrastructure on which to run experimental data challenges: the result

E. Yen (✉)
MIS Department, National Cheng-Chih University
e-mail: Eric.Yen@twgrid.org

S.C. Lin, E. Yen (eds.), *Grid Computing*,
© Springer Science+Business Media, LLC 2009

was the LCG-1. The collaboration agreed that large-scale production should begin from July 2003, with the aim of achieving real 24–7 production by the end of 2003.

Academia Sinica Grid Computing Center (ASGC)[2] is one of leading high performance computing and communication centers in Taiwan, which provides advanced services for Grid Computing from 2002, to support research by e-Science, on data intensive sciences and applications require cross-disciplinary large-scale distributed collaboration.

With more than 100 sites joining in the WLCG/EGEE [3, 4] project, Taiwan plays a leading role in Asia. ASGC provides the Grid-related technology and infrastructure support for the LHC experiments (ATLAS and CMS) in Taiwan, and has been actively participating in the WLCG/EGEE project through various activities ranging from strategic planning to infrastructure deployment and services. Serving as the EGEE Asia Federation Coordinator, ASGC (Academia Sinica Grid Computing) has provided services to 20 production sites in 8 countries with more than 1500 CPUs since 2005.

As the global e-Science infrastructure is establishing very quickly, we have to take advantage of sharing and collaboration to bridge the gap between Asia and the world, by addressing the challenges of regional cooperation in Asia Pacific Areas. Many Grid projects are commenced in this region recently but most of them have a heavy emphasis on the development of Grid middleware and technology, rather than the enabling of grid applications and real collaborations. Disparate Grids with limited operation experiences and user community engagement will make collaboration more difficult.

The objectives of ASGC at this stage are to: 1) extending e-Science infrastructure to benefit much larger scale and more resilient scientific research and applications; 2) acting as one of major e-Science Centres in the world, by serving as the coordinator for EGEE Asia Pacific Federation and WLCG Asia Center, and 3) facilitating the regional e-Science infrastructure and application development, and coordinate the regional collaborations.

In this paper, what we have achieved to serve as the e-Science gateway between Asia and Europe is described in the next section. In Section III, endeavor from production grid to self-sustainability is explored. Following are the sessions of summary and references.

2 Bridging the Gap between Asia and the World

As one of the pioneered production Grid service center and the Asia Pacific Regional Operation Center, ASGC keeps on delivering the following services to extend the e-Infrastructure and facilitate the partnerships in this region.

a. e-Infrastructure Operation services: providing continuous monitoring of grid services and automated site configuration management to maximize the availability of Grid services and resource utilization.

b. Research and Development on middleware: focusing on the technology and tools development for application integration with the underlying e-Infrastructure, and support the certification and distribution of production middleware under friendly open source license model.

c. User Support: managed process from first contact to production usage covering the site administrator, user and application developer etc. Training helpdesk and dissemination are the major efforts to support the user and attract more collaborations.

d. Interoperation: expanding geographical reach and interoperability with collaborating e-Infrastructures.

Based on the experiences of WLCG Tier-1 Center in Taiwan, ASGC joined EGEE II from 2006 and starts the support to extend gLite infrastructure in this region, engage more user communities to make use of the e-Infrastructure and services, and to foster more collaborations since then. TWGrid and APeSci two virtual organizations (VO) were set up for new application incubation and regional collaboration. Other than high energy physics applications, we also initiated the avian flu drug discovery project in March 2006, based on the Grid Application Platform (GAP) for better grid application integration and Web portal development.

In short, major achievements of ASGC are as follows, and was illustrated as the Fig. 1.

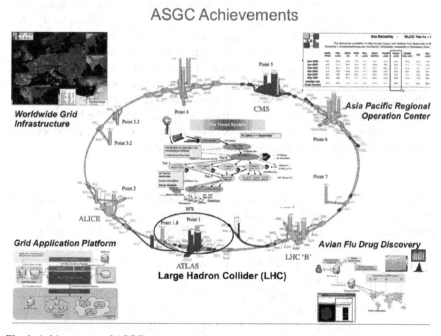

Fig. 1 Achievements of ASGC

a. WLCG Asia Tier-1 Centre: Since 2005 ASGC has formally become the first one of the 11 Tier-1 centers (the only Tier-1 in Asia) providing services, coordination and support for HEP scientists (both ATLAS and CMS experiments) worldwide (also in Taiwan). ASGC has proven to be one of the most reliable Tier-1 Centers worldwide.

b. WLCG/EGEE AP/ROC and Asia Federation Coordinator: Due to the outstanding reputation of competence and quality, ASGC was invited to join the European Union e-Science flagship project (Enabling Grid for E-sciencE, EGEE). Acting as the AP Regional Operation Centre (AP/ROC) and the Asia Federation Coordinator, ASGC coordinates the setup of resources centers and dissemination of gLite middleware in Asia Pacific region including Japan, Korea, China, Singapore, Malaysia, Philippines, Vietnam, Thailand, Australia, New Zealand, Pakistan, and India.

c. Grid Technology Development: ASGC not only facilitates WLCG/EGEE Certificate Authority and Operation Services, but also participates the technology development, including (1) GSTAT which is a Grid information monitoring system now widely used by over 200 WLCG/EGEE institutes, (2) gLite middleware certification and testing, and (3) distributed analysis tools for LHC. In addition, ASGC also leads in the development of important Grid technologies such as Grid Application Platform and the interoperability of two major Grid storage systems: SRM and SRB.

d. e-Science Infrastructure and applications: By building on WLCG's foundation and experience, we will work actively to construct Taiwan's next-generation research infrastructure to support large-scale research and cross-disciplinary programs in areas such as High Energy Physics, Digital Archives, Atmospheric Science and Bio-medical applications. In April 2006, a collaboration of ASGC, AS Genomics Research Center and other European laboratories has analyzed 300,000 possible drug candidates against the Avian Flu Virus H5N1 by using the EGEE infrastructures. Over 2000 computers were used during 4 weeks, this is equivalent to 137 years on a single computer. This is the biggest cross-continental public collaboration project ever in Drug Discovery, the story was widely reported by the international media such as BBC.

Another significant progress is the international network infrastructure of Taiwan: the first 10 gigabit network link between Asia and Europe will be operational from July 2007, built by Academia Sinica Grid Computing Center in Taiwan. ASGC is also instrumental in the promotion and dissemination of e-science and grid activities within the WLCG/EGEE framework.

However, there are still many challenges. One of the major issues for the Asia Pacific is the lack of driving e-science applications that specifically concern countries in that region. To address this issue, in spring 2006 the ASGC initiated the Avian Flu Drug Discovery Data Challenge, coordinating the participation of pioneering Asian Pacific partners alongside many European partners.

Disaster mitigation using grid technology is another area that may better represent the concerns of the Asia Pacific regions, and this and other applications will be incorporated into the future EUAsiaGrid project proposal, currently in progress. However, applications that can meet the needs of Asian Pacific scientists are crucial to the long-term sustainability of grid infrastructures in Asian and Pacific regions.

A truly global e-infrastructure will benefit hugely from rapidly growing areas such as the Asia Pacific; such benefits include not only the pragmatic advantage of running the global infrastructure from three major time zones, but also the opportunity to achieve a truly global geographic distribution.

3 From Production into Sustainability

As the EGEE is moving from production-quality grid infrastructure for e-Science in EGEE-II toward the self-sustainable state in EGEE-III. A production gLite infrastructure in Asia has been established and is composed of 21 production sites dispersed in 8 countries, with the support of APROC at ASGC. 9 sites among them joined this e-Infrastructure and passed the site certification since 2006. APROC provides deployment support and facilitates the e-Infrastructure expansion. Furthermore, grid services availability is maximized, management cost is reduced and ease-of-use is improved at the same time.

Asian Pacific partners are beginning to demonstrate a vigorous synergy. Over the last twelve months we have used 3.5 million CPU hours supporting nine virtual organizations, as in the Fig. 2. By early 2008, we will have 21 EGEE sites, more than 3,500 CPU cores and close to 2 petabytes of disk space.

Operation technology is one of the key issue of ASGC to grow the service capacity to the most while minimize the increase of operation and management cost. Typical services of APROC to support the long-term administration of each sites includes:

1. the establishment of a certificate authority (CA) domestically if none exists.
2. Increase availability and resource levels
3. Establish domestic operations structure that covers the standardized operation procedures, Tools of monitoring and notification, ticketing system for problem tracking etc., and the user an administrator support.
4. Training for administrators and users.
5. Collaborate with APROC in regional operations.
6. Support VOs of application development and production service separately.

Application will not only pull the advance of Grid services and technology but also could enhance the reliability and maturity of Grid services. Both horizontal and vertical expansions are also implemented in Asia Pacific region in accordance with EGEE. Horizontal expansion focuses on supporting more disciplines; while vertical expansion helps existing disciplines to make more intensive usages. Research

SITE	Normalised CPU time [units 1K.SI2K.Hours] by SITE and VO									
	alice	atlas	biomed	cms	dteam	lhcb	ops	Other VOs	Total	%
Australia-ATLAS	0	1	2,356	0	6	0	6	0	2,369	0.08%
Australia-UNIMELB-LCG2	0	60,125	20,970	0	47	0	43	876	82,061	2.60%
GOG-Singapore	0	0	1,875	0	13	178	38	0	2,104	0.07%
HK-HKU-CC-01	0	0	0	0	45	0	36	0	81	0.00%
IN-DAE-VECC-01	30,770	0	0	0	13	0	14	0	30,797	0.98%
INDIACMS-TIFR	0	0	0	1	32	0	13	0	46	0.00%
JP-KEK-CRC-01	0	0	0	0	71	0	50	37,449	37,570	1.19%
JP-KEK-CRC-02	0	0	0	0	34	0	35	149,789	149,858	4.75%
KR-KISTI-GCRT-01	2,030	0	0	0	3	0	0	0	2,033	0.06%
LCG_KNU	0	0	0	2,686	12	0	4	0	2,702	0.09%
NCP-LCG2	395	30	0	59	18	3,748	18	0	4,268	0.14%
PAKGRID-LCG2	18	188	18,366	339	61	7,351	52	0	26,375	0.84%
Taiwan-IPAS-LCG2	0	7,454	0	0	2	0	0	0	7,456	0.24%
Taiwan-LCG2	0	589,830	40,092	455,177	56	0	45	327,451	1,412,651	44.74%
Taiwan-NCUCC-LCG2	0	2,005	0	2,549	2	652	4	55	5,267	0.17%
TOKYO-LCG2	0	1,075,268	0	0	1,707	0	66	0	1,077,041	34.11%
TW-FTT	0	101,550	0	169,462	3	0	0	24,338	295,353	9.35%
TW-NCUHEP	0	0	0	15,267	29	0	14	0	15,310	0.48%
TW-NIU-EECS-01	0	0	0	0	45	0	56	3,827	3,928	0.12%
TW-NTCU-HPC-01	0	0	0	0	25	0	30	0	55	0.00%
TW-THU-HPC	2	10	0	12	49	81	31	1	186	0.01%
Total	33,215	1,836,461	83,659	645,552	2,273	12,010	555	543,786	3,157,511	
Percentage	1.05%	58.16%	2.65%	20.44%	0.07%	0.38%	0.02%	17.22%		

Fig. 2 Accounting of gLite sites and participated VOs of Asia Pacific Region (in terms of KSI2K-Hours) from EGEE Accounting services

applications will be chosen based on the motivation of research communities and also the scientific importance and the potential values to the advancement of Grid technology by their intensive use of existing services. Development of new high-level application oriented services need to be taken into account as well.

ASGC currently support ATLAS, CMS, Belle, Biomed, TWGrid and APeSci VOs. In addition to WLCG, high energy physics and drug discovery applications, we are also working on many projects to support them making use of Grid technologies, such as the DataGrid services for Earth Science data center, develop Grid-based long-term preservation environment for digital information and archives, integration of biodiversity resources and ecoinformatics resources, geo-mapping and earth monitoring applications and the general high performance computing applications etc. From the practical experiences, we could factorize the common grid services to flourish the generic grid application platform and porting expertise.

On the other hand, in Taiwan, the monitoring infrastructure consists of variant levels of fabrics (including the data center), Grid middleware and services and application. Alarm system is the pivot to notify the occurrence of a problem. Ticketing system would be used to tracking a problem when it happened and the whole process of the resolution. Knowledge base is used to compile the lessons learnt from daily operations, expertise and those materials of known events. Monitoring system is aiming for real time investigation of core services and should trigger the alarm once there is any critical service problem. Standard operation procedures and practices are the pragmatic expedient to make sure all the systems are working properly.

4 Summary and Future Works

Although Asia region as a whole traditionally is inexperienced in regional cooperation, but the e-Infrastructure would help us to evolve and to be beneficial from each other through easier collaborations. E-Infrastructure helps Asia countries to take advantage of sharing and collaboration to bridge the gap between Asia and the world, and additionally, assists to address the challenge of regional cooperation. Asia Pacific Region has demonstrated it's great potential to adopt the e-Infrastructure: more and more Asia countries are deploying Grid system and take part in the e-Science world. Grid in Asia is not just happening within individual countries, many regional collaboration and activities have been in real actions. However, applications of and for the Asia Pacific scientists are largely in lack which is crucial!

e-Science envisages a whole new way of doing collaborative science. For the sustainable Grid e-Infrastructure, we have to focus more on community building rather than just offering technologies. Extending from EGEE Asia Federation to EUAsiaGrid, we are widening the uptake of e-Science, by the close collaboration regionally and internationally.

Reliability is the first course to reach the sustainability. Scalability is totally another issue. Customized and advanced functionality upon user requirements is a long-term lesson, but should be a primary step to make Grid reality. At the same time, support (and service) model consistent with a sustainable grid infrastructure for both user and operation are also indispensable. The Grid will hardly succeed if it fails to reach critical mass in the absence of adequate networking and collaboration. We still need to develop a long-term strategy to manage changes, to assimilate new ideas, such as Web 2.0, and engage more communities to join.

References

1. e-Science definition by John Taylor, http://www.e-science.clrc.ac.uk.
2. Academia Sinica Grid Computing Center, http://www.twgrid.org.
3. EGEE Project, http://www.eu-egee.org.
4. WLCG Project, http://lcg.web.cern.ch.

Part II
Application - High Energy Physics, Biomedicine and Life Sciences

e-Science for High Energy Physics in Korea

Kihyeon Cho

Abstract In this paper, we report experiences and results of the integration and utilization of e-Science for High Energy Physics for ALICE and CDF in Korea. An overview is given of the current and planned uses of cyber infrastructure which contains computing, storage, network and grid service infrastructure in Korea. We will also report the experiences in operating grid farms and researches on EGEE for LHC (Large Hadron Collider) experiments.

Keywords Grid · computing · network · e-science

1 The e-Science for High Energy Physics

Now science is becoming a team sports. Easy problems are solved and challenging problems require large resources, particularly knowledge from many discipline. There is an amazing advance in information technology such as Moore's law and widespread use of IT (Information Technology) in science [1]. The e-Science is new R & D paradigm for science which is computationally intensive science that is carried out in highly distributed network environments, or science that uses immense data sets that require grid computing. HEP (High Energy Physics) has a particularly well developed e-Science infrastructure due to their need for adequate computing facilities for the analysis of results and storage of data originating from the CERN LHC (Large Hadron Collider) [2]. HEP is to understand the basic properties of elementary particles and their interactions. HEP is usually conducted at the major accelerator sites, in which detector design, construction, signal processing, data acquisition, and data analysis are performed on a large scale. The size of collaboration is 100 ~ 2000 physicists. To perform computing at the required HEP scale, the data grid is a strong requirement [3].

K. Cho (✉)
e-Science Applications Research Team, Korea Institute of Science and Technology Information (KISTI), Daejeon, 305-806, Korea
e-mail: cho@kisti.re.kr

S.C. Lin, E. Yen (eds.), *Grid Computing*,
© Springer Science+Business Media, LLC 2009

The objective of HEP data grid is to construct a system to manage and process HEP data and to support user group (i.e., high energy physicists). For the current and future HEP activities that require large scale data, the HEP data grid is indispensable and mass storage system of hard disks and tapes in a stable state is necessary. To make the HEP data transparent, CPU power should be extendable and accessible. The transparent HEP data means that the data should be analyzed even if high energy physicists as users do not know the actual place of data [1]. For e-Science for HEP, resources are computers, storage, instrument and network. Middleware resources are LCG (LHC Computing Grid), Linux OS and AIX OS. The applications are ALICE and CDF VO (Virtual Organization). KISTI has been working on e-Science for High Energy Physics. We are making ALICE Tier 2 center and CAF (CDF Analysis Farm) based on LCG farm and FKPPL (France-Korea Particle Physics Laboratory). In this paper, we introduce network, international collaborations and LCG farm for ALICE and CDF experiments.

2 Network

The first topic is network. Table 1 shows the current network between Korea and Laboratories abroad. KREONET (Korea Research Environment Open NETwork) is a national R&D network, run by KISTI (Korea Institute of Science and Technology Information) and supported by Korea government, in particular MOST (Ministry of Science and Technology) since 1988. For science and technology information exchange and supercomputing related collaboration, KREONET provides high-performance network services for Korean research and development community. KREONET has 15 regional network centers as shown in Fig. 1. It is also important to note that KREONET is connected to GLORIAD (Global Ring Network for Advanced Applications Development) which is a ring network with 10Gbps connecting Korea to Hong-Kong and the United States [4]. KISTI is directly peered to CERN via 10Gbps network. KREONET's domestic connectivity to high energy physics institutes and GLORIAD are shown in Fig. 2.

KOREN (KOrea advanced REsearch Network) also operates the domestic research and education network in Korea.

Table 1 The current network between Korea and Laboratories abroad

Laboratories	Network	Current bandwidth
KEK (Japan)	Hyeonhae-Genkai [5]	10 Gbps
Fermilab (USA)	Hyeonhae-Genkai, TransPAC2 [6]	10 Gbps
CERN (EU)	TEIN	622 Mbps
Fermilab, CERN	GLORIAD	10 Gbps

Network for HEP

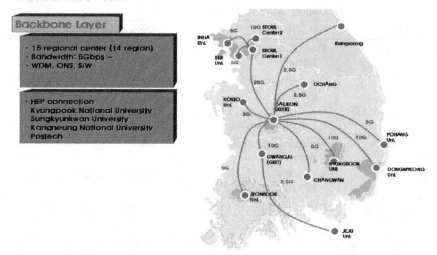

Fig. 1 KREONET for HEP institutes in Korea

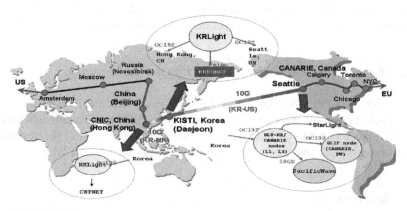

Fig. 2 GLORIAD Network

3 International Collaborations

3.1 EGEE-II Collaboration

The goal of KISTI-EGEE II collaboration is to gain experience with the EGEE middleware and operation procedures. We install and operate EGEE middleware of LCG on KISTI site. We facilitate joint research activities between Korean and Europe based on EGEE infrastructure such as High Energy Physics and Fusion grid. Currently we are working with ALICE group. We investigate the feasibility of EGEE infrastructure for researchers in other scientific and engineering areas

Table 2 The scientific programs for FKPPL

	Leading Group	
Programs	France (IN2P3)	Korea (KISTI)
Co-Directors	Vicent Breton, LPC-Clermont Ferrand	Okhwan Byeon, KISTI
ALICE	Pascal Dupieux LPC-Clemento Ferrand	Do-Won Kim, Kangnung N. Univ.
ILC Detector R&D	Jean-Claude Brient, LLR-Ecole Polytechnique	Jongman Yang, Ewha Univ.
Bioinformatics	Vincen Breton, LPC-Clermont Ferrand	Doman Kim, Chonnam N. Univ.
CDF	Aurore Savoy Navarro, LPNHE/IN2P3-CNRS	Kihyeon Cho, KISTI
Grid Computing	Dominique Boutigny, CC-IN2P3	Soonwook Hwang, KISTI

in Korea. We are involved in unfunded partners in the EGEE-II project. We are also cooperating with another partner in Korea, Chonnam National University, Kangneung National University and Sejong University. We are focusing on grid infrastructure collaboration between KISTI and EGEE-II. KISTI site has been approved as an EGEE-certified site, operating production run on a daily basis.

3.2 FKPPL (France-Korea Particle Physics Laboratory)

The object of FKPPL is to carry out, in collaboration, a scientific research program in the field of particle physics recommended by its Steering Committee between IN2P3, France and KISTI, Korea. For the first year the projects of the scientific program will be selected from the joint research proposals shown in Table 2.

4 Achievements

4.1 Grid Activities with ALICE

ALICE (A Large Ion Collider Experiment) is to study the physics of strongly inter-acting matter at extreme energy densities, where the formation of a new phase of matter, the quark-gluon plasma, is expected. ALICE will be conducted at CERN in which detector design, construction, signal processing, data acquisition, and data analysis are performed to handle PByte data. To perform computing at the required scale, the data grid is a strong requirement. In this work, we have assembled LCG farms at KISTI for ALICE experiment. We have installed ALICE VOBOX and tested it. Currently, ALICE job is running on KISTI farm. The Table 3 shows the KISTI test-bed specification and Fig. 3 shows the LCG monitoring system.

This LCG farm will be extended to 50 nodes (800 CPU) and 50 TByte at the end of this year.

Table 3 The specification of LCG farm at KISTI

OS	Scientific Linux 3.0.4
CPU	Intel Pentium-IV 2.0 GHz
Memory	2Gbyte and 4Gbyte swap memory
Disk	2TByte storage
Network	1 Gbit Ethernet

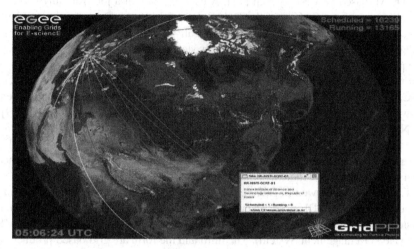

Fig. 3 LCG monitoring system shows KISTI farm in Korea

4.2 Grid Activities with CDF

Besides ALICE VO at KISTI LCG farm we will construct CDF VO, too. The CDF is an experiment on the Tevatron, USA. The CDF detector began its Run II phase in 2001. CDF computing needs are composed of raw data reconstruction and data reduction, event simulation, and user analysis. Although very different in the amount of resources needed, they are all naturally parallel activities. The CDF computing model is based on the concept of CDF Analysis Farm (CAF) [7]. To date, Run II has gathered more than $2\,\mathrm{fb}^{-1}$ of data, equivalent to 3.0×10^9 events or a couple of Pbyte of data. The increasing luminosity of the Tevatron collider will soon cause the computing requirement for data analysis and MC production to grow larger than the dedicated CPU resources that will be available [8]. In order to meet future demand, CDF is investigating in shared computing resources. The first step is DCAF (Decentralized CDF Analysis Farm) and the final step is grid. We have first embedded the CAF outside of Fermilab, in Korea called DCAF [9]. Finally we will run CDF jobs at LCG farm. Moreover, a significant fraction of these resources is expected to be available to CDF before LHC era starts and CDF could benefit from using them. In this paper we explain a detailed description of the LCG farm, including both the general idea and the current implementations.

The CAF is a large farm of computers running Linux with access to the CDF data handling system and databases to allow the CDF collaborators to run batch analysis jobs [10]. The submission uses a CAF portal which has two special things. The first one is to submit jobs from anywhere. The second thing is that job output can be sent directly to a desktop or stored on CAF FTP server for later retrieval.

However, due to the limited resources of CAF, the CDF experiment produced the concept of the CDF grid. As a first step of grid, we have first suggested and designed the DCAF based on CAF system [11]. A user can submit a job from anywhere to the cluster either at CAF or at the DCAF. DCAF in Korea is much more difficult than CAF due to data files, which are physically apart by more than 10,000 km. In order to run the remote data that is currently stored in Fermilab, USA, we use SAM (Sequential data Access via Meta-data) [12] which consist of Kerberos rcp, bbftp, gridftp and rcp as transfer methods. We use the same GUI (Graphic User Interface) of CAF. The difference is only to select the analysis farm for the DCAF in Korea. Now, DCAF around world processes 40% of total CPU of the CDF experiment [9].

Now, we are in the process of adapting and converting out work flow to the grid. The goal of movement to grid at CDF experiment is world wide trend for HEP experiment. We need to take advantage of global innovations and resources since CDF still has a lot of data to be analyzed.

CAF portal is allowed to change the underlying batch system without changing the user interface. CDF used several batch systems: 1) FBSNG (Fermilab Batch System Next Generation), 2) Condor, 3) Condor over Globus (Fig. 4), 4) gLite WMS (Workload Management System). The third and the forth are grid based production system.

The pro for Condor based grid farm is 1) that it is real fair share, globally managed user and job priorities, 2) that broken nodes kill Condor deamons, not users' job and 3) that resource selection done after a batch slot is secured. The con is 1) to use a single proxy for all jobs to enter grid sites, 2) to require outgoing connectivity, 3) not yet to be a blessed grid service. This method is more flexible so that we will use Condor based grid CAF using LCG farm at KISTI [13].

Condor based Grid CAF - Overview

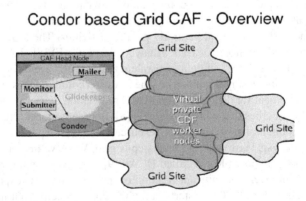

Fig. 4 The scheme of Condor based grid CAF [14]

We will also federation of LCG and OSG (Open Science Grid) farm at ASGC in Taiwan, LCG farm at Kyungpoook National University in Korea and LCG farm at University of Tsukuba in Japan. We call the federation of grid farm as Pacific CAF. This will be real grid farm. The Pacific CAF at KISTI will be extended when new supercomputer comes.

5 Conclusions

High Energy Physic is one of e-Science top brands at KISTI which is leading for e-Science for High Energy Physics in Korea. We succeeded in developing and installing HEP data grid farm in Korea. KISTI is the official ALICE Tier2 center while Kyunook National University has been working on CMS data center. KISTI has participated in CDF experiment and collaborating with Pacific CAF with Taiwan and Japan. Conclusively, KISTI has constructed ALICE Tier 2 center for CDF as well as ALICE. It will be also used for bioinfomatics VO and geo VO.

Acknowledgments We would like to thank to Jae-Hyuck Kwak and Soonwook Hwang (KISTI) for LCG farm, Yuchul Yang, Mark Neubauer (UCSD) and Frank Wuerthwein (UCSD) for CAF (Central Analysis Farm), and Igor Sfillioi (Fermilab) and Hsieh Tsan Lung (ASGC) for Pacific CAF.

References

1. In press: Kihyeon Cho, Cyberinfrastructure in Korea, Computer Physics Communications (2007).
2. A. Abashian et al. Nucl. Instr. and Meth. A 479, 117–232 (2002).
3. I. Foster et al., International J. Supercomputer Applications, 15(3), (2001).
4. G. Cole, GLORIAD (Global Ring Network for Advanced Applications). International ICFA workshop on HEP Networking, Grid and Digital Divide Issues for Global e-Science, (Daegu, 2005).
5. Y. J. Park, Korea Activities in Hyeonhae-Genkai Project. APII Workshop, (Tokyo, 2004).
6. J. Williams, CIREN/TransPAC2 Annual Report (SCI-0441096) (2006).
7. M. Neubauer, Nucl. Instr. and Meth. A 502 (2003).
8. A. Fella et al., LCGCAF the CDF Protal to the Glite Middleware, In Proc. of Conference on Computing on High Energy Physics (Mumbai, 2006).
9. K. Cho, International Journal of Computer Science and Network Security, Vol.7, No.3, 49 (2007).
10. M. Neubauer et al., Nucl. Instr. and Meth. A 502, 386–390 (2003).
11. K. Cho et al., Construction of DCAF in Korea. In Proc. 18th APAN International Conference Network Research Workshop, (Cairns, 2004).
12. A. Sill et al., Globally Distributed User Analysis Computing at CDF. In Proc. of Conference on Computing on High Energy Physics, (Interlaken, 2004).
13. G. Garzoglio, SAMGrid project. International HEP Data Grid Workshop, (Daegu, 2002).
14. I. Sffligoi, CDF Computing. Conference on Computational Physics, (Gyeongju, 2006).

Kihyeon Cho received the B.S. and M.S. degrees in Physics
from Yonsei University, Korea in 1985 and 1987, respectively.
He received the Ph.D. in Physics from University of Colorado,
Boulder, USA in 1996. During 1996–2001, he stayed in University of Tennessee, Knoxville, USA as a Post-doc. During 2001–
2006, he stayed at the Center for High Energy Physics (CHEP),
Kyungpook National University (KNU), Korea as a professor.
He is now with Korea Institute of Science and Technology Information (KISTI) as a Principal Researcher.

HEP Grid Computing in the UK: MOVING Towards the LHC Era

Jeremy Coles

Abstract The last 12 months have seen several advances in the GridPP contribution to the Worldwide Large hadron collider Computing Grid (WLCG) and the provision of over 15 million KSI2K hours of processing. This paper reviews the deployment and operations progress made in both the UK Tier-1 and Tier-2s. For the Tier-1 this includes steps taken to ensure successful implementation of CASTOR and the resolution of major issues faced with several disk procurements. For the Tier-2s the approach to storage management and the ongoing efforts being made to improve availability are described. 2007 is a critical year for WLCG and there is still someway to go in provision of an adequately resourced and stable service. The paper outlines outstanding issues and how GridPP plans to address them. Finally the status of GridPP in relation to the UK National Grid Service (NGS) and the provision of a single national infrastructure are mentioned.

Keywords Grid Computing · deployment · operations · GridPP

1 Resources

1.1 Context

The UK Particle Physics Computing Grid Project (GridPP) [1] is currently in its second stage. It was awarded £17M to build a Grid prototype from September 2001 to September 2004 and £15.9M to transform the prototype to a production Grid by September 2007.

At the time of writing, there are 19 UK Particle Physics Grid (GridPP) institutes that are providing resources to this production grid (which corresponds to 23% of

J. Coles (✉)

GridPP Production Manager, Science & Technology Facilities Council, RAL, Chilton, Oxfordshire OX11 0QX and Senior Research Associate, University of Cambridge, Cavendish Laboratory, JJ Thomson Avenue, Cambridge CB3 0HE, UK

e-mail: J.Coles@rl.ac.uk

S.C. Lin, E. Yen (eds.), *Grid Computing*,

Fig. 1 The geographical based grouping (*ellipses*) of GridPP institutes into WLCG Tier-2 centres. The London Tier-2 is separate from SouthGrid and contains the 5 sites found in the capital

the CPU resource capacity (or approximately 10,000 job slots) of the Enabling Grids for E-sciencE (EGEE) [2] project). The resources have primarily been purchased for physics exploitation of the data from the Large Hadron Collider experiments ATLAS, CMS and LHCb. There has been a steady growth in the resources since the end of 2004 and this paper presents the current status versus the Memorandum of Understanding commitments that the institutes signed with GridPP in 2004. The collaborating institutes are managed as one Tier-1 centre (based at the Rutherford Appleton Laboratory in Oxfordshire) and four Tier-2s whose formation is shown in Fig. 1.

1.2 Resources Deployed

A core consideration of any computing grid is the amount of resource deployed into it. CPU deployment in the second quarter of 2007 is shown in Fig. 2. As can be seen most sites are on target with several having deployed way in excess of their pledges.

Three histograms are shown for each site. The first represents the pledged disk in TB, the second the actual deployed from a snapshot in Q2 2007 and the third shows the disk actually being used by the LHC experiments at that snapshot time.

The picture for disk shown in Fig. 3 is less good though it is clear that some sites are playing a more significant role than others. However, what is also clear from these results is that even where a lot of disk has been deployed it is not being used.

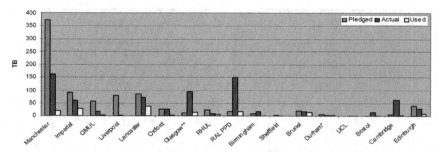

Fig. 2 Pledged and actual CPU resources in Q2 2007 at the GridPP Tier-2 sites

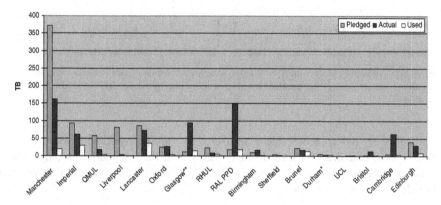

Fig. 3 Disk resources deployed across GridPP Tier-2 sites in Q2 2007

This underlies one of the concerns for sites and their need to balance efficient use against meeting pledges made on usage predictions.

While the amount of CPU and disk available is important, so to is their ratio. The ratio required by the experiments varies from 1:2 for ATLAS, through 1:4 for CMS to mainly CPU for LHCb. The current ratios across the sites vary enormously from less than 1 to more than 160! The majority of sites are in the region of 10 to 20.

This means that if and when the experiments start to use the resources as they project, the deployment of more disk is going to be critical at many of the sites.

1.3 Resource Stability

Alongside deploying resources to the Grid, another important consideration is the stability of the resources that are being provided. WLCG has relied in part on the monitoring and availability information being provided by the EGEE project. Grid-View [3] provides the graphical view of this data and provides historical information. Figure 4 shows the 2007 availability information for two of the Tier-2 sites. The significant thing to note is that the 95% targets that WLCG intends to set for site

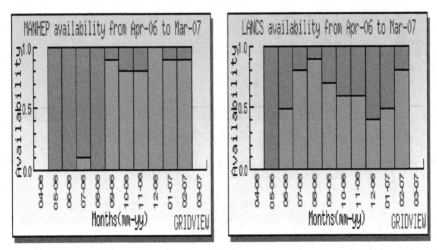

Fig. 4 Site availability plots from April 2006 to March 2007 for two GridPP Tier-2 sites. The left plot shows that achieving high availability, at least according to the ops VO SAM test results is possible

availability are indeed achievable as measured by the Site Availability Monitoring (SAM) tests. One draw back of this approach is that the tests currently only look at the operations (ops) Virtual Organisation (VO) results and do not correspond directly with user experience.

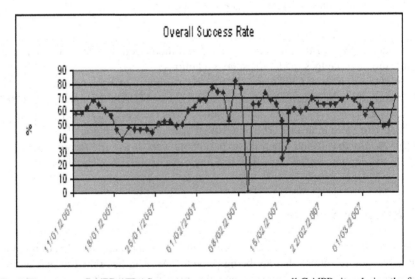

Fig. 5 The average GridPP ATLAS test success rates seen across all GridPP sites during the first months of 2007. There are a number of reasons the tests may fail, including site queues being full and the tests timing out (resource contention). The large dips correspond to failures in the testing framework and not many sites having problems simultaneously [4, 5]

Therefore, in addition to the SAM tests, GridPP elected at the start of 2007 to run user based tests under the ATLAS VO [6]. These tests first execute a precompiled Athena HelloWorld job, secondly attempt to build and run an Athena package and thirdly attempt to analyse some AOD data placed on the site Storage Element (SE). These jobs have provided sites invaluable information about where site configuration is letting user jobs down. By setting monthly increasing targets (using this information and that from SAM) good steps in performance improvement are being seen.

2 Activities

2.1 Networking

Site-to-site transfers are continuing to be run to exercise site networking ahead of more intensive experiment driven tests anticipated for later in the year or early 2008. GridPP has provided a monitoring framework called GridMon [7] that has become very useful in diagnosing site problems – see Fig. 6 for an example. GridMon relies on well defined hosts being deployed at each participating site. These hosts run regular tests between each other as defined in a site-matrix. The results are then logged centrally where they can be pulled via web-based queries.

2.2 Current Deployment Issues and Concerns

As the experiment job load has increased it has been noted that the information system has shown signs of scaling problems. One solution to this which has been discussed

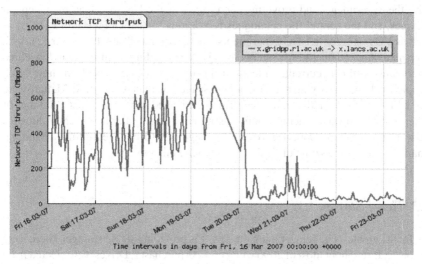

Fig. 6 An example of the information that GridMon provides to site administrators to help in the diagnosis of poor network performance

is finding better ways to deal with the information, much of which is static. Alongside this and other coding issues, there has of late been some renewed concern about the deployment of the middleware. A move last year to component based individual module updates has been beneficial to sites, but unfortunately an increasing number of releases have broken sites when picked up as auto-updates. As a consequence auto-updates are being turned off and keeping up with patches confusing to sites. Problems have also been seen in recent months with the desired configuration of sites as workarounds are used to compensate for the lack of truly VOMS aware middleware. Two cases in point were a recent attempt to rollout a job priorities mechanism and the use of Access Control Lists (ACLs) to provide required storage access for ATLAS.

On the fabric side new issues are also becoming apparent. Foremost amongst these is that the site administrators need to learn new skills to support the growing levels of resources at their sites. Improving site monitoring and the use of configuration management tools will be core topics in the year ahead. There is also scope for problems in setting up appropriate storage tokens and pools – the latter requiring careful thought as disk quotas can not be set (presently disks get full and SAM tests fail as a result). Other fabric issues are likely to arise as sites wrestle with an increasing number of cores (worker node disk space for example) and 64-bit.

3 UK Tier-1

3.1 Tier-1 Manpower and Duties

The GridPP Tier-1 has three main teams. These work in the areas of Grid Services, Fabric and Mass Storage (CASTOR). The grid services team is active in liasing with the experiments and providing such things as the UK workload management services, and the central file catalogues for various Virtual Organisations (VOs) as well as VO boxes for th LHC experiments where required. The fabric team deal with both hardware and operating system based issues including monitoring and machine interventions (this is currently a team of 6 people). On CASTOR, RAL now has 5 people working, to varying degrees, and these include management, SRM, hardware and LSF experts. In addition to these Tier-1 dedicated staff there exist a number of other staff employed in machine room operations (watching alarms and environment), networking, database support and overall management (driving recruitment, handling finances and dealing with political matters among other things).

3.2 Tier-1 Storage

By far the greatest challenge facing the Tier-1 is providing stable storage. There were problems throughout most of 2006 with new disk purchases. Drives were ejected from arrays under normal load. Many theories were put forward but it took the supplier to carry out physical tests at two sites to uncover that the problem was due to drive heads staying in one place for too long! This was fixed with a "return following reposition" firmware update. The disks are now all deployed or ready to be deployed.

CASTOR which is the mass storage system chosen by the site is still under development and as such has required intense effort to keep available. At the time of writing issues being faced include the garbage collection not always working, jobs getting submitted to the wrong servers, uneven file system filling within pools, disk-to-disk copies hanging. On the usability side there are concerns about unstable releases and the lack of administration tools provided with the release. Logging has also been inadequate and made problem resolution more difficult.

Even though there are many issues remaining, there have also been a number of successes. The computing challenges towards the end of 2006 saw good rates and the service was found to be more reliable than dCache. The disk1tape0 service has been implemented. Advertised bug-fix releases are expected to solve many of the problems mentioned above.

3.3 Tier-1 CPU Job Efficiencies

Over 2006 the Tier-1 tracked the efficiency with which supported VO jobs ran. A large variation was seen between VOs and across the months for a given VO. The results suggest that more work needs to be done on the experiments side to deal with, for example, errors that might be anticipated such as hanging gridftp connections which occur with certain batches of jobs. During 2006 the average CPU efficiencies were found to vary between 74% and 92% across the months, with individual VOs sustaining efficiencies at both high (above 95%) and low (below 10%) extremes.

4 Going Forward

GridPP has recently learnt that its proposal for GridPP3, to scale up and run the UK production grid beyond 2007 has been approved and funding of £25.9M to continue until April 2011 has been awarded.

4.1 Areas of Focus

There is a clear need to improve internal site monitoring (especially at the Tier-2 sites). Therefore, a core activity going forward will be integrating grid alarms with site fabric monitoring and ensuring that both are as automated as possible. In addition, to improve support across sites, GridPP will be encouraging greater cross-site working and cover. As users start to run analysis jobs more widely, there is also going to be a need for improved interaction between experiment users/representatives and the system administrators who run the sites.

It was noted that storage is behind CPU in terms of meeting pledged resource levels, but also that the ratios were being impacted as a result. GridPP management will be working with the Tier-2s to improve the CPU to disk ratios. In fact The Project Management Board has already initiated a series of Site Readiness Reviews whereby a management plus technical team will visit each site to assess their state ahead of further GridPP3 hardware money being allocated.

4.2 Other Work in the UK

In addition to GridPP, the UK also has a National Grid Service (NGS) which serves communities like eMinerals and BioInformatics. Longer term it is hoped that the UK will have one e-Infrastructure providing common access, tools and information with support being provided by a National Grid Initative (NGI). Ahead of this it is already apparent that much work needs to be done on policies and demonstrating increased job based interoperability. The NGS currently runs a heterogeneous hardware and middleware set with computation services based on Globus Toolkit 2 and Data Services using Oracle and Storage Resource Brokers (SRBs). A gLite-WMS was deployed in February 2007 and further EGEE components are expected to be deployed over the coming months. On the operational side there is already overlap in areas such as helpdesk support and technical strategy.

References

1. GridPP collaboration: GridPP – development of the UK computing Grid for particle physics. J. Phys. G: Nucl. Part. Phys. 32 (2006) N1–N20.
2. See http://www.eu-egee.org/
3. For current information visit http://gridview.cern.ch/GRIDVIEW/
4. http://pprc.qmul.ac.uk/~lloyd/gridpp/atest.html
5. http://pprc.qmul.ac.uk/~lloyd/gridpp/atest_info.html
6. http://hepwww.ph.qmul.ac.uk/~lloyd/gridpp/atest.html
7. http://gridmon3.dl.ac.uk/gridmon/graph.html

MediGRID – Grid Computing For Medicine and Life Sciences

Anette Weisbecker, Jürgen Falkner, and Otto Rienhoff

Abstract MediGRID has established a grid infrastructure for medical and bioinformatical research. It enhances interdisciplinary and widely location-independent collaboration of researchers by providing grid services in a controlled e-Science platform which is continually available, economically calculable and secure. As part of the German e-Science initiative D-Grid MediGRID provides access to the available D-Grid resources by the MediGRID portal. This gives an easy, secure and transparent access to a broad spectrum of applications for bioinformatics, medical image processing and clinical research. The application uses the MediGRID middleware which realizes a service oriented architecture. Services for the management of data, workflows, and resources and for enhanced security are provided. The advantages of using grid computing for medical and life sciences applications are the reduction of processing times, world-wide usage for a broad community of users and access to distributed information sources of academic and clinic providers.

1 Introduction

1.1 Requirements from Medical Research and Health Care

Grid technology provides the opportunity to fulfil the increasing requirements of medical research and health care on information technology (IT). In health care the documentation needs grow due to DRGs (Diagnoses Related Groups). The progress in genome research makes personalised medicine possible. Electronic health records for the management of the patient data disseminate quickly. Most of the medical data e.g. data vital signs or images for diagnosis are available in digital form and should be used by different institutions. Medical databases are being created e.g. for oncology and should be accessible worldwide for authorized persons. These require an IT infrastructure which supports the secure collaboration between institutions.

A. Weisbecker (✉)
Fraunhofer Institute for Industrial Engineering, Nobelstr. 12, 70569 Stuttgart, Germany
e-mail: anette.weisbecker@iao.fraunhofer.de

S.C. Lin, E. Yen (eds.), *Grid Computing*,
© Springer Science+Business Media, LLC 2009

Medical and life science research require the management of a great amount of data and high performance processing power for applications like genome sequencing, medical image processing and drug discovery.

1.2 Healthgrids

The usage of grid computing in health care and medical research leads to healthgrids, which enables the shared usage of data and applications under consideration of security and privacy [17]. Furthermore, grids support collaborative work between different organisations. Healthgrids benefit from the world wide research work in Grid Computing, for example from EGEE (Enabling Grids for E-sciencE), D-Grid (German Grid Initiative). Medical and life sciences research uses Grids to manage, analyse and evaluate exponentially growing volume of data, to reduce compute time and to achieve a higher accuracy in the results e.g. @neurIST (Integrated Biomedical Informatics for the Management of Cerebral Aneurysms) [3], ACGT (Advancing Clinico-Genomic Trials) [3], WISDOM (Initiative for grid-enabled drug discovery against neglected and emergent diseases) [9], health-e-child (an integrated health care platform for European paediatrics) [3]. For health care grids support information management and diagnostic, examples in the United States of America are caBIG (Cancer Biomedical Informatics Grids) [2] or I2B2 (Informatics for Integrating Biology and the Bedside) [6]. Furthermore grids are used to support the cooperative work in research and for education. Examples are networks like BIRN (Biomedical Informatics Research Network) [24] and EMBRACE (European Network of Excellence: A European Model for Bioinformatics Research and Community Education) [4]. The European Healthgrid [11] has established an e-health Wiki for collecting and discussing information about Grid Computing in e-health and tries to build up a knowledge base for e-health topics. The SHARE project develops a roadmap for the adoption of healthgrids in the European Union. One focus of the project is to examine the legal issues which are relevant for the usage of grid technologies in the health sector [23].

For many reasons the adoption of grid computing for health care and medical research is still in its infancy. The requirements on data protection and privacy are very high especially for data like patient data, data from biosamples, genome data [19]. The data basis is relatively inhomogeneous as the standardization of data formats (e.g. in medical imaging or clinical studies) is so far not very advanced. There is also a lack of semantic interoperability. The user group is very heterogeneous e.g. doctors from different fields, researchers for medicine or bioinformatics, assistant medical technicians. Different tasks should also be supported by the grid infrastructure. All these users have in common that they are no grid or computer experts. They expect a user friendly and task appropriate user interface in order to perform their tasks efficiently on the basis of a grid. Hiding the complexity of the grid infrastructure is therefore a basic requirement for acceptance.

2 MediGRID – Resources for Medicine and Life Science

2.1 MediGRID Software Architecture

MediGRID has established a grid infrastructure for medical and bioinformatical research. The MediGRID project is funded by the German federal ministry of education and research under the grant number 01AK803A-H. As part of the German e-Science initiative D-Grid MediGRID gains access to the available D-Grid resources by the MediGRID portal. MediGRID has a sevice oriented software architecture (Fig. 1).

The MediGRID infrastructure is based on a grid middleware layer, which uses Globus 4. This grid middleware ensures, that the resources can communicate with each other. Based on this middleware layer, the MediGRID specific services for virtualisation are implemented. Virtualisation means that the construction of the infrastructure is hidden from the user. Thus the user is not occupied with questions like on which resource the data is stored or which node is appropriate to run the application. Virtualisation comprises of compute and data resource virtualization. Compute resource virtualization means that the user shall not need to pick the hardware and storage resources. Applications and required data sources are distributed automatically to the optimal execution location. The results are automatically transferred back to the user.

Data resource virtualization gives the user access to the data without knowing where it is located. Therefore, a unified identifier is necessary that does not change in the process of migration within the grid in order to make it easier to address,

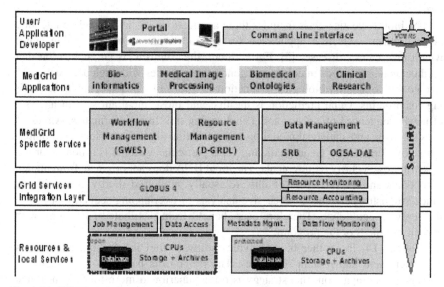

Fig. 1 MediGRID - service oriented software architecture

find and retrieve the data. For data management the Storage Resource Broker (SRB) and for data base management OGSA-DAI (Open Grid Service Architecture - Data Access and Integration) are used.

The information needed for the virtualisation is provided by the metadata management. It allows the description of the resources and their characteristics. For this description a XML based language D-GRDL (D-Grid Resource Description Language) is used. The virtualisation requires a workflow execution system which provides an automatic resolution of dependencies between applications and hardware. For this purpose the Grid Workflow Execution Service (GWES) is used [1]. It allows the definition and the description of the workflows based on Petri nets. Petri nets are well established as a model for the analysis and the design of complex discrete systems. Based on the resource description the required resources for the workflow execution are selected. At the same time the availability and capacity of the resource will be considered. The main entry point to MediGRID is a web-based portal, which allows a world wide access to the resources and application via a web browser.

2.2 *MediGRID Applications*

The medical and life sciences applications in MediGRID are grouped in classes. These classes include the areas bioinformatics, medical image processing, clinic research and ontologies [7, 10, 12, 22]. Each class consists of different applications. Additional application can be added in order to make use of the grid infrastructure and can be accessed through the portal. Currently the following applications are available.

The bioinformatics class includes three applications. A SNP (single nucleotide polymorphism) selection application for the identification of susceptible genes which may causes diseases [7]. Furthermore, the Augustus is an application that predicts gene structures in eukaryotic genomic sequences with high accuracy [22]. The goal is to identify biologically functional regions of a genome, e.g. genes coding for proteins. Gene prediction is the first and most important step in analysis of newly sequenced organisms and a challenging task in bioinformatics. Augustus uses sophisticated statistical modeling and prediction algorithms which are computationally demanding. Gene prediction for a particular genome is a non-recurrent task with low security requirements. The input DNA does not originate from human individuals and the prediction results are usually publicised shortly after analysis. Since Augustus performs a successive analysis of overlapping sequence sections, it is easy to parallelize. Therefore users benefit from distributed computing with several instances of the program.

Dialign [14] is another bioinformatics software tool for multiple alignments of nucleic acid and protein sequences. The program is based on local segment-by-segment comparison; this strategy is often superior to more traditional global alignment methods, in particular if distantly related sequences share only local homologies. However, since the original program has been slower than most global alignment methods, its applicability was limited to data sets of moderate size. Within the MediGRID portal a parallelized version of the software is used to speed up the computationally expensive procedure. In that way distributed computing allows the user to obtain high-quality alignments of bigger databases and longer sequences.

The bioinformatics applications benefit from the parallelisation in the grid. Thus more resources can be used to process larger amounts of data and to shorten the processing time.

The class of medical image processing includes application for statistical analysis of functional brain images, virtual vascular surgery and computer-aided diagnosis of prostate cancer.

The statistical analysis of functional brain images based on Magnetic Resonance Tomography (MRT) is used for preoperative planning.

The virtual vascular surgery application helps to calculate and present the animated 3D blood flow field in the brain vessels, which will be used to anticipate the pressure on the walls of the vessels in order to predict a bleeding risk (Fig. 2).

3D-Ultrasound prostate imaging application provides image processing tools for 3D reconstruction of biopsy (tissue probe) locations taken under transrectal

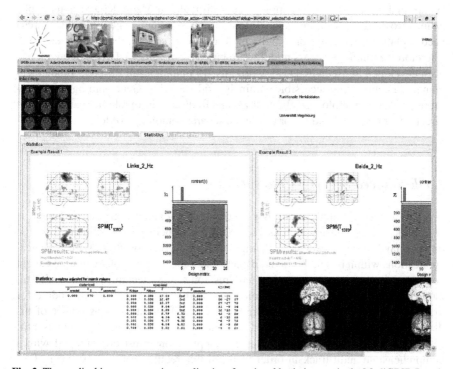

Fig. 2 The medical image processing application: functional brain images in the MediGRID Portal

ultrasound guidance for prostate cancer diagnosis. The tools encompass the detection (segmentation) of the biopsy needle on a sequence of 2D biplane 15 transrectal ultrasound images and the location (registration) of the 2D images within a prior taken 3D prostatic volume image. Even though only anonymized data is processed during the development phase of the MediGRID, all available grid security is already enabled within the application.

The usage of the grid reduces the processing time for the medical image processing applications significantly. This leads to shorter response times in diagnostics. Furthermore the applications can be used by a large number of users from different locations e.g. different hospitals.

The clinical research has two applications. One application provides algorithms for phase synchronization transitions in the human cardio respiratory system. The second application uses MediGRID for the sleep medicine. This application gathers recordings of biological signals of patients throughout the night (polysomnographic recordings) and provides algorithms for processing and analyzing the data. The main advantage of grid computing for the clinical research is the secure and fast processing of large amounts of data.

Ontologies are a key concept to support the understanding and exchange of information, especially in the life sciences. The rapid increase in the number of available ontologies in the life sciences with heterogeneous source formats and syntax make a uniform and simple access difficult. In MediGRID various applications from all application classes (bioinformatics, imaging and clinical research) need a platform for a uniform and simple ontology accessibility within the grid. Therefore an ontology access middleware based on the OGSA-DAI framework has been developed in MediGRID [8]. Currently, 15 ontologies of different biomedical domains are uniformly accessible within the grid, including GeneOntology NCIThesaurus, SequenceOntology, CellOntology and RadLex. The ontologies can be access directly from the applications or through a separate ontology portlet.

2.3 Enhanced Security Concept

The use of medical applications with personrelated data in a grid environment is constrained to certain restrictions [13, 20]. The principles of confidentiality and privacy have to be respected at all times within a grid workflow. While medical applications within hospitals still take place under the umbrella of the doctor-patient confidentiality, research computing requires some more technical effort [15, 16]. Authentication via certificates and role based authorization should be standard for grid security, while gridmap files are still in use. The patient – as owner of his data – has the right to be informed why, where and how long his data is processed and stored. Therefore medical grid applications must be equipped with a comprehensible audit track in order to fulfill this requirement (a-posteriori). Furthermore it has to be guaranteed to the patient, that his data will only be stored and processed in a trustworthy environment (Tracking, a-priori). This is a challenge in grid computing, as every grid node has to be assessed concerning the trustworthiness using trust metrics. The data itself is mostly represented as database content or as files. Current grid security systems allow to control access on file level or on database entry level. Concerning structured medical documents this is not sufficient, as a fine granular access control is needed in order to grant access to certain parts of a document only.

2.4 MediGRID Portal

The MediGRID applications are available through a portal. The portal is implemented with the GridSphere Portal Framework. For each application a portlet is prepared, which allows the users to access the applications without any previous knowledge about the architecture of MediGRID (Fig. 2). The portlets have been developed for the GridSphere Portal Framework and are compliant with to the JSR168 standard. The portal allows a worldwide, secure access to the resources and applications via a web browser [5]. In order to ensure a secure grid usage, a PKI (Public Key Infrastructure) based authentication and authorization is used.

The users log on to the portal with PKI certificates. Using the MyProxy upload tool (MPU) lifetime-restricted credentials are generated for the first medical grid applications (Fig. 3). All actions in the portal are subjected to a strict usage policy, which reflects the paramount legal basis for medical grid applications.

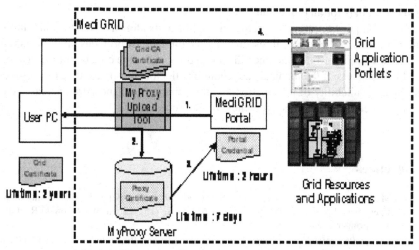

1. Login at the portal and download the MPU tools via java webstart
2. Creation of a proxy certificate and Upload on the MyProxy Server
3. Creation of Credentials via the MediGRID portal
4. Usage of portal applications, which need credentials

Fig. 3 Certificate based usage of MediGRID over the portal

By using PKI certificates the user identity can be proves reliably and the strong security requirements of the medical community can be ensured. The user management is based on a role-based virtual organisation management. It uses the Virtual Organisations Management and Registry Service (VOMRS) provided by D-Grid.

The portal was developed according to the method of User Centered Design (UCD) (ISO 1999) and the Portal Analysis and Design Method (PADEM) [21]. UCD always keeps the requirements of the users in the centre of attention and is based on the design of interaction between users and the system referred to as interaction design. Its basic approach is to model a system from the user's perspective and to focus on the usability of the software system with which the user interacts.

3 Discussion and Conclusion

The MediGRID project set up an enhanced grid infrastructure for medical research and health care. It shows the advantages of grid computing for different application classes. These advantages of grid computing in medicine and life science are a substantial reduction of overall processing times and an easy-to-use access to applications together with a transparent access to various distributed information sources of academic and clinical providers. grid computing supports patient centric integration of information across different institutions and health sectors under consideration of data protection and privacy [18]. It enables the development of new medical applications and services. The challenge is to define and provided grid services and business models for an on-demand usage.

Grid computing offers a promising opportunity for the support of future collaborative work in medical research and health care. It provides an information technology basis for integrated health care and enhances the collaboration between the different parts of the medical care chain like doctors, hospitals, care centres etc. The better availability of information and the enhanced collaboration increases the quality in health care and the efficiency of the processes.

References

1. Alt M., Hoheisel A., Pohl H.-W., Gorlatch S. (2006). A grid workflow language using high-level petri nets. In PPAM2005, volume 3911 of LNCS, 715–722, ed. Wyrzykowski R. et al., Berlin: Springer 2006
2. Beck R. (2006). caBIG^{TM}: Concept, Cachet, or Cornerstone? Proceedings American Medical Informatics Association Annual Symposium, Washington, 11.-15.11.2006
3. Blanquer I., Breton V., Hernandez Y., Legree Y., Olive M., Solomonides T. (2006). SHARE: Technology Baseline Report. FP6-2005-IST-027694 SHARE-D3.2_final.doc 2006
4. Embrace (2007). http://www.embracegrid.info. Accessed December 2007
5. Falkner J., Weisbecker A. (2006). Integration of Applications in MediGRID. Integration of Applications in MediGRID. In: Cracow 2006 Grid Workshop Proceedings, eds. Bubak M., Turala M., Wiatr K, 511–518. Krakow: Academic Computer Centre Cyfronet AGH

6. Goryachev S. (2006). A Suite Of Natural Language Processing Tools Developed for the I2b2 Project. Proceedings American Medical Informatics Association Annual Symposium, Washington, 11.-15.11.2006

7. Hampe J., Franke F., Rosenstiel P., Till A., Teuber M., Huse K., Albrecht M., Häsler R., Sipos B., Mayr G., De La Vega FM., Briggs J., Günther S., Prescott NJ., Onnie CM., Fölsch UR., Lengauer T., Platzer M., Mathew CG., Krawczak M., Schreiber S. (2007). A genome-wide association scan of non-synonymous SNPs identifies a susceptibility variant for Crohn disease in the autophagy-related 16-like (ATG16L1) gene. Nat. Genet. in press.

8. Hartung, M., Rahm, E. (2007). A grid middleware for ontology access. Presentation. German e-science Conference, 02–04 May 2007, Baden-Baden

9. Hofmann M. (2007). Relevance for Pharma Research. Special Interest Session "Grid for Health", e-Health Week Berlin, 18 April 2007, http://www.medigrid.de ISO 13407 (1999). Human-centred design processes for interactive systems. International Standardization Organisation

10. Kottha S., Peter K., Steinke T., Bart J., Falkner J., Weisbecker A., Viezens, F., Mohammed Y., Sax U., Hoheisel A., Ernst T., Sommerfeld D., Krefting D., Vossberg M. (2007). Medical Image Processing in MediGRID. German e-science Conference, 02–04 May 2007, Baden-Baden

11. Legree Y. (2007). EU-HealthGrid Initiative – Current International State of the Art. Spec ial Interest Session "Grid for Health", e-Health Week Berlin, 18 April 2007, http://www.medigrid.de

12. Luchtmann M., Baecke S., Lützkendorf R., Naji L., Bernarding J. (2006). Accelerated fMRI data analysis using parallelized SPM on a cluster architecture. Submitted to 13th Annual Meeting of the Organization for Human Brain Mapping.

13. Mohammed, Y., Viezens, F., Sax, U., Rienhoff, O. (2006). Rechtliche Aspekte bei Grid-Computing in der Medizin. Health Academy, 2:235–245

14. Morgenstern, B., Prohaska, S.J., Pöhler, D., Stadler, P.F. (2006). Multiple sequence alignment with user-defined anchor points. Algorithms for Molecular Biology 1, 6.

15. Pommerening K., Reng M.(2004). Secondary use of the ehr via pseudonymisation. Stud Health Technol Inform., 103:441–6

16. Pommerening, K. et al. (2005). Pseudonymization in medical research - the generic data protection concept of the TMF. GMS Medizinische Informatik, Biometrie und Epidemiologie, 3:1

17. Rienhoff O. (2000). A legal framework for security in European health care telematics. Studies in health technology and informatics, v. 74. Amsterdam, Washington: ISO Press

18. Sax U., Weisbecker A., et al. (2007). Auf dem Weg zur individualisierten Medizin - Grid-basierte Services für die EPA der Zukunft. Telemed Conference 17 April 2007, Berlin

19. Sax U. (2006). Stand der generischen Datenschutz-Konzepte sowie deren technischen Realisierungen in biomedizinischen Grids. In Grid-Computing in der biomedizinischen Forschung, eds. Sax U, Mohammed Y, Viezens F, Rienhoff O.: Datenschutz und Datensicherheit, 38–43. München: Urban und Vogel

20. Sax U. et al. (2006). Medigrid - medical grid computing. In EGEE'06 - Capitalising on e-infrastructures

21. Spath D, Hinderer H. (Eds.) (2005). Marketreview Portal Software. In German. Stuttgart, Fraunhofer IRB

22. Stanke M., Keller O., Gunduz I., Hayes A., Waack S., Morgenstern B. (2006). AUGUSTUS: ab initio prediction of alternative transcripts. Nucleic Acids Res.34, W435–W439

23. Wilson P., Andoulis I., Solomonides T., Herveg J., Breton V. (2006). Data Protection and Confidentiality in Healthgrids: The SHARE Project – A Framework for Developing a Roadmap for the Adoption of Grid Technology in Healthcare. In Grid-Computing in der biomedizinischen Forschung, eds. Sax U, Mohammed Y, Viezens F, Rienhoff O.: Datenschutz und Datensicherheit, 16–24. München: Urban und Vogel

24. BIRN project (2007). http://www.nbirn.net/. Accessed December 2007

Porting Biological Applications in Grid: An Experience within the EUChinaGRID Framework

Giuseppe La Rocca[1], Giovanni Minervini[1], Giuseppe Evangelista,
Pier Luigi Luisi, and Fabio Polticelli

Abstract The number of natural protein sequences is infinitely small as compared to the number of proteins theoretically possible. Thus, a huge number of protein sequences, defined as "never born proteins" or NBPs, have never been observed in nature. The study of the structural and functional properties of NBPs represents a way to improve our knowledge on the fundamental properties that make existing protein sequences so unique. Protein structure prediction tools combined with the use of large computing resources allow to tackle this problem. The study of NBPs requires the generation of a large library of non-natural protein sequences (105–107) and the prediction of their three-dimensional structure. On a single CPU it would require years to predict the structure of such a library of protein sequences. However, this is an embarrassingly parallel problem in which the same computation must be repeated several times and the use of grid infrastructures makes feasible to approach this problem in an acceptable time frame. Here we describe the set up of a simulation environment within the EUChinaGRID [1] infrastructure that allows non expert users to exploit grid resources for large-scale proteins structure prediction.

Keywords Proteins · structure prediction · EUChinaGRID

1 Introduction

Trivial calculations show that the number of natural proteins is an infinitesimal fraction of all the theoretically possible protein sequences. In fact approx. 300,000 natural protein sequences are known so far, many of which evolutionary related, while, considering random proteins of just 100 amino acids in length, with the 20 natural amino acids it is possible to obtain 100^{20} chemically and structurally different proteins. This leads to the consideration that there is an enormous number of protein sequences which have never been exploited by nature. We named these

---

[1] These two authors contributed equally to the present work

G.L. Rocca (✉)
INFN Catania, 95123 Catania, Italy
Department of Biology, University Roma Tre, 00146 Rome, Italy

S.C. Lin, E. Yen (eds.), *Grid Computing*,
© Springer Science+Business Media, LLC 2009

"never born proteins" or NBPs. A fundamental question in this regard is if the ensemble of natural proteins possesses particular properties in terms for example of particular thermodynamic, kinetic or functional properties. The key feature of natural proteins is their ability to form a stable and well defined three-dimensional structure from which their specific biological function derives. Thus, the structural study of NBPs can be useful to understand if natural protein sequences were selected during molecular evolution because of their peculiar properties or if they are just the product of contingency. It is not feasible to approach this problem experimentally, as this would require the structural characterization of an enormous number of random proteins. Thus we chose to tackle this problem using a computational approach. We generated a large number of random protein sequences (approx. 10^5) without any homology with natural proteins and studied their structural properties using the *abinitio* protein structure prediction software, Rosetta *abinitio* [2]. From a computational viewpoint this is a highly demanding problem in that on a single CPU it would require years to predict the structure of such a large library of protein sequences. On the other hand, this is an embarrassingly parallel problem in which the same computation (prediction of the three-dimensional structure of a protein) must be repeated many times (for a large number of proteins). Grid infrastructures are one of the best tools to approach these problems as a large number of computing resources can be used to execute relatively simple calculations. Here we describe the porting of the Rosetta *abinitio* protein structure prediction software in the EUChinaGRID Infrastructure and the development of a user friendly job submission environment within the GENIUS Grid Portal [3].

2 Methods

2.1 Generation of the Random NBPs Sequences Library

To generate the NBPs sequences library an utility has been developed, called RandomBlast, which generates random amino acid sequences and checks that sequences have no significant similarity to known natural proteins. RandomBlast consists of two main modules: a pseudo random sequence generation module and a Blast software interface module. The first module uses the Mersenne Twister 1997 pseudo-random number generation algorithm [4] to generate pseudo-random numbers between 0 and 19. A free implementation of this algorithm, available in C programming language from Matsumoto and Nishimura [5], was used in RandomBlast. Random numbers are then translated in single character amino acid code using a simple "random number-amino acid type" conversion table. Single amino acids are then concatenated to reach the sequence length specified by the user in input (usually 70). Each sequence generated is then given in input to the second RandomBlast module, an interface to the Blast blastall program [6] which checks if similar sequences are already present in the database of natural proteins. If this is the case the sequence is rejected by RandomBlast. The RandomBlast utility has been written in C programming language and it's available, upon request to the authors, for Windows operating systems.

2.2 Rosetta Abinitio Method Details

Rosetta *abinitio* [2] is an *abinitio* protein structure prediction software based on the assumption that in a polypeptide chain local interactions influence the conformation of sequence segments, while global interactions determine the actual, energetically favourable, three-dimensional structure compatible with the local interactions. For a each query sequence, Rosetta derives the local sequence-structure relationships from known protein structures stored in the Protein Data Bank [7] extracting the distribution of conformations adopted by short sequence segments. The set of conformations is then taken as an approximation of the distribution adopted by the query sequence segments during the folding process. Rosetta workflow can be divided into two phases:

Input generation – The query sequence is divided in fragments and the software extracts from the Protein Data Bank the distribution of three-dimensional structures adopted by these fragments, based on their specific sequence. The generated fragments data base contains all the possible local structures adopted by each fragment of the entire sequence. The procedure for input generation requires the output generated by the auxiliary programs Blast [6] and PSIPRED [8] in addition to the access to non redundant NCBI protein sequence database [9]. However, this procedure is not computationally expensive (a few minutes of CPU time on a Pentium IV 3,2 GHz). Thus the fragments database is generated locally with a script that automatizes the procedure for a large dataset of query sequences. About 500 input datasets are currently generated in one week with this procedure.

Abinitio protein structure prediction – For each query sequence, Rosetta assembles the sets of fragments in a high number of different combinations using a Monte Carlo procedure. The resulting protein structures are subjected to an energy minimization procedure using a semi-empirical force field in which the principal non-local interactions considered are hydrophobic and electrostatic interactions, hydrogen bonds and excluded volume. The structures which are compatible with both local biases and non-local interactions are then ranked on the basis of the total calculated energy. Rosetta *abinitio* has been deployed on the EUChinaGrid infrastructure and a user friendly job submission environment environment has been developed within the GENIUS Grid Portal [3], allowing non grid-expert users to run large-scale protein structure prediction.

3 Results

A single Rosetta *abinitio* run consists of two different phases. First an initial model of the protein structure is generated using the fragment libraries and the PSIPRED secondary structure prediction. Then the initial model is used as input for a second Rosetta run in which it is stereochemically idealized. A shell script registers the program executable (pFold.lnx) and the input files (fragment libraries and secondary structure prediction file) on the LFC File Catalog, calls the Rosetta *abinitio* executable and proceeds with workflow execution. A JDL file was created to run Rosetta *abinitio* on a Grid environment.

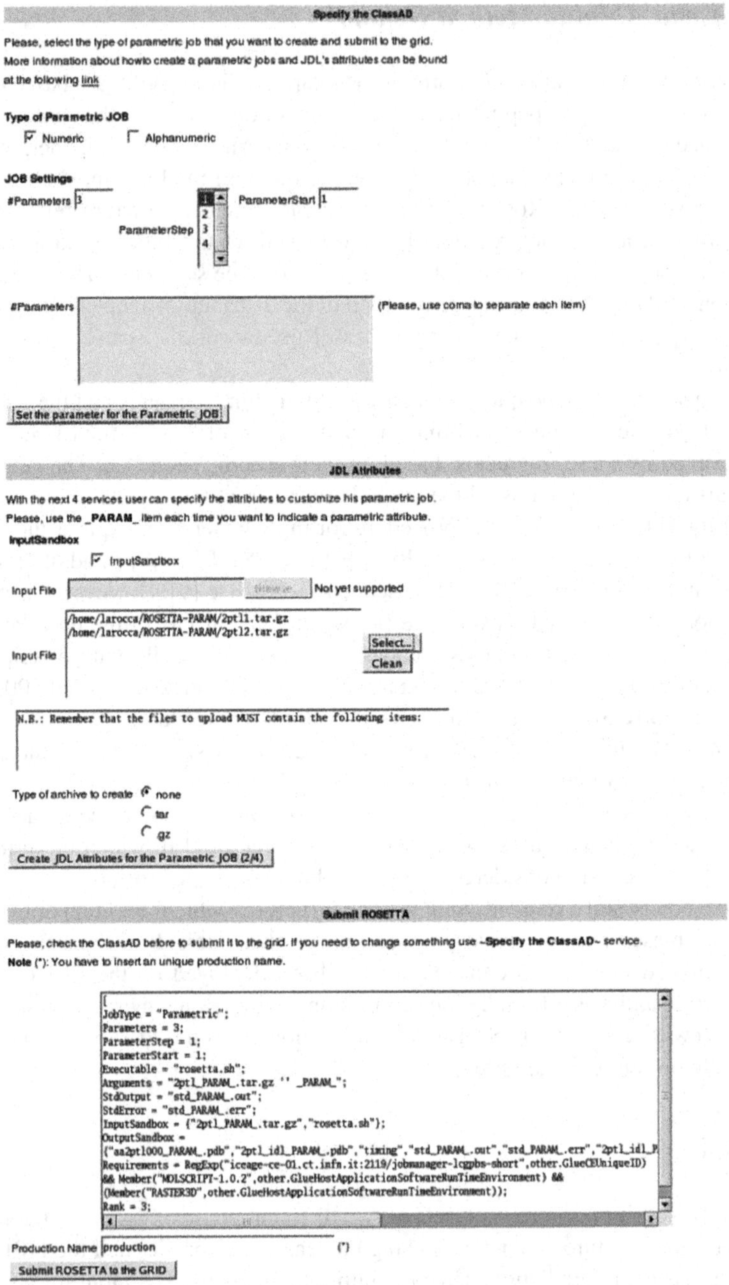

Specify the ClassAD

Please, select the type of parametric job that you want to create and submit to the grid.
More information about how to create a parametric jobs and JDL's attributes can be found
at the following link

Type of Parametric JOB
☑ Numeric   ☐ Alphanumeric

JOB Settings
#Parameters 3   ParameterStart 1

ParameterStep 3

#Parameters   (Please, use coma to separate each item)

Set the parameter for the Parametric JOB

JDL Attributes

With the next 4 services user can specify the attributes to customize his parametric job.
Please, use the _PARAM_ item each time you want to indicate a parametric attribute.

InputSandbox
☑ InputSandbox

Input File   Remove   Not yet supported

/home/larocca/ROSETTA-PARAM/2ptl1.tar.gz
/home/larocca/ROSETTA-PARAM/2ptl2.tar.gz

Input File   Select...
                  Clean

N.B.: Remember that the files to upload MUST contain the following items:

Type of archive to create ⦿ none
                           ○ tar
                           ○ gz

Create JDL Attributes for the Parametric JOB (2/4)

Submit ROSETTA

Please, check the ClassAD before to submit it to the grid. If you need to change something use ~Specify the ClassAD~ service.
Note (*): You have to insert an unique production name.

```
[
JobType = "Parametric";
Parameters = 3;
ParameterStep = 1;
ParameterStart = 1;
Executable = "rosetta.sh";
Arguments = "2ptl_PARAM_.tar.gz '' _PARAM_";
StdOutput = "std_PARAM_.out";
StdError = "std_PARAM_.err";
InputSandbox = {"2ptl_PARAM_.tar.gz","rosetta.sh"};
OutputSandbox =
{"aa2ptl000_PARAM_.pdb","2ptl_id1_PARAM_.pdb","timing","std_PARAM_.out","std_PARAM_.err","2ptl_id1_P
Requirements = RegExp("iceage-ce-01.ct.infn.it:2119/jobmanager-lcgpbs-short",other.GlueCEUniqueID)
&& Member("MOLSCRIPT-1.0.2",other.GlueHostApplicationSoftwareRunTimeEnvironment) &&
(Member("RASTER3D",other.GlueHostApplicationSoftwareRunTimeEnvironment));
Rank = 3;
```

Production Name production   (*)
Submit ROSETTA to the GRID

Fig. 1 Screenshots of the GENIUS grid portal showing services for the specification of the number of NBPs structure predictions to run (*top panel*), of the input and output files (*middle panel*), and for the inspection of the parametric JDL file (*bottom panel*)

A key issue for the exploitation of the Grid paradigm is to overcome the difficulty in using the Grid middleware by users who are not familiar with it. In our case, to achieve this goal and allow non grid trained biologists to run the software, Rosetta *abinitio* application has been integrated on the GENIUS (Grid Enabled web eNvironment for site Independent User job Submission) Grid Portal. Using GENIUS portal, non-expert users can access the grid, run Rosetta *abinitio* jobs and monitor their progress using a conventional web browser, with little or no knowledge of the gLite middleware. In fact, the complexity of the underlying grid Infrastructure is completely hidden to the end user. In addition, given the huge number of NBP structures to be predicted, an automatic procedure for the generation of parametric JDL files has been set up within the GENIUS Portal. Screenshots of the GENIUS grid portal showing services for the specification of the number of Rosetta *abinitio* jobs to run, of the input and output files, and for the inspection of the parametric JDL file created are shown in Fig. 1.

A first data challenge has been successful submitted to the EUChinaGRID infrastructure with a total of approx. 10,000 submitted jobs and a performance[2] (total submitted jobs/total aborted jobs) of 10,3.

Acknowledgments This work has been supported by a European Commission grant to the project "EUChinaGRID: Interconnection and Interoperability of grids between Europe and China" (contract number: 026634).

References

1. The EUChinaGRID project, http://www.euchinagrid.org
2. Rohl, C.A., Strauss, C.E., Misura, K.M., Baker, D.: Protein structure prediction using Rosetta. Methods Enzymol. 383, 66–93 (2004)
3. GENIUS Grid Portal, https://genius.ct.infn.it/
4. Matsumoto, M., Nishimura, T.: Mersenne Twister: A 623-dimensionally equidistributed uniform pseudo-random number generator. ACM Transactions on Modeling and Computer Simulation 8, 3–30 (1998)
5. Source code for MT19937 available at the URL: http://www.math.sci.hiroshima-u.ac.jp/~m-mat/MT/emt.html
6. Altschul, S.F., Gish, W., Miller, W., Myers, E.W., Lipman, D.J.: Basic local alignment search tool. J. Mol. Biol. 215, 403–410 (1990)
7. Berman, H.M., Westbrook, J., Feng, Z., Gilliland, G., Bhat, T.N., Weissig, H., Shindyalov, I.N., Bourne, P.E.: The Protein Data Bank. Nucleic Acids Res. 28, 235–242 (2000)
8. McGuffin, L.J., Bryson, K., Jones, D.T.: The PSIPRED protein structure prediction server. Bioinformatics 16, 404–405 (2000)
9. National Center for Biotechnology Information, http://www.ncbi.nlm.nih.gov

---

[2] Performance evaluated as by the 24th. of October 2007.

Grid Computing at Peking University in EUChinaGRID Project

Weibin Gong, Sijin Qian, Bin Xia, and Shulei Zhu

Abstract Grid computing promotes the sharing of massive computer resources, so that many applications can be greatly benefited from this technology to proceed to the level which was unreachable in the past. Peking University (PKU) is one of 10 partners in the EUChinaGRID project funded by European Commission. In the scope of this project, the BEIJING-PKU site (based on the middleware gLite of European grid project EGEE) in the EUChinaGRID infrastructure has been established and with it some promising results of grid application (on biological and experimental high energy physics researches) have been obtained by two subgroups (Biology and Physics groups) of PKU respectively. This article briefly introduces the EUChinaGRID project, the PKU group in the project, the BEIJING-PKU grid site and the application result via this grid site to access the global grid system.

Keywords EGEE · LCG · gLite3 · EUChinaGRID · protein structure

1 Introduction

The EUChinaGRID project has been funded by European Commission under the 6th Framework Programme (FP6) for Research and Technological Development. It aims on extending the European GRID infrastructure for e-Science to China and on strengthening the collaboration between China and Europe in computing grid field [1]. It is also to foster the creation of an intercontinental e-Science community by training people and supporting the existing and new grid applications.

Peking University (PKU) has been ranked as one of the top universities for many decades in China. It is one of 10 partners in the EUChinaGRID project. PKU group is consists of two subgroups, one is the biology group led by Prof. Bin Xia, another is the High Energy Physics (HEP) group led by Prof. Sijin Qian. Among 5 Working Packages (WPs) of EUChinaGRID project, PKU group participated in WP3 (pilot

S. Qian (✉)
Peking University, Beijing, China
e-mail: sijin.qian@cern.ch

S.C. Lin, E. Yen (eds.), *Grid Computing*,
© Springer Science+Business Media, LLC 2009

73

infrastructure operational support), WP4 (grid application) and WP5 (dissemination). Within the scope of WP3, a grid site (with the name of BEIJING-PKU) has been established since the beginning of 2007. PKU group's activities in WP4 include the biology and HEP applications. We have heavily engaged in the dissemination work in WP5, including to host a grid user tutorial at PKU in November of 2006.

In this paper, Section 2 is to briefly describe the EUChinaGRID project; Section 3 is to explain the status of grid site BEIJING-PKU and some results from the HEP application; Section 4 shows the biology application by PKU group; the summary is given in Section 5.

2 Grid Computing and EUChinaGRID Project

Grid computing is an evolution of related development in information technology, such as p2p (Peer to Peer), distributed computing and so on. It shares many common grounds with these technologies and works as a combination to climb to a level which the individual precedent technology could not reach. Grid computing has many features such as distributed, dynamical, diversity, self-comparability, autonomic and multiple management, etc. Therefore, Ian Foster "defined" the grid computing as "Flexible, secure, coordinated resource sharing among dynamic collections of individuals, institutions and resources (i.e. "Virtual Organizations", VO) [2]. Here the resource includes computers, data storages, databases, sensors, networks and software, etc. A "VO" can be conceived as a group of people (and resources) belonging to the same or different real organizations that want to share common resources in order to achieve the goals which are unreachable by each individual alone.

2.1 LCG, EGEE Projects and Grid Applications

Currently being built and soon-to-be one of the largest scientific instrument in the world, the Large Hadron Collider (LHC) will hopefully be completed and be operational at the beginning of 2008; it will produce roughly 12–14 Petabytes (1Petabytes = 1 million Gigabytes, if being stored in normal CDs, the accumulation of CDs for 1 PB of data will be piled up to several kilometers tall) of data annually, which will be distributed around the globe and analyzed by thousands of scientists in some 500 research institutes and universities worldwide that are participating in the LHC experiments. About 100 000 CPUs at 2004 measures of processing power are required to simulate and analyze these data. No any single computer or supercomputer center in the world can satisfy the requirement to analyses and store the data.

LCG (LHC Computing Grid) project emerged in2002. The data from LHC experiments will be distributed around the globe according to a four-tiered model. The Tier-0 centre of LCG is located at CERN; those data which arrive at Tier-0 will be quickly distributed to a series of Tier-1 centers after initial processing, then continuously to Tier-2s and Tier-3s. BEIJING-PKU site [3] will act as one of Tier-3s, which can consist of local clusters in a Department of University or even of individual PCs, and which may be contributed to LCG on a regular basis [4]

The core task of implementing LCG project is the development of grid middleware. Nowadays, the heterogeneous IT systems are not compatible with the model of computing grid; therefore we need an extensible system, called as grid middleware, to enable the interaction of grid and existing network. The "grid middleware" refers to the security, resource management, data access, instrumentation, policy, accounting, and other services provided for applications, users, and resource providers to operate effectively in a Grid environment. Middleware acts as a sort of 'glue' which binds these services together [5]. LCG project had studied and deployed the grid middleware packages which were developed by other projects and organizations. The middleware widely distributed at CERN and the LHC community latter gradually has been replaced by the "gLite" middleware that is maintained and developed by EGEE (Enabling Grids for E-Science in Europe) project.

EGEE is an important European project which was started in April 2004 and aims to establish a Grid infrastructure for e-science (in Europe first, then later beyond Europe), and its goal is to provide researchers with access to a geographically distributed computing grid infrastructure, available around clock. LCG contributed to the initial environment for EGEE: the gLite3 middleware of EGEE comes out as the fruit of convergence of LCG 2.7.0 and gLite 1.5.0 in the spring of 2006. One major difference between two middleware is that LCG middleware focused on data handling but gLite3 does on data analysis. The site of BEIJING-PKU has been upgraded to gLite3 from the initial installed LCG middleware by following the general trends.

2.2 EUChinaGRID Project and Peking University Group

EUChinaGRID project funded by European Commission under the FP6 (as a part of the specific programme "Structuring the European Research Area") started from the beginning of 2006 with the duration of 2 years. There are 10 partners (6 from Europe and 4 from China) plus 2 third parties in the project. The coordinator of project is INFN (Instituto Nazionale di Fisica Nucleare) of Italy, 5 other European partners are CERN (European Organization for Nuclear Research), University of Roma Tre (Department of Biology), Consortium GARR of Italy, GRNET (Greek Research and Technology Network), Jagiellonian University Medical College of Poland. 4 Chinese partners are IHEP (Institute of High Energy Physics) of Chinese Academy of Science (CAS), CNIC (Computer Network Information Center) of CAS, Beihang University and Peking University. 2 third parties are ASGC (Academia Sinica Grid Computing Center) in Taiwan and University of Roma Tre (Department of Physics).

The main objectives of EUChinaGRID project are:

1. Support the Interconnection and Interoperability of Grids between Europe and China.

2. Main focus is on two specific Grid infrastructures, i.e. CNGRID in China (with the middleware of GOS) and EGEE in Europe (with the middleware of gLite)
3. Dissemination of advanced knowledge in Grid technology is also an important part of the activity.
4. Strengthening the collaboration between scientific groups in both regions, supporting existing and new Grid applications

EUChinaGRID project is aiming to foster the integration and interoperability of the Grid infrastructures between Europe and China for the benefit of eScience applications and worldwide Grid initiatives. The project studies and supports the extension of a pilot intercontinental infrastructure using the EGEE middleware. It promotes the migration of existing and new applications on the Grid infrastructures between Europe and China by training new user communities and supporting the adoption of grid tools and services for scientific applications.

As introduced in Section 1, Peking University group has been mainly engaged in 3 among 5 Working Packages of EUChinaGRID project. Within the scope of WP3 (pilot infrastructure operational support), we have set up a fully functional grid site BEIJING-PKU which is going to be described in rather details in Section 3.

Two subgroups in PKU are participating in WP4 (grid application) of EUChinaGRID pertaining to different disciplines of sciences: Biology and Physics. The Beijing Nuclear Magnetic Resonance Center (BNMRC) is a national center for biomolecular structural studies in China located at PKU; this group makes use of new grid technology to enhance the quality of Never-Born-Protein (NBP) applications. The PKU high energy physics (HEP) group has participated in the CMS experiment on LHC at CERN since 12 years ago; it uses the computing grid on the huge amount of Monte-Carlo event generation and data analysis. Some results obtained by HEP group will be shown in Section 3.3.

In WP5 (dissemination) of EUChinaGRID, we have taken part in organizing the training and other activities (e.g. to briefing the journalists and medias for their participation in the project conference, to making the presentations at various international grid conferences, etc.). In November of 2006, PKU has hosted a Grid user tutorial taught by all Chinese tutors (in its first time) and it got one of the highest feedback scores evaluated by the trainees.

3 BEIJING-PKU Site and Application on HEP in Peking University

Along with the development of grid computing technology, the grid computing team of Peking University mainly considers itself as a grid user. Our aim is to run a stable site, to exploit more computing and data storage resources when needed, to offer our spare resources (whenever available) to other users and to make full use of the grid for the tasks in the high energy physics and biology researches. This quite coincides to the objectives of EUChinaGRID project.

3.1 BEIJING-PKU Computing Grid Site

The construction of BEIJING-PKU site was started in the middle of 2006, and become almost fully functional in the Spring of 2007 after the bottleneck problem of international network connection has been solved. It should be emphasized that the construction of this site would not be successful if without the help from experts of EUChinaGRID project. Figure 1 shows the layout of the site. The assignment of computer hosts is listed in Table 1. The site now can be constantly detected by and shown at the GridICE monitoring system (Fig. 2)

The site has been tested regularly. As a small-scale site, at this stage we have not installed all components of gLite3 yet, but only some key components which will be helpful for the robustness and stableness.

3.2 Grid Application on HEP in Peking University and our Physics Goal

Due to the huge amount of data going to be collected from LHC which is scheduled to collide the proton beams with the highest energy in the world in less than 6 months from now, the PKU physics group must be ready for analysing these data, not only the real data collected by CMS detector from the middle of 2008, but also the Monte-Carlo (MC) data (with the similar amount as the real experimental data) from now on. The PKU physics group has worked on this application in following aspects established the BEIJING-PKU site for getting access to the LCG system;

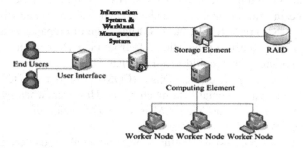

Fig. 1 Topological layout of BEIJING-PKU site

Table 1 The assignment of hosts in BEIJING-PKU site

Host	Components	Middleware version	system	Remark
grid. $MYDOMAIN	UI	GLite3_0_0	SLC308	–
grid01.$MYDOMAIN	SE + MON	GLite3_0_0	SLC308	–
grid03.$MYDOMAIN	WN1	GLite3_0_0	SLC308	no host certificate
grid04.$MYDOMAIN	CE + SB	GLite3_0_0	SLC308	–
grid06.$MYDOMAIN	WN	GLite3_0_0	SLC308	no host certificate
grid07.$MYDOMAIN	RB	GLite3_0_0	SLC308	–

Where $MYDOMAIN=phy.pku.edu.cn SLC=Scientific Linux CERN

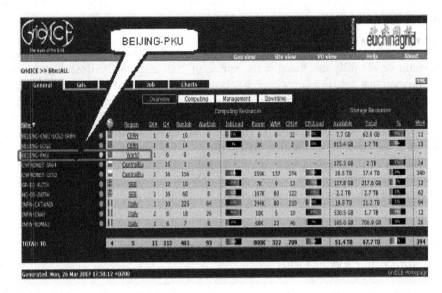

Fig. 2 BEIJING-PKU site is detected by the GridICE monitoring system

used the above system to have analysed a large MC dataset stored in Italy and USA, and have produced some result; provided a configuration file for CMS collaboration in order to generate at least 1 million prompt J/ψ events; The physics goal of PKU-CMS group is to use the heavy Quarkonia (J/ψ or Y) for verifying the Non-Relativistic Quantum ChromoDynamics (NRQCD). In the past, normally the p-p colliding beam experimental data can be explained approximately by the Color Singlet Model (CSM) of NRQCD, but CSM has large discrepancy (Fig. 3) on the high transverse momenta J/ψ production rate from the CDF experimental data on Tevatron (a proton-antiproton collider) at Fermilab (USA).

In contrast, if a Color Octet Mechanism (COM) is introduced, CSM + COM together can fit the experimental data much better. However, when use the COM to predict the J/ψ polarization, the COM is still not coincide the data from CDF experiment (Fig. 4)

With LHC's high luminosity (100 times higher than Tevatron) and high energy (factor 7 higher than Tevatron), the larger statistics of data are hopefully to help to solve the J/ψ polarization puzzle.

3.3 Result of Analysing the Large Bs Event Data Set

The huge amount (expected in the order of several PetaBytes per year) of CMS data have been (and are going to be) distributed at many places around world, We have used the BEIJING-PKU grid site to submit the jobs for analysing a large data set stored in Italy (as shown in Fig. 5 below).

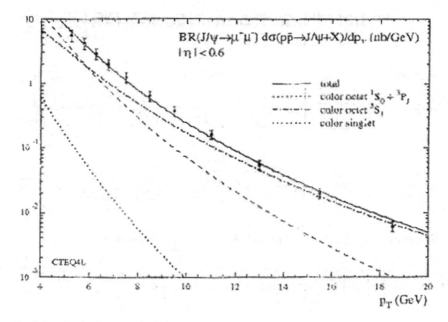

Fig. 3 J/ψ Production rates & NRQCD

J/ψ Polarization

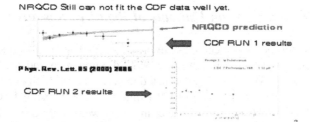

Fig. 4 J/ψ Polarization

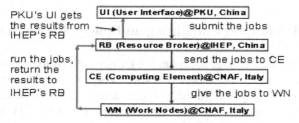

Fig. 5 The latest Procedure via the IHEP LCG Tier-2 facility After analyzing nearly 20,000 events in a Bs → J/ψ+ event data set (stored in Italy), some results have been obtained, an example is shown in Fig. 6 below

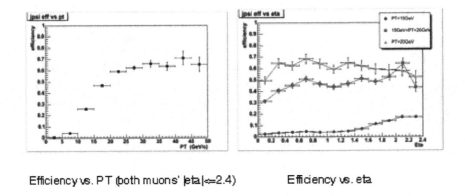

Efficiency vs. PT (both muons' |eta|<=2.4)   Efficiency vs. eta

2

Fig. 6 The sample results from the physics analysis with the grid tool

There results have been summarized into a CMS Notes [6] which has been approved by CMS in July of 2007.

3.4 Ongoing Work and an Estimate of Required Resource

The next steps for us are to generate 1 million prompt J/ψ and 1 million prompt Υ events, then to put them through the CMS full simulation and reconstruction software chain (CMSSW). We have estimated that, for each million events, it needs about 24,000 hours (or 1000 days) of CPU time (for one P4 Xeon 1.5GHz computer), and about 1.1 TB of storage space; in result, we would need $\sim$ 2800 days (i.e. $\sim$ 9 years) of CPU time and $\sim$ 3.1 TB of storage space for such 2 million J/ψ and Υ events plus 40% of background events

4 Application of Grid Computing on Biology Research at PKU

The Peking University biology subgroup in EUChinaGRID is located at the Beijing Nuclear Magnetic Resonance Center (BNMRC) which is sponsored by Ministry of Science and Technology and Ministry of Education of Chinese government, also by Chinese Academy of Science and Chinese Academy of Military Medical Sciences. BNMRC is managed by Peking University and is a national NMR (Nuclear Magnetic Resonance) facility established on November 4th, 2002. BNMRC homes the first 800 MHz NMR spectrometer in China, along with two 600 MHz and a 500 MHz NMR spectrometer equipped with a cryoprobe. The center is for research and training in bio-molecular NMR studies. Massive computing is needed to process and analyze NMR data for solution structure calculation and for molecular dynamic simulation.

The NMR Spectroscopy is a major method for obtaining high resolution structure in addition to X-ray structure. It is operated at the physiological temperature and condition which are closer to native functional state. The structure calculation is very time consuming for multiple structures and multiple rounds. Figure 7 is the procedures for calculation of 3D structure of protein molecules. Figure 8 is a sketch to show how the structures are formed from constrains.

The structure calculation includes the energy minimization. The empirical energy (which is from experimental data) contains all information about the primary structure of the protein and also data about topology and bonds in proteins in general. Figure 9 is an example of structure calculation and refinement, each round of calculation involves many structures, normally 200 structures per round, and each protein may need 10–30 (or more) rounds of calculations. Some structures calculated recently are shown in Fig. 10.

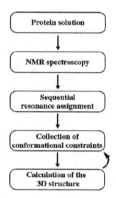

Fig. 7 NMR structure determination

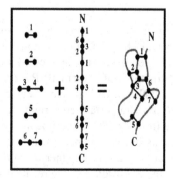

Fig. 8 Restrained molecular dynamics and simulated annealing

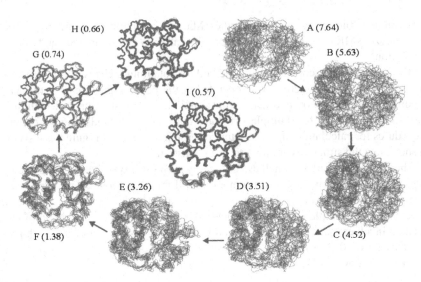

Fig. 9 Structure calculation and refinement

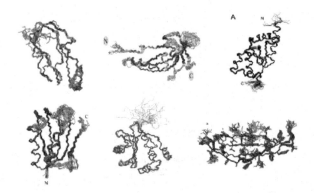

Fig. 10 Examples of some structures calculated recently

The analysis software for protein structures is "Amber" which is commercial software and the licenses need to be granted on all computers involved. University Rome III and PKU have procured the license and tested it lately. Some preliminary results for analyzing the structures of protein PHPT1/Pi with the work-node at BEIJING-PKU site and at INFN-ROMA3 site have been obtained as following.

Distance constraints are most important constraints in protein structure calculation, and they are mainly from NOESY experiment. Hydrogen bond constraints and dihedral angle constraints are important in structure calculation, and can be derived from secondary structure analysis, together with initial structure calculation. Statistics of violation show the consistence of the resulted structure with the experimental data. No violation or few violations mean that the structure is consistent with the experiment and can represent the native structure of the protein. Statistics of PROCHECK are another evaluation standard of the protein structure by analyzing the dihedral angles of the residues. The value of core region is bigger and of the disallowed region is smaller; the protein structure is better refined and better represent the native state of the protein. If the value of RMSD (root mean square deviation) is smaller, the convergence of the structures is better, and the resolution of the structures is higher.

Figrue 11 (a) composes of 20 protein structures. All 100 structures are calculated for PHPT1 bound with Pi. 20 of them with lowest energy, which means that these 20 structures are most native-like, are selected and superimposed to represent the structure of PHPT1/Pi. In NMR results, the protein structure is usually represented by such an ensemble structures (20 structures, for example), which exhibits the dynamics of different parts. Figure 11 (b) is the mean structure of the 20 structures. Ribbon diagram is a displaying model for protein structure. Red represents alpha helix, cyana represents beta strands. Helix and strand are typical structural types

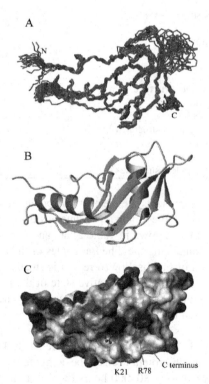

Fig. 11 The bound Pi is displayed as *ball/stick* model. (**a**) Superimposition of 20 PHPT1/Pi structures with most favorite energies from total 100 structures. (**b**) Ribbon diagram of the mean PHPT1/Pi structure. (**c**) Electrostatic potential surface of the mean PHPT1/Pi structure with bound phosphate displayed in *ball/stick* mode

Table 2 Structural statistics of PHPT1/Pi structures

	PHPT1/Pi
Distance constraints	
intra-residue	1329
Sequential	616
Medium	308
long-range	743
Ambiguous	906
Total	3902
Hydrogen bond constraints	37
Dihedral angle constraints	
Φ	38
Ψ	39
X_1	28
Total	105
Violations	
NOE violation (> 0.3 Å)	3
Torsion angle violation ($> 2°$)	1
PROCHECK statistics (%)	
core regions	83.0
allowed regions	15.7
generously allowed regions	1.1
disallowed regions	0.2
RMSD from mean structure	
Backbone heavy atoms	
All residues (Å)	1.15 ± 0.21
Regular secondary structure (Å)	0.27 ± 0.06
All heavy atoms	
All residues (Å)	1.67 ± 0.18
Regular secondary structure (Å)	0.69 ± 0.11

in protein. Figure 11 (c) represents the electrostatic potential surface of PHPT1/Pi. Red represents negatively-charged, blue represents positively-charged.

Statistics of PROCHECK (shown in Table 2) are another evaluation standard of the protein structure by analyzing the dihedral angles of the residues. The value of core region is bigger and of the disallowed region is smaller; the protein structure is better refined and better represent the native state of the protein. If the value of RMSD (root mean square deviation) is smaller, the convergence of the structures is better, and the resolution of the structures is higher.

The computing resources needed by PKU-Biology group have been estimated: By using the Intel 2.4 GHz Xeon CPU Each structure needs 4 hours, each round to compute 200 structures Each protein needs to be computed for 10 rounds Totally if 10 proteins to be analyzed $\rightarrow \sim 80,000$ hours (> 9 years) CPU time and > 1TB storage space.

The real calculation for the above protein PHPT1/Pi structure costs about 15579 seconds on BEIJING-PKU work-node and about 14297 seconds on INFN-ROMA3 work-node.

5 Summary

EUChinaGRID project has mostly achieved its goals during last two years: to foster the creation of an intercontinental eScience community by training people and by supporting the existing and new applications; to establish an interoperable infrastructure for grid operations between Europe and China.

Peking University group has accumulated some experience on the grid computing within the scope of EUChinaGRID project, But much more work are needed to be done, for example,

> To maintain and upgrade the BEIJING-PKU site for providing more complete and stable services.
> To further explore the biology application by analyzing more varieties of protein structure.
> To gear up the readiness of HEP application for analyzing the huge amount of MC and real data which shall pour in when LHC to start the operation in 2008;

It has been evident that with the collaborative effort from all relevant fields, the grid computing technology has been and will be more mature, and will produce more application results which were unthinkable in the past.

Acknowledgments We appreciate very much the helps and supports from all partners of EUChinaGRID project which are essential for our achievement in last two years. The construction of BEIJING-PKU site has been a collective effort from all members of PKU group; we particularly thank the contribution from Ms. K. Kang, Mr. L. Zhao, D. Mu, Z. Yang, S. Guo and L. Liu. Finally, we are very grateful for the warm hospitality of ASGC during the ISGC,2007 symposium and for their great help on solving some technical problems of BEIJING-PKU site in 2007.

References

1. Foster, and C. Kesselman (editors). The Grid: Blueprint for a New Computing Infrastructure, 2nd edition. Morgan Kaufmann (2004)
2. http://euchina-gridice.cnaf.infn.it:50080/gridice/host/host_summary.php?siteName=BEIJING-PKU
3. http://lcg.web.cern.ch/lcg/overview.html
4. http://www.ncess.ac.uk/learning/start/faq/
5. Z. Yang and S. Qian, "J/$\psi \to \mu^+\mu^-$ reconstruction in CMS", CMS Notes 2007/017, (7/2007)
6. http://www.euchinagrid.org/

Part III
Grid Middleware & Interoperability

ReSS: A Resource Selection Service for the Open Science Grid

Gabriele Garzoglio, Tanya Levshina, Parag Mhashilkar, and Steve Timm

Abstract The Open Science Grid offers access to hundreds of computing and storage resources via standard Grid interfaces. Before the deployment of an automated resource selection system, users had to submit jobs directly to these resources. They would manually select a resource and specify all relevant attributes in the job description prior to submitting the job. The necessity of a human intervention in resource selection and attribute specification hinders automated job management components from accessing OSG resources and it is inconvenient for the users.

The Resource Selection Service (ReSS) project addresses these shortcomings. The system integrates condor technology, for the core match making service, with the gLite CEMon component, for gathering and publishing resource information in the Glue Schema format. Each one of these components communicates over secure protocols via web services interfaces.

The system is currently used in production on OSG by the DZero Experiment, the Engagement Virtual Organization, and the Dark Energy. It is also the resource selection service for the Fermilab Campus Grid, FermiGrid. ReSS is considered a lightweight solution to push-based workload management.

This paper describes the architecture, performance, and typical usage of the system.

Keywords Resource Selection · large distributed computing · open science grid

1 Introduction

The Open Science Grid (OSG) [1]s a consortium of US National Laboratories and Universities that provides a US-wide Data Grid to address the computing needs of scientific communities. OSG makes available to its collaborators hundreds of computing and storage resources. For such large distributed system, the selection

G. Garzoglio (✉)
Fermi National Accelerator Laboratory Pine st. And Kirk Rd. 60510 Batavia, IL, USA
e-mail: garzogli, tlevshin, parag, timm@fnal.gov

of an appropriate set of resources to run user applications can become a complex problem. Even when such selection occurred, the Grid middleware and the application environment often need to be informed about the characteristics of the selected resource, in order to dispatch and run the application appropriately.

In September 2005, the Resource Selection Service (ReSS) Project [2] was charged with developing and integrating an end-to-end solution to these problems for the OSG. The project was sponsored by the DZero experiment [3] and the Fermilab Computing Division in collaboration with the Open Science Grid, FermiGrid [4], the CEMon gLite Project (PD-INFN), and the Glue Schema Group.

There were five main goals that the project set for itself:

- Implement a light-weight cluster selector for push-based job handling services
- Enable users to express requirements on the resources in the job description
- Enable users to refer to abstract characteristics of the resources in the job description
- Provide registration for clusters and mechanisms for automatic expiration of the registration
- Use the standard characterizations of the resources via the Glue Schema

Being the sponsoring Virtual Organization (VO), DZero provided most of the initial requirements. However, the resulting system is now adopted on the Open Science Grid as a general service and used by the DZero experiment, the Engagement VO, and the Dark Energy Survey. In addition, the ReSS system is the resource selector for the FermiGrid Campus Grid.

This paper presents the Architecture of ReSS, the Resource Selection model utilized, the current deployments of the system, and discusses the results of different studies and evaluations.

2 Architecture

The ReSS system is composed by two components:

1. an information provider and publisher service, deployed at the resources
2. an information repository and resource selector, deployed semi-centrally.

Figure 1 shows a diagram of the system architecture.

1. Information providing and publishing is implemented by the CEMon service, a component of the gLite software. CEMon collects information at the resource by invoking local commands, logically grouped using the abstraction of "Sensors". The sensor developed for OSG invokes and parses the output of the Generic Information Providers (GIP), a suite of scripts that present resource information organized according to the Glue Schema [5]. For each sensor, the information can be presented in different formats, currently, LDIF, XML, new classad, and old classad. Each format is implemented according to the specifications of Glue Schema mapping documents. The ReSS project has driven the

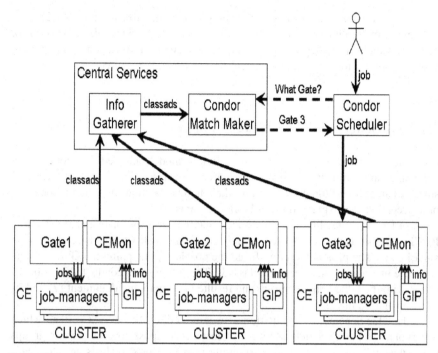

Fig. 1 The architectural diagram of the Resource Selection Service

definition of the Glue Schema to old classad format mapping. ReSS uses the old classad format, to use Condor software for resource selection.

CEMon can publish information synchronously or asynchronously. Clients can access information synchronously, by invoking web services interfaces directly, or they can subscribe to CEMon in order to receive periodic asynchronous events. Alternatively, administrators can configure CEMon with a pre-defined list of subscribers, so that specified clients can be periodically notified with asynchronous events.

2. ReSS uses asynchronous event notification to publish resource information to the central information repository. The Condor [6] Information Collector implements this repository, which is used by the Condor Match-Making service to implement resource selection.

Information is routed from CEMon to the Condor Collector by the Information Gatherer (IG) component. Effectively, IG acts as an interface adapter between the two services. In ReSS, IG is deployed as a central stateless service. The service can be configured to apply simple transformations to the incoming information. This feature is used to add attributes containing expressions that, when evaluated, validate the semantics of the attributes for the OSG use case. These expressions check, for example, the presence of "critical" attributes, the consistency of attribute values (e.g. the number of nodes in a cluster cannot be negative), etc. Since resource selection is implemented using Condor components, the infrastructure provides for a seamless integration of condor-based job scheduling services, like Condor-G. In addition, Condor provides interfaces to query the central information repository, in case users prefer to adopt ad-hoc algorithms for selecting resources.

2.1 Glue Schema to Old Classad Mapping

The Glue Schema is a resource description model adopted by commercial companies and Grid organizations. Resources are described in terms of entities, such as Clusters or Storage Areas, and their logical relationships, like association or aggregation, are expressed using UML diagrams.

In order to use readily available match-making services for resource selection, ReSS describes resources in old classad format, an unstructured list of [attribute, value] pairs. The project therefore faced the problem of mapping the Glue Schema structure into a set of unstructured classads. The activity was conducted in collaboration with the Glue Schema group and resulted in a mapping document [7] and its implementation in CEMon.

In the Glue Schema, a computational resource is described by a "Cluster", which is part of a computing center or "Site". A Cluster is composed by one or more groups ("Subclusters") of homogeneous computing nodes ("Hosts"). Hosts are characterized by parameters related to the processor type, memory, operating system, etc. Access to the Cluster can be achieved by one or more gateways or queues ("Computing Elements" or CE). The Computing Element is described by informational parameters, such as the gateway address, state parameters, such as the number of running or idle jobs, policy parameters, such as the maximum wall clock time allowed by the local scheduler, etc. In addition to total values for these parameters, like the total number of running jobs at the CE, the model also allows for VO-specific values ("VOView"), like the number of running jobs for a specific VO.

Figure 2 shows a schematic UML representation of a computational resource. The mapping between this structure and a set of old classads is built considering all possible combinations of inter-related CE, Cluster, and Subclustrer entities. In other words, each combination (classad) contains a single CE, Cluster, and Subcluster entity. In addition, if VO-specific parameters are available to characterize the CE (VO View entity), these are used instead of the general CE attributes.

Each resulting classad can be thought of as a virtual homogeneous cluster with one access gateway, described from the point of view of the VO. The ReSS system matches each job to one of these "virtual" computational resources. Storage descriptions are "flattened" using similar rules and are added to their associated Cluster classad.

Being combinatorial, this algorithm could in principle produce a very large number of classads for each site. In practice, typical OSG installations consist of one storage resource and one cluster, considered homogeneous for simplicity (i.e. one Subcluster), with a few Computing elements and up to a couple dozen supported

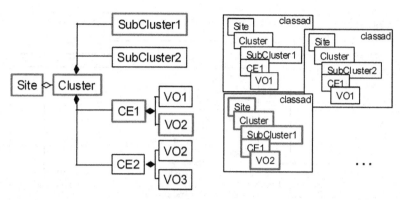

Fig. 2 Mapping the Glue Schema "tree" (*left*) into a set of "flat" classads (*right*): the algorithm navigates through all possible combinations of (Cluster, Subcluster, CE, VO)

VOs. In the current system, complex sites advertise 48 classads, while simple sites advertise 1. With this multiplicity, we expect the system to scale up to a few hundreds sites before incurring into scalability limitations of the condor system. This limit is deemed acceptable considering that the current number of OSG sites is about 80 and the annual growth is typically of a few sites per year.

2.2 Typical Uses of the System

ReSS provides a direct and indirect mechanism to access resource information from the system.

The direct mechanism consists in querying the ReSS information repository. Queries are a set of constraints on the resource attributes (e.g. "List all clusters that support the DZero VO"). Filters can be applied to display specific information only. Resources that meet the specified criteria are returned to the user in bulk, appropriately formatted according to the given filters. The user can then run ad hoc algorithms to narrow down her selection and submit the job using standard Grid interfaces.

The indirect mechanism consists in accessing the ReSS information repository through the Condor-G system. Users specify their resource requirements and rank criteria using the condor job description language. Attributes can be dereferenced to enhance the job environment or to send directives the job handling middleware.

Figure 3 show an example of a simple job description and how it references attributes from a resource classad.

A popular way of using the ReSS system is a hybrid between the direct and indirect methods described above. A VO queries the ReSS information repository directly, getting an initial coarsely-selected list of resources. Each classad in this list is enhanced with VO-specific attributes. For example, the Engagement VO of OSG adds parameters from test jobs run periodically at resources. The enhanced list

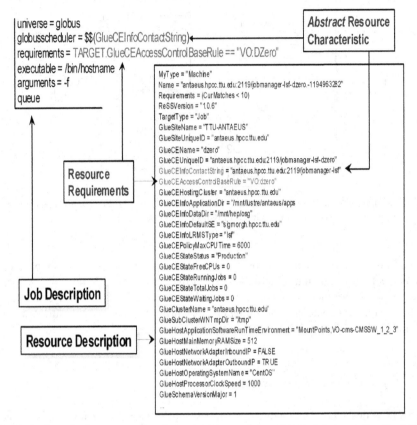

Fig. 3 Attributes in the resource description (*right*) are referenced in the job description (*topleft*)

is then uploaded to a Condor matchmaker, controlled by the VO. Users of the VO configure the schedulers of their Condor-G deployments to point to the VO match maker. Thus, users can access the VO matchmaker indirectly, specifying resource and VO-specific attributes in the condor job description language.

The DZero experiment adopts a direct mechanism to submit jobs to OSG resources. DZero jobs are logically grouped in units of computation. In general, these units consist of several jobs. An example of such computation, called data processing, applies a data transformation algorithm to an input dataset, consisting of multiple files. Because of the typically long processing time, each file is input to a single job. The jobs that process a whole input dataset define the unit of computation.

By policy, jobs belonging to the same unit of computation are executed at the same cluster. Resources are selected for the whole unit by querying directly the ReSS system. For each cluster, the resource-ranking algorithm computes the ratio of the number of Idle jobs (jobs queued at the cluster's local scheduler) over the number of Running jobs. The whole unit of computation is submitted to the resource with the lowest ranking value or, in other words, to the resource that has the least Idle jobs per Running job. The algorithm also strongly penalizes clusters with Idle jobs, but no Running jobs.

Variations of this simple algorithm are used in production by DZero to select OSG resources.

3 ReSS Deployments

The ReSS system has been deployed at two major Grid infrastructures: the Open Science Grid and FermiGrid, the Fermilab campus Grid.

ReSS central services are deployed for OSG and FermiGrid on Xeon 3.2 GHz 4-CPU machines with 4 GB of RAM. These machines run the services at a very low load (< 1).

On FermiGrid, the ReSS publishing services (CEMon) have been deployed on 8 of the campus clusters, advertising a total of almost 750 classads for a total of more than 12,000 job slots. The campus grid can be accessed through a single gateway via the GRAM protocol. Jobs are locally queued up using Condor-G, before being routed to the resource that meets the job requirements.

On OSG, CEMon is deployed at about 64 sites, producing short of 2000 classads.

4 Validations and Evaluations

The ReSS project has undergone 2 independent evaluations processes:

1. a study of the resources utilized by CEMon when running on a typical OSG machine: this study compared CEMon to other popular information publishing services (MDS2) [8]
2. an evaluation of the use of ReSS to meet the Workload Management requirements of the US-CMS VO: this evaluation compared several workload management technologies [9].

In (1), we studied the resource requirements of two information-publishing services, CEMon and GRIS/MDS2, on a typical OSG node under two different conditions. The first condition simulated a heavily loaded environment, where information on resources was required continuously by several external services. The idea was investigating the difference in resource utilization between the CEMon model, where information is pushed to a central collector, versus the MDS2 mode, where information is pulled directly from the site monitoring services by external services. The second condition compared the two publishing services queried at the same slow frequency, one every 10 minutes.

The machine characteristics studied were load, percentage of CPU utilized, and memory consumption. The conclusions of the study are

- Running only CEMon does not generate more load than running only GRIS, or CEMon and GRIS together.
- CEMon uses less %CPU than a GRIS that is queried continuously, simulating a heavily loaded environment (0.8% vs. 24%). On the other hand, CEMon uses more memory (%4.7 vs. %0.5). This is not surprising because CEMon offers web services interfaces, a technology well known to be memory intensive.
- The average load to the machine is smaller when running CEMon alone (avg. 0.5) than when running a GRIS that is queried continuously (avg. 1.1). Both servers generate lesser load than when running the Generic Information

Providers (GIP) scripts by hand continuously (avg. 1.8): this is expected because both servers cache data.

Figure 4 shows a typical load average profile, running only CEMon. In (2), US CMS evaluated several Workload Management Technologies. The goal was measuring characteristics such as scalability and robustness, in order to select a technology

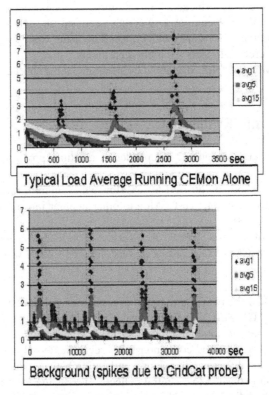

Fig. 4 The load average of the machine vs. time; the measurements of the load resulting from running the CEMon process vs. time (*top*) are compared to the load when no user processes are running on the machine (*bottom*). The spikes on the bottom plot result from periodic processes being run for monitoring purposes

that could meet the requirements of the VO. The study evaluated Condor-G and ReSS on a large test system, submitting thousands of jobs running the sleep command for a random time between 30 minutes and 6 hours. The test system consisted of 4 Grid sites that agreed to run the sleep jobs on the same nodes where "production" jobs where also running, virtually doubling their job slot capacity. Each cluster provided about 2000 slots for the sleep jobs.

Condor-G was evaluated submitting 40,000 jobs at a rate of about 8 Hz to 4 Condor-G schedulers. The system scaled well to this limit and resulted robust with a 0.5% failure rates. This rate could be in principle reduced by automatically resubmitting failed jobs. In some cases, it was observed crashes of the gateways.

Gateway crashes resulted in discrepancies between the status of the jobs at the site and at the Condor-G scheduler.

Configuring the Condor-G scheduler to interact with the ReSS system did not change the scalability or robustness properties.

The conclusion of the study was that ReSS is a lightweight, scalable, and robust infrastructure. A criticism was that ReSS does not handle out-of-the-box user fair share among the VO, leaving this responsibility to site batch systems. Also, the ReSS model, which consists in pushing jobs to resources, does not allow for changes in user priorities after the job has been submitted. To overcome these limitations, US CMS decided to adopt the GlideIn Factory WMS technology and integrate it with ReSS for global-level resource selection.

5 Conclusions

The Resource Selection Service (ReSS) project provides cluster-level resource selection for the Open Science Grid and FermiGrid Campus Grid. The system uses the Glue Schema model to describe resources and the Condor classad format to publish information. ReSS integrates the Condor match making service, for resource selection, with gLite CEMon, for information gathering and publishing. The system naturally interfaces with the Condor-G scheduling system. ReSS is a lightweight, scalable, and robust infrastructure for resource selection of push-based job handling middleware.

Acknowledgments We want to thank the developers of CEMon, in particular Massimo Sgaravatto and Luigi Zangrango, for their collaboration and promptness in addressing our concerns; the members of the OSG Integration Test Bed for their help in the validation of ReSS; the members of the Virtual Data Toolkit for their help in packaging CEMon; Igor Sfiligoi and Burt Holzman from US CMS for their evaluation of ReSS; University of Oklahoma, in particular Karthikeyan Arunachalam and Horst Severini, for spearheading the study on CEMon resource utilization; Marco Mambelli, UChicago, and MatsRynge, Renci, John Weigand, Fermilab, for their feedback.; the Glue Schema Group for their help with the Glue Schema to old classad document; FermiGrid for their interest in and contribution to the ReSS project. This paper was written at Fermilab, a US National Laboratory operated by Fermi Research Alliance, LLC under Contract No. DE-AC02-07CH11359 with the United States Department of Energy.

References

1. The Open Science Grid home page: http://www.opensciencegrid.org
2. The Resource Selection home page: https://twiki.grid.iu.edu/twiki/bin/view/ResourceSelection
3. The D0 Collab., "The D0 Upgrade: The Detector and its Physics", Fermilab Pub-96/357-E.
4. D.R. Yocum et al.: "FermiGrid", FERMILAB-CONF-07-125-CD, May 2007. 5pp. Presented at TeraGrid '07: Broadening Participation in TeraGrid, Madison, Wisconsin, 4–8 Jun 2007.
5. The GLUE schema home page: http://glueschema.forge.cnaf.infn.it
6. J. Frey, T. Tannenbaum, M. Livny, I. Foster, and S. Tuecke, "Condor-G: A Computation Management Agent for Multi-Institutional Grids", in Proceedings of the 10th International Symposium on High Performance Distributed Computing (HPDC-10), IEEE CS Press, Aug. 2001.
7. The Glue Schema to Old Classad Mapping document: http://glueschema.forge.cnaf.infn.it/SpecV13/OldClassAd
8. K. Arunachalam, G. Garzoglio, "Performance Measurements of CEMon on an OSG Test Environment", OSG White Paper OSG-doc-521-v1. https://twiki.grid.iu.edu/twiki/bin/view/ResourceSelection/CEMonPerforman eEvaluation
9. I. Sfiligoi, B. Holzman, "Evaluation of Workload Management Systems for OSG", Talk at the OSG council meeting on Mar 07 https://indico.fnal.gov/contributionDisplay.py?contribId=65& sessionId=13& confId=468

A Model for the Storage Resource Manager

Andrea Domenici and Flavia Donno

Abstract The Storage Resource Manager had been proposed as a standard interface for high-end storage systems deployed on Grid architectures. In this paper we propose a conceptual model for the SRM that should supplement its API specification with a clear and concise definition of its underlying structural and behavioral concepts. This model would make it easier to define its semantics; it would help service and application developers, and provide for a more rigorous validation of implementations. Different notations are used as appropriate to define different aspects of the model.

1 Introduction

The Woldwide LHC Computing Grid (WLCG) is the infrastructure that will provide the computational and storage facilities needed to process the data collected by the four experiments at the Large Hadron Collider (LHC) at CERN, amounting to several Petabytes each year.

One of the critical issues that WLCG has to face is the provision of a Grid storage service that allows for dynamic space allocation, the negotiation of file access protocols, support for quality of storage, authentication and authorization mechanisms, storage and file management, scheduling of space and file operations, support for temporary files, and other storage management functions.

The *Storage Resource Mananger* (SRM) has been proposed [1] as a standard interface for high-end storage systems deployed on Grid infrastructures. In particular, a significant effort by an international collaboration coordinated by the WLCG has led to the definition of the SRM 2.2 protocol and to its implementation on all storage solutions deployed in WLCG.

The SRM is specified primarily as an application programming interface (API). In this paper we propose a conceptual model for the SRM that should supplement the API and other specifications with an explicit, clear and concise definition of its underlying structural and behavioral concepts. This model would make it easier to

A. Domenici (✉)
DIIEIT, University of Pisa, v. Diotisalvi 2, I-56122 Pisa, Italy

S.C. Lin, E. Yen (eds.), *Grid Computing*,

define the service semantics; it would help service and application developers and provide for a more rigorous validation of implementations.

The proposed model is meant to strike a satisfactory compromise between clarity and formality. Different notations (e.g., basic set-theoretic and logical formalism, UML [2] diagrams, and plain English) are used as appropriate to define different aspects of the model.

2 The Storage Resource Manager

A *Storage Element* (SE) is a Grid Service implemented on a mass storage system (MSS) that may be based on a pool of disk servers, on more specialized high-performing disk-based hardware, or on a disk cache front-end backed by a tape system, or some other reliable, long-term storage medium. Remote data access is provided by a GridFTP service [3] and possibly by other data transfer services, while local access is provided by POSIX-like input/output calls.

A SE provides *spaces* where users create and access *files*. A file is a logical set of data that is embodied in one or more physical *copies*.

Storage spaces may be of different qualities, related to reliability and accessibility, and support different data transfer protocols. Different users may have different requirements on space quality and access protocol, therefore, besides the data transfer and file access functions, a SE must support more advanced resource management services, including dynamic space allocation.

The *Storage Resource Manager* (SRM) is a middleware component that provides the resource management services through a standard interface, independent of the underlying MSS. The interface is defined by the S*RM Interface Specification* (IS) [4] that lists the service requests that a client application may issue, along with the data types for their arguments and results.

Request signatures are grouped by functionality, such as *space management* requests that allow clients to reserve, release, and manage spaces, specifying or negotiating their quality and lifetime, ad *data transfer* requests that get files into SRM spaces either from a client's space or from other storage systems, and retrieve them. Other groups are *directory, permission*, and *discovery* functions.

3 A Model for the Storage Resource Manager

The main SRM specification are the above mentioned IS and the *Storage Element Model for SRM 2.2 and GLUE schema description* [5]. Other relevant documents are [1, 6, 7]. We proposed a model to extend the specifications with a synthetic description of the basic entities, their relationships, and their behaviors.

We have chosen to use two sub models, with different levels of formality. The semi-formal model uses plain English and UML diagrams, and it is meant to give an overall view of the system, identifying its main components, their relationships and behavior, and to define and clarify the terms used in the IS. A more formal model uses set-theoretic and logical notations to express constraints. This model is meant to resolve ambiguities that might remain in the semi-formal model, and to support the design and testing of SRM implementations.

3.1 Describing Concepts and Properties

In the *static model*, the SRM concepts are represented as object classes, their properties and reciprocal relationships being modeled by attributes and associations subject to various constraints. Figure 1 shows a partial UML class diagram for the SRM static model.

Some of the attributes represent important properties: *retention policy, access latency,* and *(file) storage type*. Retention policy describes the likelihood that a file copy may be list in a given storage space. This likelihood may be high (REPLICA retention policy), intermediate (OUTPUT), or low (CUSTODIAL). The OUTPUT policy is currently not implemented. Access latency describes data accessibility: a space where data are immediately accessible is ONLINE, otherwise it is NEAR-LINE. A NEARLINE space is supported by mechanical media, such as tape, that require data to be staged to temporary disk storage for access. A third latency, OFFLINE, is currently not implemented. The *storage type* refers to file lifetime. A FOLATILE file is deleted automatically after a given time. A DURABLE file also has a limited lifetime, but it must be removed explicitly by its owner. A PERMANENT file has an unlimited lifetime, until removed by its owner. Durable files are currently not implemented. A *Site URL* (SURL) identifies the file within the SE, and the SE itself.

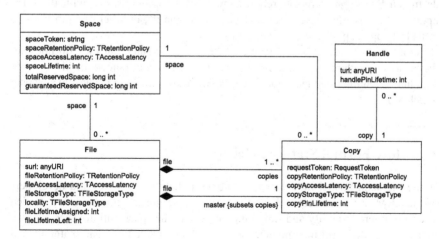

Fig. 1 Static model of the SRM

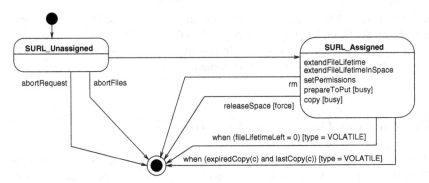

Fig. 2 State machine for File (1)

The associations in the diagram show that a space hosts zero or more files, that each file has one or more copies, one of which is the master copy, that each copy resides on a space, and it has one or more handles.

3.2 Describing Behavior

The dynamic model of the SRM is described by UML state diagrams. Figure 2 shows a part of the model, related to files.

A file is created with a *prepareToPut* or a *copy* request. A request can be served asynchronously, so a file may remain for some time in a waiting state (*SURL_Unassigned*) before it is assigned a SURL. In this state, the file can be destroyed by an *abortFiles* or *abortRequest* operation. Otherwise, eventually a SURL is assigned and the file enters a state (*SURL_Assigned*) where it can be destroyed by an *rm* (remove) request, by a *releaseSpace* request with the *force* option, when its lifetime expires and the file is volatile, or when the pin lifetime of its last copy expires and the file is volatile.

Some requests are accepted in the *SURL_Assigned* state, but they do not alter the behavior. Such requests are listed as *internal transitions* (shown inside the state icon in the diagram) and leave the file in *SURL_Assigned* and in its current substate, whichever it is.

4 A More Formal Static Model

While the semi-formal model exposed above is helpful for users and developers of the SRM, a finer level of detail and a greater degree of formality are needed to ensure interoperability and full compliance with the specification. Therefore we propose an initial, still incomplete, formal model expressed in basic mathematical notation. Since the SRM is still evolving and several issues are still open, the model is limited to fundamental features, upon which further extensions and refinements can be built.

An elementary mathematical notation was chosen instead of some more specialized language, such as the UML *Object Constraint Language* [8] or the *Z Specification Language* [9], but it should be easy to translate the notation adopted here to those formalisms, if needed.

First, we introduce some *basic sets* whose members are unstructured values, such as atomic symbols (meant to represent names of objects or discrete values for their attributes) or numbers. Then we define the *constructed sets* of *storage elements, spaces, copies, handles,* and *files* as Cartesian products of some previously defined sets.

Functions are used to represent various properties and relationships. *Constraints* on properties and relationships are expressed as predicate logic formulas.

For example, two of the basic sets are the set of space or file sizes, defined as identical to the set of natural numbers ($Sz = $ IN), and the set of retention policies, defined as a set of three values ($Rp = \{$REPLICA, OUTPUT, CUSTODIAL$\}$).

The set of spaces is defined as $S = T \times L \times Prop \times Sz \times R_s$, where T is the set of space tokens (i.e., identifiers), L the set of lifetimes, $Prop$ a set of tuples of space properties, and R_s is the set of request issued for each space.

As an example of a constraint, the statement that *"a file cannot outlive its space"* is expressed as

$$\forall_{f \in F, t > stime(f)} 0 < lleft(f, t) < lleft(mspace(f), t)$$

where F is the set of files, t is a time value, *stime(f)* is the time of file creation, *lleft(f, t)* is the file or space lifetime remaining at time t, and *mspace(f)* is the space holding the master copy of file f.

5 Validation of Existing SRM Implementations

The SRM has been implemented for five different MSSs, namely CASTOR [10], developed at CERN and based on tape libraries and disk servers, dCache [7], developed at DESY, used with multiple MSS backends, DPM [11], a disk-only MSS developed at CERN, DRM/BeStMan, a disk-based system developed at LBNL, the first promoter of SRM, and StoRM [12], a disk-based system developed at CNAF, based on parallel file systems such as GPFS or PVFS.

All these systems are being tested for compliance with the SRM IS. Using various techniques of black-box testing [13], five families of test cases have been designed: *Availability* to check the availability of the SRM end-points; *Basic* to verify basic functionality of the implemented SRM APIs; *Use Cases* to check boundary conditions, function interactions, and exceptions; *Exhaustion* to exhaust all possible values of input and output arguments such as length of filenames, SURL format, and optional arguments; *Stress* tests to stress the systems, identify race conditions, study the behavior of the system when critical concurrent operations are performed, and in other exacting conditions.

The SRM model proposed in this paper has been used to derive several test cases in the *Basic* and *Use Cases* test suites.

6 Conclusions

A comprehensive model of the SRM is being developed to support the development and verification of SRM implementations, using different notations and levels of formality in order to satisfy the needs of different stakeholders in the SRM development.

The first draft of the model is available, and feedback from its users is awaited. In fact, the model has already contributed to the validation of existing implementations by assisting in the design of a few families of tests, and its development has helped in identifying unanticipated behaviors and interactions. The testing campaign itself has helped the developers to find solutions that better satisfy the needs of the users.

Acknowledgments The work of the many people in the SRM collaboration is gratefully acknowledged. In particular we would like to thank Arie Shoshani, Alex Sim and Junmin Gu from LBNL, Jean-Philippe Baud, Paolo Badino, Maarten Litmaath from CERN, Timur Perelmutov from FNAL, Patrick Fuhrmann from DESY, Shaun De Witt from RAL, Ezio Corso from ICTP, Luca Magnoni and Riccardo Zappi from CNAF/INFN, for their valuable input in the specification definition process. Finally, we would like to thank the WLCG project for giving us the opportunity to collect the requirements and test the proposed protocol for real use-cases. The authors have been supported by CERN and INFN, respectively.

References

1. Shoshani, A. Sim and J. Gu: Storage Resource Managers: Middleware Components for Grid Storage. Proceedings of the 9th IEEE Symposium on Mass Storage Systems (MSS '02). (2002)
2. J. Rumbaugh, I. Jacobson, I. Booch: The Unified Modeling Language Reference Manual, 2nd edn. Addison-Wesley (2004)
3. W. Allcock et al.: Grid FTP protocol specification. Document, GGF GridFTP Working Group (September 2002)
4. The Storage Resource Manager Working Group: The Storage Resource Manager Interface Specification, Version 2.2, http://sdm.lbl.gov/srm-wg/doc/SRM.v2.2.pdf (December 2006).
5. P. Badino et al.: Storage Element Model for SRM 2.2 and Glue schema description, v3.5. Technical Report, WLCG (Oct. 27, 2006)
6. Shoshani et al.: Storage Resource Management: Concepts, Functionality, and Interface Specification, Future of Grid Data Environments: A Global Grid Forum (GGF) Data Area Workshop, Berlin, Germany (March 9–13, 2004)
7. M. Ernst et al.: Managed data storage and data access services for data grids, Proceedings of the Computing in High Energy Physics (CHEP) conference, Interlaken, Switzerland (September 27 – October1, 2004)
8. J. Warmer, A. Kleppe: The Object Constraint Language: Getting Your Models Ready for MDA. 2nd edn. Addison-Wesley (2004)

9. J. Woodcock, J. Davies: Using Z – Specification, Refinement, and Proof. Prentice Hall (1996)

10. Barring et al.: Storage Resource Sharing with CASTOR, 12th NASA Goddard/21st IEEE Conference on Mass Storage Systems and Technologies (MSST2004), U. of Maryland, Adelphy, MD (Apr. 13–16, 2004)

11. J.P. Baud, J. Casey: Evolution of LCG-2 Data Management, Proceedings of the Computing in High Energy Physics (CHEP'04) conference, Interlaken, Switzerland (September 27 – October 1, 2004)

12. E. Corso et al.: StoRM, an SRM Implementation for LHC Analysis Farms, Proceedings of the Computing in High Energy Physics (CHEP'06) conference, Mumbai, India (Feb. 2006)

13. G.J. Meyers, (rev. by) C.S., (rev. by) T.B., T.M.T.: The Art of Software Testing, 2nd edn. John Wiley & Sons (2004)

The Session Based Fault Tolerance Algorithm of Platform EGO Web Service Gateway

Xiaohui Wei, Yuan Luo, Jishan Gao, and Xiaolei Ding

Abstract Although grid computing has adopted Web services technology to deal with platforms heterogeneity and to enhance service and application interoperability, it is still a challenge to build web service applications with high reliability and availability to meet the requirements of grid communities. The paper discusses the design of Platform EGO WSG with high reliability. To support a huge user base and reduce the response time, WSGs work in cluster model and the loads are dynamic balanced among them. Besides, a lightweight notification mechanism is implemented to provide better interoperability between WSG and WSCs. Moreover, we designed a session-based a-synchronized recovery algorithm to achieve WSG fault tolerance, which has short freezing time and is able to isolate the recovery process for each WSC. This approach can rebuild the service sessions and the notification mechanism after restart, to handle Notification failure, and WSG failure report, etc.

Keywords Grid · web service gateway · fault tolerance · session · load balance

1 Introduction

From OGSI to WSRF, grid computing has gradually adopted Web services and SOA technologies to solve the resource sharing problems in heterogeneous environments of science, engineer and commerce [1]. Unlike traditional cluster computing environments such as LSF, PBS, and SGE etc., Platform Enterprise Grid OrchestratorTM (EGO) is a SOA based grid platform newly released by Platform Computing Inc. to manage the shared resources across geographically dispersed sites for diverse enterprise applications, services and workloads. Platform EGO Web Service Gateway (WSG) is a grid middleware to enable the applications, called web service clients (WSC), to access Platform EGO services as web services. However, it is a challenge to realize web service based grid services with high performance,

---

X. Wei (✉)

College of Computer Science and Technology, Jilin University, China

e-mail: {weixh@jlu.edu.cn, pp.jordan@email.jlu.edu.cn, gjs0064114@126.com, dxlxiaolei@163.com}

S.C. Lin, E. Yen (eds.), *Grid Computing*,

reliability and availability to meet the requirements of grid communities. As grid computing becomes widely adopted, there is a fresh need for web service technologies to combine with recovery-based techniques and parallel processing technologies to achieve fault-tolerance and high performance.

2 Related Works

Although many works have been done in the field of distributed system recovery, the research on web service fault-tolerance is very new in this area. Currently there are no standard specifications dealing with fault tolerance in web services.

Normally a web server does not maintain the active connections with its clients, which is called stateless. Hence, in many cases, people just use very simple protocol to handle the web service crashes. A service monitor mechanism would be used to detect the service fault and the future requests from clients will be re-directed to redundant servers. For example, paper [2, 3] deliver fault tolerance on web services based on the passive replication approach and implement basic fault detection mechanisms on primary server. Paper [4] proposes a general architecture to realize fault-tolerance web services, which have components responsible for calling concurrently the service replicas, wait for processing, analyze the responses processed, and return them to the client. Moreover, paper [4] supports the use of the active replication technique in order to obtain fault tolerance in service oriented architectures.

Paper [3] is also capable of tolerating for requests being processed at the time of server failure. However, its implementation need modifications to the Linux kernel and to the Apache web server. While paper [5] presents an implementation of a fault tolerant TCP that allows a fault tolerance server to keep its TCP connections open until either it recover the TCP connection or fail to backup. Working with rollback recover, the failure and recovery of the server process are completely transparent to client processes connected with it via TCP.

In Platform EGO, the pattern of Web Service Gateway is used to trap and map service requestors to its target services. To support a huge grid user community, Platform Ego WSG can be deployed in cluster model in that a bunch of WSGs work concurrently with dynamic load balancing to provide a much higher performance. As the numbers of WSGs could be large and their locations are not fixed, it is not practical to setup a backup for each WSG, due to the performance overhead [6]. Hence, in this paper, we use rollback recovery to realize a lightweight fault-tolerance mechanism for WSGs. It works well with the WSG cluster model to be able to provide both high reliability and high performance to end users.

Rollback recovery achieves fault tolerance by saving the recovery information (called checkpoints) of processes periodically in stable storage, which has many flavors. It can be transparently to users via supported by OS kernel, like on Cray or SGI, or implemented as a library, like Condor [7]. It can also be embedded in applications to let users decide when and what to save on stable storage, which is called application level rollback recovery.

In the paper, the application level rollback recovery is realized in WSG. Since the most critical information in a WSG is the active sessions between WSG and its WSCs, and the sessions between WSG and EGO internal services, we designed a session based a-synchronized recovery algorithm which has short freezing time and is able to isolate the recoveries of different WSCs. Moreover, the load balancing algorithm for WSG cluster is also based on sessions, which is consistent with the recovery algorithm. When a WSG is down, the system can either restart a new instance if there is an available host, or select another WSG to take over the failed WSG's workload.

3 Paper Organization

The rest of this paper is as follows. In Section 2 we introduce the overview of EGO platform. Section 3 presents the EGO WSG, including WSG architecture, WSG session, WSG security, etc. Section 4 gives out the WSG fault tolerance approach and recovery algorithm based on Reliable Notifications, WSG failure report, etc. In Section 5, we make the conclusion.

4 EGO Overview

To discuss Platform EGO is out of the scope of the paper. However, in order to understand WSG's functionality, we will give a brief introduction to Platform EGO first. Platform EGO is a SOA based grid platform to offer a single, cohesive management environment that centrally allocates the shared resources across geographically dispersed sites for diverse enterprise applications, services and workloads. It allows developers, administrators, and users to treat a collection of distributed software and hardware resources on a shared computing infrastructure (cluster) as parts of a single virtual computer. Platform EGO uses Information, Allocation and Execution as key concepts in its Enterprise Grid Architecture. While many technologies effectively deal individually with Information and Execution activities associated with resource management, none take a comprehensive approach to the Allocation component. To accomplish this, Platform EGO uses a single common agent on each server to orchestrate the sharing of enterprise resources across application and organizational domains. Figure 1 illustrates Platform EGO as the foundation for a grid platform. The traditional computing resources, like hosts and clusters, are virtualized by a bunch of loose-coupled services, such as resource allocation service, execution service, security service, etc.

In a traditional cluster, like LSF or SGE, the users submit their jobs to the cluster. Then, the cluster will allocate resources and execute the jobs. A couple of EGO services provide the similar functionality but with better flexibility and extensibility. For example, in EGO, a user may first ask for resources from Allocation Service. Once the resources are allocated, Allocation Service will send a notification to the user. Then the user can ask for Execution Service to execute the task on allocated resources. If the resources allocated to a user are reclaimed by the system, or the status of a task change, the user will also get the notifications from EGO services.

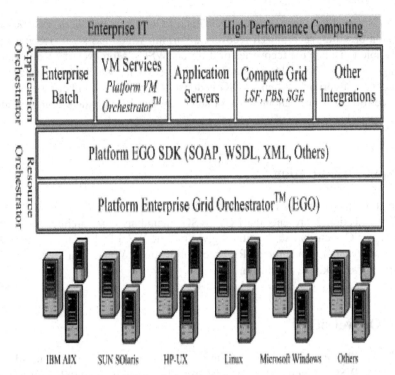

Fig. 1 Platform EGO as the foundation for a grid platform

5 EGO Web Service Gateway

EGO Web Service Gateway (WSG) that provides a standards-based web services interface for web service clients (applications) to contact Platform EGO.

6 EGO WSG Architecture

WSG is a special EGO service to enable the users to access EGO via web service interface, and itself is also under the control of Service Director. The WSG is able to (a) transfer a WSC's request to the proper EGO services; (b) send the notifications from EGO services back to WSCs; (c) support role-based access control; (d) has no effect on the WSCs after a restart, (e) provide EGO Platform with high performance. In the paper we introduced the WSG Cluster model to enable multiple WSGs to work together to provide higher performance and scalability. Figure 2 shows the WSGs Cluster Architecture.

In this model, multiple WSGs are working in parallel to handle WSC requests, and balance the load among them to further improve the scalability and performance, which is similar to WebSphere's Web Service Gateway Cluster (WSGC). A new component, Request Director is introduced to distribute the load among

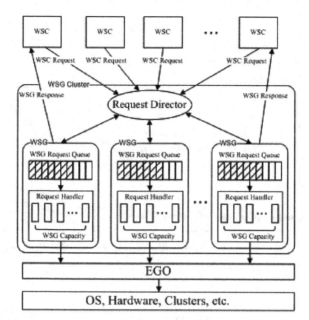

Fig. 2 WSGs Cluster Architecture

WSGs. Request Director contains two sub components: Load Balancer and Load Info Manager. The Distributor of each WSG will periodically send its load info L to Load Info Manager. If the load of a WSG is too high, it even can send an unavailable message to Load Info Manager to block Balancer to distribute more loads to it.

Load Balancer is a mediator between WSCs and WSGs, and its load distributing policy is also session based. At the beginning of a new client session, WSC will query Load Balancer to get an available WSG. Then, Load Balancer will check Load Info Manager and return a proper WSG's URL to WSC. After that, the WSC will contact the WSG directly during the session. If there is no WSG available, Load Balancer may start a new WSG. Hence, the WSG Cluster size is dynamic adjusted due to the real load.

WSG uses the thread pool pattern to process WSC requests in parallel. There is a Request Queue to hold the requests from WSCs, and there is a bunch of working threads, called Request Handlers, to handle the requests in Request Queue concurrently. Distributor is responsible for dispatching the requests to the Handlers. The handlers access the proper EGO services on behalf of WSCs and send back the results to WSCs. Figure 3 shows the WSGs workloads.

Each Handler processes the WSC's requests by transforming them into a series of accesses to EGO services using internal APIs. Some EGO services require the clients to maintain the session context, and the related communications must use the same session Handle. However, WSCs have no knowledge about the EGO services. Hence, WSG implements a Session Manager to manage the EGO service sessions for WSCs. While accessing EGO services, Session Manager will decide whether to

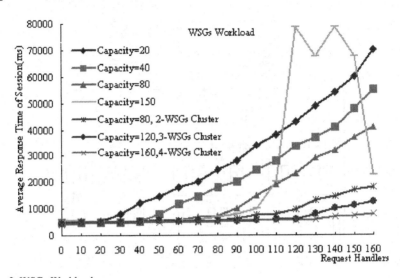

Fig. 3 WSGs Workload

use an existing session or to create a new one. If a session will not be used any more, it will be closed by Session Manager immediately.

The WSG supports notifications by following WS-Notification specification [8]. Notification Manager integrates the functionalities of Notification Broker and Subscription Manager. EGO services work as Notification Publishers, while WSCs are both Notification Subscribers and Notification Consumers. The WSCs who want to receive notifications should register themselves to WSG Notification Manager first. Then, Notification Manager will listen to the active sessions maintained by Session Manager, collect the notifications from EGO services, and deliver them to registered WSCs respectively.

Due to the Notification Manager and Session Manager, WSG could not be designed as a stateless component. After restart, WSG must rebuild all the live sessions with EGO services, and recover the notification context for all registered WSCs. Hence, Data Manager is designed to save/restore the necessary running contexts related to notifications and sessions. We will discuss WSG's recovery algorithm in Section 4.4.

7 WSG Sessions

Session is an important concept in WSG, as it relates to WSG's recovery, notification, and performance tuning etc. WSG has two kinds of sessions. One is the sessions between WSCs and WSG, which are called client sessions. The other is the sessions maintained by WSG and EGO services, which are called service sessions. After a client session is created, multiple service sessions would be setup by WSG and specific EGO services to perform the requests from the client session. Once a

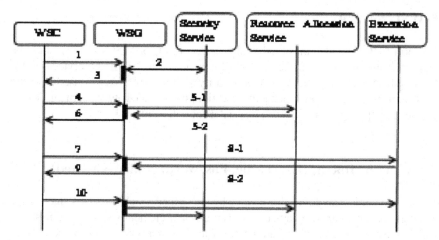

Fig. 4 A Client Session

client session is closed by the WSC, all the corresponding service sessions will be closed immediately by WSG. The following example will show how WSC run a task on Platform EGO via WSG.

Commonly, a client session contains multiple operations, and Fig. 4 gives out an example. First, the WSC starts the client session with WSG by providing the role name and password (step 1). WSG will authenticate the role name and password via accessing EGO security service (step 2), and return a session credential to WSC on success (step 3). The WSC should ship the credential in its subsequent requests to identify itself during the session. In step 4, WSC sends the resource requirement for the job execution to WSG and waits for resource allocation notifications. Then, WSG will create a service session with EGO Allocation Service and send the resource allocation requests to it (step 5-1). After the required resources are allocated successfully, a notification will be returned by Allocation Service to WSG (step 5-2). Once received the resource allocation notification forwarded by WSG (step 6), the WSC will start the job execution request (step 7). After that, WSG will create another service session with Execution Service to start the job (step 8-1). During the job running, the notifications will be sent to WSC once the job status changes (step 8-1). After the job finish, WSG will send a job finish notification to WSC (step 9). Then, WSC will close its session with WSG (step 10), and WSG will cancel the credential and close all the relevant service sessions.

As there are dependencies between some operations in a session, such operations have to be executed in proper order. For example, the job execution operation must be issued after its resource allocation operation. In real life, the operations from different client sessions (WSCs) will compete for EGO resources. If an operation of a session is delayed, all its consequent operations are delayed too.

8 WSG Security

Platform EGO provides the role-based access control for WSCs. A user could be mapped to multiple roles inside of EGO. Before accessing any EGO service, a WSC must authenticate itself to EGO. WS-Security's Username Token is used between WSG and WSCs to support such authentication. In WS-Security's Username Token profile 1.0 [9], a user name token consists of four elements as below:

9 UsernameToken: (Username, Password, Nonce, Created)

Nonce element is a random value created by the sender which is used as an effective countermeasure against replay attacks. The *Created* element specifies a timestamp which is used to indicate the creation time. The *Username* and *Password* pair is used to authenticate the WSC's identity. Inside Platform EGO, there is a table to map the usernames to role names. Besides normal users, there are some special users are defined by Platform EGO, such as EGO_admin, which has privileges to re-start the EGO system or change the system configuration.

As the internet is an unsafe communication channel, even WSG supports SSL to protect the SOAP message from being intercepted by eavesdroppers, it is still not recommended to use Username/Password frequently. Hence, we enhanced the Ws-Security Username Token profile to support credential based authentication. A credential is an encrypted string token that consists of the user information and a time stamp. Normally, a WSC gets its credential from WSG by providing the username and password when it starts a new client session with WSG. After that, WSC is able to use Credential instead of Username/Password to authenticate itself to WSG. Since each credential has a life time like a Kerberos ticket, it needs to be renewed before it expires during a session. With the above enhancement, a username token is extended as the following:

UsernameToken: ((Username, Password)|(Credential),Nonce, Created)

The above enhancement does not only improve the protection for sensitive information but also provide more flexibility. For example, the system admin does not need be mapped to privilege roles for all his operations. He can start a session as a normal user and get the credential. In most cases, he just uses the normal user's credential to perform the tasks, and the system admin's username/password is only used when necessary.

10 WSG Fault Tolerance

The communications among WSCs, WSG and EGO services are not simple request-response model. Notifications play very important roles so that the WSCs are usually designed as event-driven applications. Therefore, WSG must have its own fault tolerant approaches, such as rebuild the service sessions and the notification mechanism after restart, to handle the failures. Otherwise, it could cause deadlocks or WSG crashes.

11 Reliable Notifications

A deadlock may be caused when a WSG have already sent the allocation notification to the WSC but the WSC do not receive any notification. In this scenario, the allocated resource will not be released unless the WSC calls the WSG to do so. But the WSC has not even been notified that the required resources have been allocated.

In this case, A WSG has the responsibility to notify its WSCs with any status change, such as Allocation Notification, et al. In this scenario, the WSG is an A WSC, in another hand, have the responsibility to inform the WSG when the notifications of resources allocation have been received.

Firstly, the WSG disseminates information as a Notifications Publisher by sending one-way messages to the WSC as a Notification subscriber that are registered to receive it. Secondly, the WSC plays a role of Notification Publisher to send the notification back to the WSG while WSG is a Notification Subscriber. If a WSG doesn't hear from a WSC about the notification for a while, a copy of this notification will be sent again. But if the WSG crashes in the middle of this resend procedure, the deadlock will show up again. In Section 4.3, we will introduce Session Recovery to prevent this deadlock caused by WSG failure.

12 WSG Failure Report

Previously, The WSG Director has no instrument to be informed if a WSG is disabled to connect to its Clients. Here we report a proper method for the WSC client to inform the WSGs Director about WSG failures. When a WSC has a problem when connecting to a WSG, it reports an error code to WSGs Director with this failure. With this report in hand, the WSGs Director evaluates the failure and restart the WSG if needed.

An API to this method is implemented on the Client side of WSG. The Failure Report method consists of 3 parameters: 1) Client Session ID; 2) WSG handle; 3) Error Code.

Using this method, the WSCs group can partially be a WSGs status monitor, and significantly increase the reliability of the WSG system.

13 Sessions Recovery

In Fig. 4, WSG crashes and restarts at some time between step 5 and 6. After restart, WSG cannot build the service sessions for WSC by itself as it doesn't know either the session's credential or WSC's user-name/password. However, the WSC will

Table 1 Recovery table

Client	Flag	Notification End point	Service	Notification		
ClientSession1	VALID	http://wsc1.jlu.edu.cn/8800	EGO service1			
			EGO service2	Note1		Note2
ClientSession2	VALID	http://wsc2.jlu.edu.cn/8801	EGO service1	Note1		
			EGO service2	Note2	Note3	Note4

not send any further request unless it receives the resource allocation notification. Unfortunately, due to the notification failure caused by service sessions lost, a deadlock comes up. Moreover, the resources allocated for the WSC will not be used or released. In this scenario, we recover the client session and service session when restart the WSGs (Table 1).

As WSG decides when and what should be saved, only necessary information is saved for the recovery, which is one of the advantages of application level checkpointing. The below table, Recovery Table, will be maintained by WSG Data Manager in the disk. The table records all the active client sessions identified by session ID, WSCs' endpoint to receive notifications, the EGO services that a WSC is accessing, and Allocation Notifications which are not received and reported back from WSCs. After restart, the recovery algorithm will recover all the existing client and service sessions. When the sessions between WSCs and WSGs rebuilded, the WSGs will send again the Allocation Notifications exist in the table, to the WSCs. The Allocation Notifications will be removed from the recovery table when the WSG get the reply from the WSC. If all the Notifications have been received by WSCs, the Column "Notification Not Received" in the recovery table will be blank.

14 Recovery Algorithm

As the WSCs are designed by the different users, they could have different working models. Hence, the WSG's recovery algorithm must consider all the possible behaviors of WSCs. And we should isolate the recovery procedures for different WSCs so that they will not affect each other. The checkpointing/restart algorithms are embedded in WSG's source code.

The recovery algorithm consists of six parts.

Algorithm Part 1: After restart, WSG will rebuild the Recovery Table and start a dedicated recovery thread to do the recovery as below.

{

       Build the **Recovery Table** *from disk;*
       Mark all the client sessions in the Table as **INVALID**;
       Create the recovery thread dedicated for recovery, then:
              The **Main thread** *will execute algorithm part 2;*
              The dedicated **recovery thread** *will execute algorithm part 3;*

}

Algorithm Part 2: At normal runtime, all the active client sessions in the Recover Table are marked as VALID, and WSG will execute this part of Algorithm.

While (true) {

    Get a Request from WSC;

    If (the Request is from an **INVALID client session***) Then {*

        //this "branch" will only be executed after WSG restart.

        Get session credential from the request's SOAP message header;

        Rebuild all the service sessions with the services in the Service

    Name List;

    Mark the client session as **VALID***;*

    };

    Handle the Requests;

    If (the Request is **created a new client session***) Then {*

    Append a new item in the recovery table;

    Fill the WSC's Notification Endpoint and the client session ID;

        Mark the new client session as **VALID***;*

    };

    If (the Request is **closed a client session***) Then {*

    Remove the item from the recovery table for the client session;

    };

    If (the Request is **created a new service session***) Then {*

    Execute algorithm part 4;

        Append the service name into the Service **Name List for the proper**

    client session;

    }

    If (the Request is **closed a service session***) Then {*

        Remove the service name from the Service Name List

    for the proper client session;

    };

    Get a message from WSC;

    If (the message is **Notification Received***) Then {*

    Remove the Notification from the **Recovery Table***;*

    }

    If (the contents of the **Recovery Table** *changes) Then {*

        Save the Recovery Table into the disk;

    }

Algorithm Part 3: The recovery thread will execute the following algorithm.

Do {

    Send WSG **Restart notification** *to all the WSCs with an client session marked as* **INVLAID** *in Recovery Table;*

    //WSCs will execute algorithm part 5 while get the notification

    While (there are replies from WSCs) {

        //handle WSCs' replies for WSG Restart notification

        Get the reply from next WSC;

If (the WSC's client session is marked **INVALID***) Then {*
    Get the session credential from the reply's SOAP message header;
    Rebuild all the service sessions with the services in the
Service Name List;
      Mark the client session from this WSC as **VALID***;*
   } Else {//ignore the redundant replies.
    Discard the reply;

  }

}
} Until (all the client sessions are **VALID***)*
Exit the thread;

Algorithm Part 4: This part of algorithm is executed by Request Director to return a lightest workload WSG to the WSC, or restart a failed WSG.
{

  *If (***create a new service session** *request) Then {*
  If (No WSG avaiable) Then {
    Start a new WSG and return the WSG URL to WSC;
  } else {
    Return a lightest workload WSG to WSC;
  }

  }
  *If (***WSG Recovery Request***) Then {*
  Go to Algorithm part 3;//Restart the failed WSG;
  }

}

Algorithm Part 5: This part of the algorithm is executed by the WSCs notification handlers, to report back any information.
{

  If (it is a **WSG Restart notification***) Then {*
  Put client session's credential in the reply's SOAP message header;
  Send the reply to WSG;
  }
  If (it is a **Resource Allocation Notification***) Then {*
  Send a message to WSG that the Notification has been received;
  }
  If (. . .) – . . . . . . ˜

}

Algorithm Part 6: This part of algorithm is invoked by the WSC when unable to connect to a WSG.
{

  *If (***Unable to Connect to WSG***) Then {*

Send to Request Director a **WSG Recovery Request**;
//WSG will execute algorithm part 4;
}
If (Connecting to WSG **Timeout***) Then {*
If (Timeout over 3 times) Then {
    Set the status to **Unable to Connect to WSG**;
    } else {
    Reconnecting to WSG;
}
}
}

The algorithm works in a-synchronized model so that after restart WSG can accept the WSCs' requests immediately without waiting for the recovery process to finish. Hence, the WSG's recovery is almost invisible to WSCs. As the recovery process for each WSC is handled separately, different WSCs will not affect each other during the recovery stage. Moreover, the algorithm works well with the WSG cluster model which will be discussed in next section. In Platform EGO, all WSGs have a share file system to save the configuration and the Recovery Tables so that if a WSG cannot restart somehow, its Recovery Table can be taken over by another WSG. Hence, WSGs can be backups for each other in cluster model.

15 Conclusion

The paper discussed the design and implementation of the web service gateway for Platform EGO. The pattern of Web Service Gateway to trap and map service requestors to its target services can be found in other commercial products, like WebSphere Application Server. Compared with these products, Platform EGO WSG is an enhanced implementation, as it provides more advanced functionalities, such as notification, fault-tolerance, and can work in cluster model with dynamic load balancing.

In the paper, the application level rollback recovery approach is used in WSG. Since the most critical information in a WSG is the active sessions between WSG and its WSCs, and the sessions between WSG and EGO internal services, we designed a session based a-synchronized recovery algorithm which has short freezing time and is able to isolate the recoveries of different WSCs. This fault tolerant approach can rebuild the service sessions and the notification mechanism after restart, to handle the WSG failures. Moreover, a lightweight notification mechanism is implemented to enable the EGO services to send messages to web service clients (WSCs) in a-synchronized model without any change to the underneath SOAP stack.

Acknowledgments The authors would like to acknowledge support from the China NSF under Grant No.60703024, Platform Computing Inc. under Grant 3B6056721421, and Jilin Department of Science and Technology under Grant No.20070122 and 20060532.

References

1. I. Foster (2006) Globus Toolkit Version 4: Software for Service-Oriented Systems. IFIP International Conference on Network and Parallel Computing, Springer-Verlag LNCS 3779, pp 2–13.
2. Aghdaie, N., Tamir, Y. (2002) Implementation and Evaluation of Transparent Fault-Tolerant Web Service with Kernel-Level Support. Proceedings of the IEEE International Conference on Computer Communications and Networks, pp 63–68.
3. Dialani, V., Miles, S., Moreau, et al. (2002) Transparent Fault Tolerance for Web Services Based Architectures. Proceedings of 8th International Euro-Par Conference on Parallel Processing, Paderborn, Germany Proceedings. Volume 2400.
4. G. Teixeira Santos, L. Cheuk Lung, C. Montez (2005) FTWeb: A Fault Tolerant Infrastructure for Web Services. Proceedings of the 2005 Ninth IEEE International EDOC Enterprise Computing Conference (EDOC'05).
5. Alvisi, L. Bressoud, T.C. El-Khashab, and et al. (2001) Wrapping server-side TCP to mask connection failures. Proceedings of INFOCOM 2001.Twentieth Annual Joint Conference of the IEEE Computer and Communications Societies.
6. P. Townend and J. Xu (2004) "Replication-based Fault Tolerance in a Grid Environment", in Proceedings of U.K. e-Science 3rd All-Hands Meeting, Simon J. Cox Eds., Nottingham Conference Center, U.K., 31st August - 3rd September, 2004, ISBN 1-904425-21-6..
7. Condor Team, University of Wisconsin-Madison (2002) Condor Version 6.8.2 Manual, http://www.cs.wisc.edu/condor/manual/v6.8/ref.html. Accessed January 2006.
8. A. Nadalin IBM, C. Kaler Microsoft, R. Monzillo Sun, et al. (2006) wss-v1.1-os-UsernameTokenProfile. http://docs.oasis-open.org/wss/v1.1/. Accessed May 2006.
9. S. Graham, P. Niblett, D. Chappell et al (2004) Publish-Subscribe Notification for Web services, 1.0. http://www-128.ibm.com/developerworks/library/ws-pubsub/WS -PubSub.pdf Accessed May 2006.

Experiences with Using UNICORE in Production Grid Infrastructures DEISA and D-Grid

M. Rambadt, R. Breu, L. Clementi, T. Fieseler, A. Giesler, W. Gürich, P. Malfetti, R. Menday, J. Reetz, and A. Streit

Abstract The early stages of Grid Computing focussed on developing concepts and prototype software. Grid middleware is now at a phase of some maturity and today the focus has shifted to providing production ready Grid environments for scientists. DEISA and D-Grid aim for this production scope. DEISA is the consortium of leading national European supercomputing centres that currently deploys and operates a persistent, production quality, and distributed supercomputing environment in Europe. D-Grid is the German Grid initiative that builds up and operates a sustainable Grid infrastructure and establishes methods of e-science in the German scientific community. UNICORE is used in DEISA and D-Grid as the interface to heterogeneous production resources, and hides the complexity of resources from users. UNICORE is one of the leading Grid middleware systems used in production Grid infrastructures worldwide. This paper describes the experiences with UNICORE as Grid middleware in e-infrastructures comprising production systems in production use.

1 Introduction

Since "The Grid: Blueprint for a New Computing Infrastructure" [1] many national and continental Grid projects around the world exist and the number of funded projects even seem to increase every year. While in the beginning the projects concentrated on building a working Grid middleware, today we observe more and more projects targeting production ready Grid environment for scientists. Among others this production scope is defined in DEISA and D-Grid, too.

The DEISA (Distributed European Infrastructure for Supercomputing Applications) project [2] started in May 2004 to provide a persistent and production quality, distributed supercomputing environment. The members of the consortium wish to improve the level of exploitation of their systems and, at the same time, to provide

M. Rambadt (✉)
Forschungszentrum Jülich GmbH, Germany
e-mail: m.rambadt,r.breu,t.fieseler,a.giesler,w.guerich,r.menday,a.streit@fz-juelich.de,
l.clementi@cineca.it, johannes.reetz@rzg.mpg.de

S.C. Lin, E. Yen (eds.), *Grid Computing*,
© Springer Science+Business Media, LLC 2009

a higher Quality of Service to the users, by being able to offer them a larger joint resource pool [2]. When building such an infrastructure the DEISA partners considered several applications and middleware technologies that are providing the functionalities necessary to integrate their high-performance computing systems.

The DEISA consortium decided to use UNICORE (UNiform Interface to Computing REsources) [3] to establish a Grid infrastructure. UNICORE is one of the leading Grid middleware systems used in for production usage at a number of supercomputing centres and Grid infrastructures [4]. It hides the complexity of the underlying systems and architectures providing users with a seamless environment to work in and it uses a single sign-on mechanism based on X.509 certificates from a Public Key Infrastructure (PKI).

D-Grid [5] started as the national German Grid initiative in September 2005 combining seven community projects dealing with astronomy, climate research, high energy physics, engineering, medical research, humanities, and energy meteorology. In D-Grid the available middleware is Globus [6], LCG/gLite [7] and UNICORE. Thus the scientists are free to choose the best middleware for their application or just the middleware they are familiar with. This paper describes the experiences with UNICORE in production within DEISA and D-Grid and the features of a Grid middleware to meet the user requirements.

2 UNICORE

UNICORE provides a seamless interface for preparing and submitting jobs to a wide variety of heterogeneous distributed computing resources and data storages. It supports users for running scientific and engineering applications in a heterogeneous Grid environment.

The UNICORE software was initially developed in the UNICORE and UNICORE Plus projects [4, 10] funded by the German Ministry of Education and Science (BMBF) until the end of 2002. After that, its functionalities and its robustness were enhanced within several EU-funded projects, for example, EUROGRID [7] and OpenMolGRID [8]. Since 2004, several supercomputing centres are employing UNICORE in production.

In UNICORE every job is represented by a Java based abstract job formulation, the so-called Abstract Job Object (AJO). This gives the user the possibility to prepare jobs on an abstract level without having to know specific details of a particular target system. With the abstract formulation, the job can be submitted to different target architectures running different batch schedulers without changes.

3 UNICORE Components

UNICORE possesses a vertically integrated architecture. It provides both client and server components. In the current, production ready version, UNICORE 5, the server-side consists of the Gateway, Network Job Supervisor (NJS) including an

Incarnation Database (IDB), the UNICORE User Database (UUDB), and the Target System Interface (TSI). All components are written in Java and Perl allowing UNICORE to be installed on a large variety of operating systems.

The user only has to install the UNICORE client, and apart from some simple location configuration, has to know little regarding the functionality of the server components.

The UNICORE client GUI is used for the preparation, submission, monitoring, and administration of complex multi-site and multi-step jobs. It provides the user with an extensible application support, resource management of the target system, and integrated security mechanism.

Every submitted abstract job request (AJO) is signed using the personal X.509 certificate of the user. Thus, other UNICORE server components can perform authentication and authorisation relying on the public key infrastructure (PKI) in use. The NJS translates the abstract job information to a concrete job which is executed on the target system then. The client also provides data management and transfer functionality through an intuitive GUI.

4 Monitoring of UNICORE Servers with SIMON

For production Grids it is crucial to monitor the functionality of all involved components. Administrators should always be aware of problems before the user is. Therefore, DEISA developers implemented SIMON (Site Monitor for UNICORE Grids). SIMON is based on implementations coming together with DESHL (see Section 2.3) from the DEISA JRA7 group. It monitors the state of a UNICORE based Grid deployment by executing user-defined test suites periodically and automatically against selected sites. SIMON provides both availability and functionality tests of the UNICORE server components.

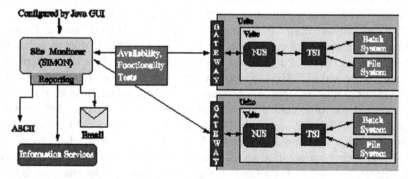

Fig. 1 Schema of SIMON functionality

Functionality tests include job execution monitoring as well as file imports to remote file systems. SIMON is easy to install and to configure via a Java based graphical user interface and thus is very flexible to add UNICORE sites or extend the parameters of an already existing site. SIMON records both expected and unexpected outcomes. That information can be used to build detailed reports regarding the health status of the Grid. The test results might be extracted and prepared in various final presentation formats or for instance they can be emailed to the UNICORE administrators. SIMON is used in both DEISA and D-Grid to monitor the UNICORE components. Currently this is in a pilot phase, but will move to full production status very soon.

5 DESHL (DEISA Services for the Heterogeneous Management Layer)

DESHL is a set of tools which allow users and their applications to manage batch jobs and data across a computing Grid. DESHL offers a command line environment to users. The option of having command line access to Grid infrastructures is extremely attractive for many users, but often not at the expense of the graphical option, and DESHL nicely compliments the full featured UNICORE graphical client. The development of DESHL takes place within the JRA7 activity of the DEISA project and whilst DEISA users are currently the main DESHL users, there is no impediment preventing the software being used on other infrastructures, such as D-Grid.

DESHL is currently used across the UNICORE 5 based infrastructure of DEISA, and does not require any additional software installation or configuration on the server-side, on top of the normal UNICORE installation and configuration. Thus, the seamless environment enjoyed by a GUI UNICORE user is also available to the DESHL user.

In addition to the command line API support DESHL can be used from within applications through an implementation of the SAGA API. Finally, DESHL is distributed with excellent documentation and a graphical installer.

Two key software abstraction layers further enhance the portability of DESHL. From the implementation perspective, the Roctopus [12] API is used to isolate the specific characteristics of a particular Grid middleware, and this will be exploited in future to provide DESHL support for Web-Service based UNICORE 6 Grid deployments. From an application developer and command line user perspective, file and job management use the emerging SAGA (Simple API for Grid Applications) [13] Grid standard. This includes using SAGA directives as the basis of the job description document. The programmer API which users can use within their own applications is based on the SAGA API. It is noteworthy that DESHL was the first available Java implementation of the emerging SAGA standard.

6 Production Environment in D-Grid and DEISA

A Grid middleware can only be as powerful as the underlying software, hardware and network is. So it is essential to achieve a smoothly functioning combination of all aspects. How this fits into the production character of D-Grid and DEISA will be shown in the next sections.

7 D-Grid User Management Infrastructure

In order to make Grid resources available to users via UNICORE or other middleware, a Grid infrastructure is required. For this, a point of information comprising a user portal and a provider portal has been installed for D-Grid users and resource providers. Users obtain the information to get a user Grid certificate, to register for a Virtual Organization (VO), to install and to use Grid middleware clients (i.e. the UNICORE client). Certificates can be obtained from Registration Authorities (RAs) run by all partners of the core D-Grid, by the DFN and by GridKA. The registration of users is done using VOMRS [14]. For each community and for the core integration project an own VO with an own instance of a VOMRS server has been configured. Users register to the VOMRS server of the corresponding VO. The UNICORE client is provided in a version which is specially pre-configured for the use in D-Grid.

For resource providers information is supplied to install the Grid middleware and to integrate the resources into the D-Grid infrastructure. The integration comprises the registration of a resource to the D-Grid resource management system, where a database with information about all resources is stored. To help the local administrator in managing D-Grid users at his site, the mapping of certificate DNs (Distinguished Names) to Unix accounts for D-Grid users of all VOs which are allowed to access these resources, can (regularly) be generated by a script which contacts the D-Grid resource management system. The information concerning which VOs have access to a resource is stored in the database of the resource management system. This information is used as a pointer to find the corresponding VOMRS database which obtains the information about users who are allowed to access the resources of the VO. Additionally the resource management system provides the DNs of the Grid server certificates of the UNICORE Network Job Supervisor (see Section 2.1) of other installations within D-Grid. The information about user mapping together with the DNs of NJS server certificates are used to update the UNICORE User Data Base (UUDB) of the local installations.

8 DEISA User Management Infrastructure

To achieve a higher level of interoperability between the different resources, the DEISA partners decided to harmonise their user management systems and to establish a DEISA user administration system by deploying a distributed network of

LDAP [15] servers. They are used to propagate information about DEISA users from the user's home site to all the partner sites. A standardisation of the naming schema for DEISA users and the assignment of site-specific ranges of UIDs and GIDs ensure that DEISA user accounts are replicable on every system belonging to the DEISA infrastructure.

A user who wants to use DEISA resources needs to apply for an account only at his home site. The user record information (user name, UID, GID, the subject of his certificate, etc.) propagates via LDAP from his home site to all the other DEISA sites.

Every night the local UUDB is updated automatically with the new user information coming from LDAP. As an improvement of the UNICORE authorization system the DEISA consortium requested to implement a modification in the UUDB internal management. The standard UUDB implementation maps the complete public part of the user's certificate to a user's account, while the modified DEISA UUDB checks only whether the Distinguished Name (DN) of the certificate used to sign the UNICORE Job (see Section 2) is present in the UUDB. With support of the UNICORE developers, the implementation of the UUDB authorisation mechanism has been adapted accordingly. A new release of the UUDB also allows the mapping of one DN to more than one user ID and/or project. This is interesting for users working in several projects and who do not want to apply for a new certificate each time.

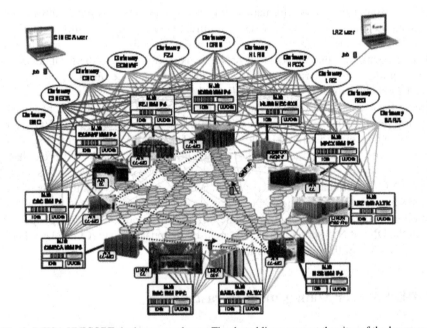

Fig. 2 DEISA UNICORE deployment schema. The dotted lines connect the sites of the homogeneous super-cluster. These sites employ the multi-cluster LoadLeveler that allows migrating jobs directly from site to site

Nearly all the resources of the DEISA infrastructure are now integrated also by means of a shared file system (Fig. 2). GPFS-MC (General Parallel File System-Multi Cluster) [11] allows achieving a transparent high-performance data access over the Wide Area Network.

When submitting a job, UNICORE creates a temporary working directory (called USPACE) at the target system where, among others, batch scripts, input, output and error files are placed. At first, DEISA partners did not require a common path for the USPACE. It was simply located on a site local file system. However, when submitted UNICORE jobs are to be migrated to other clusters by the Multi-Cluster LoadLeveler, the USPACE at the originating cluster needs to be transparent.

As a solution, the different partners have decided to configure UNICORE in order to use a common USPACE path on the GPFS-MC. In this way, UNICORE jobs submitted to the homogeneous super-cluster (see the dotted lines in Fig. 2) have always a consistent reference to the USPACE and thus to the files needed by the NJS at the originating site for monitoring the job status and fetching the output. The implementation of this solution required the modification of some TSI scripts.

9 Experiences from UNICORE in Production Grid Infrastructures

For more than three years now, UNICORE has been used in production in several European universities, companies and research centres. Mid 2005 the DEISA Extreme Computing Initiative (DECI) was launched aiming at enabling new challenging supercomputer applications. This initiative was set up to enable a number of those "grand challenge" applications in all areas of science and technology. These leading, pioneering applications depend on the DEISA infrastructure because they are dealing with complex, demanding and innovative simulations, and benefit from the exceptional resources provided by the Consortium.

10 User Requirements to a Grid Middleware

From the DEISA and D-Grid experiences first of all users need a working Grid middleware and infrastructure. The software has to be stable and available preferably all the time. In DEISA and D-Grid the UNICORE developers established fall back options e.g. for the UNICORE Gateway. As the central entry point for every user request, the Gateway plays a crucial role. In DEISA every partner site has installed a Gateway and all target systems are available via all those Gateways. So, if one Gateway should crash, the user is still able to connect to another one to submit his jobs successfully. In D-Grid there are two identically configured Gateways running at different institutions to avoid a single point of failure, too.

In case of any trouble with the server components a monitoring tool for Grid components detecting problems like SIMON is essential, as problems should be fixed as soon as possible.

Furthermore scientists have to be interested in protecting their data from unauthorized access. It would have dramatic consequences, if, for example, patent details would be stolen while the job is submitted to the Grid. Hence, security is essential for a production Grid middleware. UNICORE uses the standard X.509 PKI for authentication, authorisation, and data integration. Authentication is done in the UNICORE gateway which does the following checks:

- Is the user's certificate still valid?
- Is the certificate on the current Certification Revocation List (CRL) of the signing CA?
- Has it been signed by a trusted CA?

Both DEISA and D-Grid only accept certificates signed by an EU-GridPMA [16] trusted national Grid CA. The UNICORE security model for authentication is implemented in the UNICORE NJS which operates as a UNICORE scheduler. All public user certificates are stored in the UNICORE UUDB and they are mapped to an existing account on the target system. Every time the NJS receives an AJO, it checks if the signer's certificate distinguished name (DN) is stored in the UUDB, and if so the job is forwarded to the target system and assigned to the corresponding user account.

In addition scientists submitting their jobs to a Grid often want their jobs not only to be computed on one computing platform but on different ones. They want to use an as much abstract job description as possible in their Grid client. UNICORE provides this with the AJO model which allows the user to generate his jobs and workflows very easily and platform independent.

Often only initial hurdles prevent users from using Grid middleware. So difficulties occur even before the Grid middleware is used the first time. e.g. a criterion for users is how easy it is to adapt applications or to deal with and manage certificates. In order to deal with the first aspect, UNICORE provides the plug-in concept to adapt user's applications into UNICORE in a comfortable way. Many Scientist are not familiar with certificates as user credentials. With the integrated UNICORE Keystore Editor the user can easily manage all his certificates or request for new ones.

The acceptance of a Grid Middleware looms large with the convenience to access distributed resources regarding getting user accounts etc. The user administration of DEISA and D-Grid reduces the user's administrational efforts to a minimum.

Users' customs differ e.g. concerning graphical user interfaces and command line tools for job submission. So it is precious to provide both with the same functionality like with DESHL and UNICORE.

Our experiences with Grid infrastructures like DEISA and D-Grid show that fulfilment of functional requirements is not sufficient. Users want 24 hours a day and 7 days a week availability of the Grid infrastructure 24 hours a day 7 days a week availability of the Grid experts. Even if this is a ideal scenario which can't be established at every Grid providing site for cost reasons DEISA and D-Grid established multiple ways to provide multiple ways of user support. Both projects introduced a user and administrator help desk, central mailing lists and support hotlines at each participating site. In case of any problems the user contacts the list at their home site to solve the problem locally or to forward the request to another site. The quality of problem management is up to the time needed to solve the request.

User support is absolutely essential but not only after a problem has occurred but also before. So, detailed documentation of all used Grid middleware is necessary. Job examples have to be available and an additional FAQ section. DEISA and D-Grid provides this information on their web pages http://www.deisa.org and http://www.d-grid.de.

11 Conclusions

Grid has to mature more and more into a production status as it gets more and more desirable for scientists. There are various numbers of established Grid middleware systems which already satisfy the production interests of scientists and there is still much effort and funding to be spend on further development and integration of additional features, etc. However, in all those activities the developers should always focus on the user requirement; Grid middleware can only be successful if it is accepted and used by the end users, i.e. the scientists.

Scientists have to be stimulated and encouraged to use Grid middleware for applications, computations, data transfer and access to resources. They also have to be encouraged to adapt and integrate their applications to/into Grids. But once convinced, they likely use it further on.

In the meantime developers focus on Grid interoperability as a user should be able to submit his job transparently and independently of the underlying Grid middleware.

Acknowledgments A special thank goes to all the DEISA and D-Grid partners that contributed their effort, solutions, and ideas to the current deployments and configurations.

References

1. I. Foster and C. Kesselman (Eds.). The Grid 2: Blueprint for a New Computing Infrastructure. Morgan Kaufmann Publishers Inc. San Fransisco (2004)
2. http://www.deisa.org – Distributed European Infrastructure for Supercomputing Applications
3. http://www.unicore.eu
4. D. Erwin (Ed.): UNICORE Plus Final Report – Uniform Interface to Computing Resources. Forschungszentrum Jülich (2003)
5. A. Streit, D. Erwin, Th. Lippert, D. Mallmann, R. Menday, M. Rambadt, M. Riedel, M. Romberg, B. Schuller, and Ph. Wieder. UNICORE – From Project Results to Production Grids. L. Grandinetti (Edt.), Grid Computing: The New Frontiers of High Performance Processing, Advances in Parallel Computing 14, Elsevier, 2005, pages 357–376

6. I. Foster: Globus Toolkit Version 4: Software for Service-Oriented Systems. International Conference on Network and Parallel Computing, Springer LNCS, (2005)
7. https://www.d-grid.de – German Grid Initiative
8. K. Nowinski, B. Lesyng, M. Niezgódka, and P. Bala: Project EUROGRID. Proceeding of the PIONIER 2001, Poznan (2001)
9. S. Sild, U. Maran, M. Romberg, B. Schuller, and E. Benfenati: OpenMolGRID: Using Automated Workflows in GRID Computing Environment. Proceedings of the European Grid Conference 2005, Amsterdam, (02/2005)
10. D. Erwin and D. Snelling: UNICORE: A grid computing environment. Proceedings of Euro-Par 2001, Springer, Machester (08/2001)
11. F. Schmuck and R. Haskin: GPFS: A Shared-Disk File System for Large Computing Clusters. Proceedings of the FAST, Monterey, (01/2002)
12. B. Hagemeier, R. Menday, B. Schuller, and A. Streit A Universal API for Grids. Proceedings of Cracow Grid Workshop (CGW'06), Cracow, Poland, 2006
13. http://forge.ogf.org/sf/projects/saga-core-wg
14. http://computing.fnal.gov/docs/products/vomrs/vomrs1_2/pdf/booktitle.pdf
15. K. Zeilenga and OpenLDAP foundation: Lightweight Directory Access Protocol (LDAP): Technical Specification Road Map. RFC 4510, (06/2006)
16. Profile for Traditional X.509 Public Key Certification Authorities with secured infrastructure. EUGridPMA, Version 4.0 (10/2005)

Dashboard for the LHC Experiments

Julia Andreeva, Benjamin Gaidioz, Juha Herrala, Gerhild Maier,
Ricardo Rocha, Pablo Saiz, and Irina Sidorova

Abstract In this paper we present the Experiment Dashboard monitoring system, which is currently in use by four Large Hadron Collider (LHC) [1] experiments. The goal of the Experiment Dashboard is to monitor the activities of the LHC experiments on the distributed infrastructure, providing monitoring data from the virtual organization (VO) and user perspectives. The LHC experiments are using various Grid infrastructures (LCG [2]/EGEE [3], OSG [4], NDGF [5]) with correspondingly various middleware flavors and job submission methods. Providing a uniform and complete view of various activities like job processing, data movement and publishing, access to distributed databases regardless of the underlying Grid flavor is the challenging task. In this paper we will describe the Experiment Dashboard concept, its framework and main monitoring applications.

1 Introduction

The LHC experiments ALICE, ATLAS, CMS and LHCb are preparing for data acquisition planned to start in 2008. The LHC will produce about 15 Petabytes of data annually and access to this data has to be provided to 5000 scientists in about 500 scientific institutions all over the world. These numbers allow to estimate the scale and complexity of the LHC computing task. For their computing systems all LHC experiments had chosen the globally distributed tiered model. The LHC experiments are relying on several Grid infrastructures: LCG/EGEE, OSG, NDGF. At the current stage, the improvement of the performance and reliability of the Grid sites and services is becoming a very important task and various monitoring systems are contributing to achieve this goal. At the same time the overall operation depends not only on the Grid's performance and reliability, but also on the quality of the experiment specific software and services. The monitoring system focused on the needs of the LHC user community has to provide monitoring information in a transparent way across several Grid infrastructures and has to combine data

J. Andreeva (✉)
European Organization for Nuclear Research CERN G06910, CH-1211 Geneva 23, Switzerland.
e-mail: Julia.Andreeva@cern.ch

related to the performance of the Grid infrastructure and data that is experiment/ activity/application specific. Such a monitoring system should be able to satisfy users in various roles like production manager, coordinator of data transfer, site administrator supporting a given experiment at the local site or simply an analysis user submitting analysis jobs to the Grid. Finally, it should be capable not only to detect different kinds of problems or inefficiencies, but also to assist in understanding the underlying reasons.

The goal of the Experiment Dashboard is to satisfy the requirements mentioned above. In the first section of this paper we will describe the concept of the Experiment Dashboard monitoring system and its framework. The next sections will provide an overview of the main Experiment Dashboard monitoring applications, including examples of the usage of the tools by the LHC experiments. The two final sections will focus on the future work and draw some conclusions.

2 Overview of the Architecture

The Experiment Dashboard provides a view of the Grid infrastructure focused on the needs of the users of the LHC VOs. The dashboard developers took into account the requirements of the LHC experiments and analysed monitoring data collected by existing monitoring systems and by the experiment specific tools and services. This data was analysed in order to understand how various sources can complement each other and how information coming from multiple sources can be correlated and merged.

The main components of the Experiment Dashboard are: information collectors, data storage, (currently implemented for an Oracle backend) and the web applicaton (presentation layer). In general, the system is using multiple sources of information. Information can be transported to the Experiment Dashboard via various protocols and data collectors are implemented in either push or pull modes.

2.1 Introduction to the Experiment Dashboard Framework

The schema of the Experiment Dashboard framework is presented in Fig. 1. The framework is implemented in Python and covers the functionalities common to all monitoring applications: collection of information, access to the database and presentation of the information to the user (Apache and mod_python).

2.1.1 Information Collectors (Dashboard Agents)

Providing a reliable monitoring system rely on data collectors running permanently and recovering in case of failure. The Experiment Dashboard framework provides all the necessary tools to implement, manage and monitor these permanent processes (called "agents"). Their status is automatically reported to the maintainers (by three

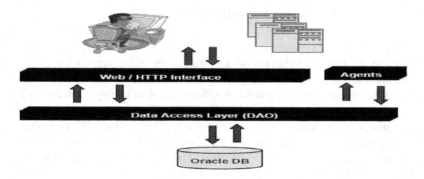

Fig. 1 Experiment dashboard framework

means: a web application, an e-mail or an SMS). Dashboard services are also used to implement other kinds of permanents tasks like the computation of daily statistics.

2.1.2 Database Access

To ensure a clear design and maintainability of the system, the definition of the monitoring application queries is decoupled from the internal implementation of the data storage. Every monitoring application implemented within the framework comes with the implementation an interface called "Data Access Object" (DAO): a set of public methods for the update and retrieval of information. Access to the database is accomplished by using a connection pool to reduce the overhead in creating new connections, therefore the load on the server is reduced and the performance increased.

2.1.3 Data Presentation Layer

The Experiment Dashboard requests are handled by a system following the Model-View-Controller (MVC) pattern. They are handled by the "controller" component, launched by the mod_python Apache extension, which keeps the association between the requested URLs and the corresponding "actions", executing them and returning the data in a format requested by the client. All actions process the request parameters and execute a set of operations (e.g. retrieve data with the DAO). The output of an action is then transformed into the required format (HTML page, plain XML, CSV, image) by the "view" components. The controller applies automatically the view to the data.

This flexibility in the output format allows the system to be used not only by users but also by other applications. For example, apart the access through a web browser, the system provides command-line tools and python API. CLI and API are relying on the available rendering in XML which they use internally to fetch data and present to the user (text mode for the CLI or Python object for the API).

HTML pages are rendered using XSL transformation applied to the XML output.

3 Experiment Dashboard Applications

Experiment Dashboard monitoring applications are now covering a wide range of activities of the LHC experiments on the Grid. Some of the applications, like job monitoring and site reliability, are generic and in production for all LHC experiments, others are specific to a given experiment, like data management monitoring [6], developed on the request of the ATLAS experiment. As a general rule, the development of a new application starts on the request of one of the LHC experiments, but in case when no experiment specific information sources are involved, this application can be reused for other experiments. The overview of currently available applications is shown in Fig. 2. The main applications are described in this chapter.

3.1 Job Monitoring

The goal of the job monitoring is to follow job processing of the LHC experiment on the distributed infrastructure. The Experiment Dashboard keeps track of all jobs submitted by the experiment users and stores the main monitoring indicators, such as resource usage and sharing, Grid behavior, application robustness and data access quality. Information related to the job processing is aggregated and depending on the users's request can be shown as a function of different attributes. The dashboard also helps to keep record of resource sharing between physics activities within an experiment, such as production and analysis, between different analysis groups and between individual users.

For job monitoring the Experiment Dashboard uses multiple sources of information (grid information systems and VO information). Information from the Logging and Bookkeeping system is not retrieved directly. The Experiment Dashboard uses RGMA [7], ICRTM [8] and GridICE [9]. The application-specific information is gathered throughout the job lifetime – submission, runtime and output retrieval – via the MonALISA [10] monitoring system (VO jobs are instrumented to report their meta information and progress).

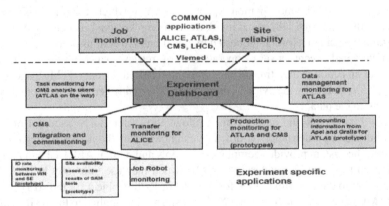

Fig. 2 Experiment Dashboard applications

Regarding the user interface, job monitoring applications provide a snapshot of the job processing status, the so called "interactive view", which allows to see what is happening now and provides the straight forward way to detect any inefficiencies related to job processing, like the misconfiguration of Grid services at sites or corrupted data. A historical view, which shows job processing evolution over any given time range, is also provided.

Currently, the job monitoring application is used by all 4 LHC experiments and by the VLEMED VO [11] (outside the LHC community).

3.2 Site Reliability

The site reliability application [12] was developed to facilitate the task of the site administrators, to estimate the site performance regarding job processing and data transfer and to detect and understand eventual problems at the site. Site reliability related to job processing uses the same information sources as the job monitoring application, but allows to analyze what happened to every individual job submitted via a Resource Broker in more details and presents the results of this analysis in different formats. One of the main features of the site reliability application is that it estimates the job processing success rate by taking into account the success of every individual job submission attempt (every individual job can be resubmitted by a Resource Broker several times). This application generates daily reports for the number of successful or failed attempts for all sites, serving a given VO and provides a ranking of the sites based on these reports.

3.3 Task Monitoring

The task monitoring application can be regarded as a supplement of the job monitoring application, but focused on the needs of the LHC analysis users submitting their jobs to the Grid. The application provides a consistent way of following a user's analysis tasks regardless of the job submission tool, which was used for the job generation and submission, under the condition that the job submission tool was instrumented for reporting to the dashboard. Using the web interface, the user can browse the analysis tasks, which have been submitted over the chosen period of time, see meta attributes of the task or of the individual job, check the success or failure of jobs belonging to a given task in real time without the necessity of opening the log files. Currently, the task monitoring application is in production for the CMS and ATLAS users.

3.4 ATLAS Data Management Monitoring

Data distribution is one of the most challenging tasks for the LHC experiments, in particular due to very strong requirements regarding data safety and large-scale data replication. Practical management issues with the storage systems and wide-area networks increase the complexity of the data management task. The LHC experiments need reliable monitoring, capable of following the large scale distribution of the experiment datasets as well as the transfer of individual files.

3.4.1 Information Sources

The main sources of the monitoring information for ATLAS data management applications are ATLAS data management services (one instance running per site). (For a detailed description of the ATLAS system, please refer to [6].) The services provide transfer and file placement information. To understand the reasons of data management problems, the application uses the results of SAM tests and correlates results of these tests with the eventual failures detected by the monitoring system.

3.4.2 Monitoring Transfers

The flow of monitoring data starts as soon as a new dataset request - a subscription - is made and picked up by the system agents on the sites, marking it as queued. It is then marked as incomplete as soon as the first file starts to be transferred, and will eventually get to the status complete, once all the dataset files are available on the destination site. A similar flow exists for each individual file transfer, from the moment the site transfer agents try to find a suitable replica to be used as a source to the registration of the file in the local file catalog, so that end users can retrieve it. Meanwhile, there are interactions with file transfer services with possible retrials in case of failure. The Experiment Dashboard keeps track of every single event in both, the dataset and the file workflows, storing also the errors or reasons of every state change. This information is kept during (at least) the time of the whole dataset transfer. The global view provides a site overview covering different metrics, for example, the throughput or a list of completed files/datasets, a summary of the most common errors (transfer and placement), etc. Via a detailed view, the user can navigate through the complete history of the dataset transfer, starting from the dataset state to the state of each of its files and to the history of each single file placement following all status changes.

3.5 Monitoring of the Production Activity for ATLAS and CMS

Production activities of all LHC experiments are fully relying on the distributed Grid infrastructure. Even though there are a lot of similar features in the organization of the production activity in the LHC experiments, there are a lot of differences as well. These differences have an impact on the implementation of the production monitoring systems [13, 14]. Both ATLAS and CMS are using several Grid infrastructures and a variety of job submission methods for production. The functionality, which is provided by the Experiment Dashboard for the production monitoring of ATLAS and CMS is different, but for both experiments the production monitoring systems are developed as a joined effort from the Experiment Dashboard team and the developers of the production systems in ATLAS and CMS experiments.

3.5.1 ATLAS Production Monitoring

The ATLAS production system is based on a central database, holding information about the job status (waiting submission, scheduled in a resource, running, being aborted and many other). In particular, the production system manages job definitions which are then dispatched to different processing back-ends: LCG/EGEE, OSG and NDGF. The main users of the production monitoring system are production managers and operators, and the user interface should allow them to follow the production progress and to detect problems in a straight forward way.

ATLAS had already a monitoring system which maintenance could not be ensured. A dashboard application was thus implemented. The re-implementation was a good opportunity to factorize multiple functionalities at once, identifying critical views, and optimizing the navigation. Moreover, the integration with ATLAS data management monitoring is natural since the same framework is used at the back. The major improvement for the production operators coming along with the new interface, is the direct way to identify the problematic tasks, which require to take action, to detect sites with wrong software installations (in order to send a GGUS ticket) and to get the top errors for each site/task/submission tool. Production managers and site administrators can benefit from the very flexible interface for generating performance plots, which is provided by the new interface. The future development foresees the interaction between data management and production monitoring systems with the possibility of data exchange between two database back-ends. Another important direction of the future development is defining alarm conditions and enabling alarms in case of problems.

4 Future Plans

There are several directions regarding the future development of the Experiment Dashboard, but the main goal is to improve the reliability and completeness of the provided monitoring information. To achieve this goal we are adding the new sources of the monitoring information. For example, for improving data reliability in the job monitoring application the Experiment Dashboard team is collaborating with Condor-G [15] developers in order to instrument Condor-G submitter to report information related to job status changes to the Experiment Dashboard. At the same time, for jobs submitted via a gLite Resource Broker we explore the possibility to receive job status changes information from the gLite Logging and Bookkeeping system via a subscription mechanism.

The Experiment Dashboard is following the modifications of the work flow and data management organization of the LHC experiments. Some of the experiments are using pilot submission systems, where several user applications can run in a single Grid job. This is not currently supported by the Experiment Dashboard database schema. We are planning to modify the Experiment Dashboard schema and user interface to be able to cope with this submission mode.

We are working on improvements of the user interfaces, for example, the enabling of secure access to certain types of information based on X509 authentication, where relevant.

Another important direction of the development is the improvement of effectiveness for troubleshooting. For instance, we analyze collected statistics on the job failures trying to define mechanisms, which would allow to decouple application failures, caused by the errors in the user code from the failures related to the problems of sites or Grid services.

Finally, we are working on the development of new applications, for instance, the production monitoring applications for ATLAS and CMS.

5 Conclusions

The Experiment Dashboard is currently in production for all four LHC experiments. The core part of the job monitoring functionality is also used by the VLEMED VO outside the LHC community. While most of the existing Grid monitoring tools are coupled to a given infrastructure or a given middleware, the Experiment Dashboard works across various Grid infrastructures. It uses multiple sources of monitoring data including other Grid monitoring systems or services specific to the experiments. This increases the reliability and completeness of the provided information.

The Experiment Dashboard framework defines the overall structure of the project, provides common ways for managing the components of the system and contains a lot of generic methods, which can be used for the development of new applications. These functionalities of the framework facilitate a lot the new developments and everyday support of the system.

Close collaboration with the experiments allows to create the system focused on the exact needs of the users regarding monitoring, providing complete views of how the distributed infrastructure is used by the LHC experiments, and covering different areas of their activities.

Acknowledgments The authors would like to express their gratitude to the developers of the monitoring, accounting and job submission systems, in particular MonALISA, Imperial College Real Time Monitoring, RGMA, GridIce, SAM [16], Apel, Gratia, and Condor-G for the fruitful collaboration, to our colleagues in the LHC experiments who contributed a lot to the progress of the Experiment Dashboard project, to the Oracle support team at CERN for excellent DB support and useful advices, and to EIS and FIO in CERN IT for their help and prompt response to our requests. Special thanks to Stefano Belforte - the initiator of the Experiment Dashboard project, Massimo Lamanna and Iosif Legrand without their support and valuable guidance the progress of the project would not be possible.

This work is funded by EGEE. EGEE is a project funded by the European Union under contract INFSO-RI-031688.

References

1. LHC home page, http://lhc.web.cern.ch/lhc/
2. The LCG Editorial Board, "LHC Computing Grid Technical Design Report", LCG-TDR-001, CERN-LHCC-2005-024, June 2005

3. Enabling Grid for E-sciencE (EGEE), http://www.cern.ch/egee
4. Open Science Grid (OSG) Web Page, http://www.opensciencegrid.org/
5. Nordic Data Grid Facility (NDGF) Web Page, http://www.ndgf.org/
6. R. Rocha et al., "Monitoring the Atlas Distributed data Management System", Conference on Computing in High Energy and Nuclear Physics (CHEP07), September 2007, Victoria (Canada)
7. R-GMA home page, http://www.r-gma.org/
8. Imperial College Real Time Monitor home page, http://gridportal.hep.ph.ic.uk/rtm/
9. GridIce home page, http://gridice.forge.cnaf.infn.it//
10. Monitoring Agents Using a Large Integrated Services (MonALISA), http://monalisa.cern.ch/monalisa.html
11. VLEMED virtual organization. http://www.vl-e.com.
12. P. Saiz et al., "Grid reliability", Conference on Computing in High Energy and Nuclear Physics (CHEP07), September 2007, Victoria (Canada)
13. S. Campana et al., "Experience with the gLite Workload Management System in ATLAS Monte Carlo Production on LCG, Conference on Computing in High Energy and Nuclear Physics (CHEP07), September 2007, Victoria (Canada)
14. J. Hernandez Calama et al., "CMS Monte Carlo production in the WLCG Computing Grid", Conference on Computing in High Energy and Nuclear Physics (CHEP07), September 2007, Victoria (Canada)
15. Condor-g home page, http://www.cs.wisc.edu/condor/condorg/
16. SAM home page, http://sam-docs.web.cern.ch/sam-docs/

Characteristics of a Novel Grid Resource Broker cum Meta-Scheduler

B. Asvija, K.V. Shamjith, Henry Sukumar, R. Sridharan, Mohanram N, and Prahlada Rao

Abstract Modern Service Oriented Grids seamlessly integrate huge sets of distributed, heterogeneous resources that are spread across different administrative and business domains. The authors, in this paper bring out the characteristics of a Novel Grid Broker cum Meta-Scheduler that efficiently manages and harnesses resources in the grids. The requirements of this Federated & Autonomous Resource Management System include handling policy enforcements of Resources, Jobs and Users, addressed at Grid/Community/Site/Individual resource levels. It addresses the requirements with respect to Administrative, User, and Community (Virtual Organization) views. It highlights the requirements from an Application/Domain specific perspective, for maximizing the throughput through fine-tuning and optimizing communication and data storage patterns. The requirements are abstracted for various resource types like Compute, Storage, Data, Memory, Network, and Software in a grid. The need of a Descriptive Language (to formulate these requirements in an unambiguous manner), using Request-Response model is also presented. The features of the popular meta-schedulers available today are compared.

1 Introduction

Modern grid infrastructures house very large sets of heterogeneous resources that are widely distributed over geographical locations and administrative domains [1, 2]. This heterogeneity and distributed nature of resources necessitate for an efficient management system that can aid in their optimum utilization. Nevertheless, such a system has to face new challenges that are unique to this realm. Hence, understanding these challenges becomes extremely important in our endeavor of building successful Grid infrastructures.

In this paper, we begin with the discussions on the broader goals of a Resource Broker cum Scheduler. The following sections list the expectations from a general

B. Asvija (✉)
Centre for Development of Advanced Computing (C-DAC), Bangalore, India
e-mail: asvijab, shamjithkv, henrys, rsridharan, mohan, prahladab@cdacb.ernet.in

S.C. Lin, E. Yen (eds.), *Grid Computing*,
© Springer Science+Business Media, LLC 2009

user's perspective and administrator's perspective of the system. A detailed analysis of each of these requirements is presented. Finally, a short discussion is given on the popular Grid brokers and schedulers in the market.

2 Broader Goals

At a broader level, it can be seen that any such system is expected to achieve the following goals. These goals form the basic requirements of the complex system.

a. The foremost requirement would be to aggregate the heterogeneous resources and manage the workload at a global level.
b. It would also be expected to provide unattended, reliable, and efficient execution of jobs on heterogeneous and dynamic resources in a grid.
c. A less discussed, but equally important requirement is to offer a unified interface for managing these loosely coupled resources, maintaining scalability and autonomy.

As it can be seen from the above discussion, these goals comprise of both administrative and user level requirements of the system. These two sets of users form the basic actors in forming the use cases of the overall system. Hence, as a possible better approach to understand these requirements, the following discussion captures them from these two perspectives.

3 Administrative Requirements

Administrative requirements encompass most of the issues related to the management of resources in the grid. It also becomes essential to monitor and manage the users, belonging to various domains and Virtual communities in a grid. Another common issue is to manage the jobs themselves. Accounting and Logging for all these services forms a core requirement from administrators. A secure framework, which encompasses all these services, is also of prime concern. A detailed analysis of each of these requirements is presented below.

3.1 Resource Management

Resource Management [3] is a generic term that is applied to the monitoring and management of various types of resources available in the grid. Although each type of resource may require a different approach for achieving this, it is desirable to have a **virtual, unified framework**, comprehensive enough to push down the translated global parameters and actions into individual resource managers. A logical extension of this issue is to have the system capable of interacting with popular, existing

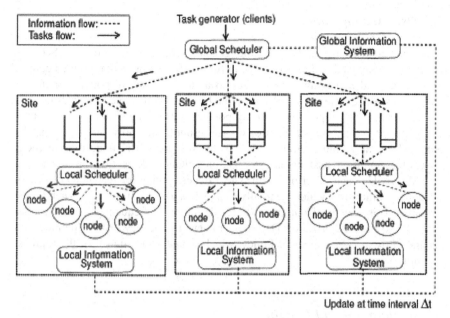

Fig. 1 The 'Push' Model of Resource Manager [7]

resource managers such as the batch schedulers available at the cluster level such as the PBS [4] LSF [5], Load Leveler [6] etc. (See Fig. 1)

Another important requirement is to have a uniform framework to enforce **Policy settings** amongst various resources in the grid. The policy settings can govern a variety of parameters on the resources including valid users, user groups, resource priorities, scheduling classes, job-preemption policies and others, to name a few. These policy settings can be enforced at different levels –

a. Global or Grid Level
b. Virtual Organization/Community Level
c. Site or Cluster Level
d. Individual resource Level.

As an extension of the policy settings, **Resource Quotas** can also be enforced at these various levels. Typical quota parameters on compute resources include number of Jobs, Nodes, Processors, Wall clock time etc., and Limits on CPU, Physical Memory, Virtual Memory, Disk utilizations.

Another issue to consider in this context is related to the **Resource Lifetime Management**. The system, with the aid of notifications from an Information infrastructure, should be capable of handling the resource breakdowns and perform **Adaptive scheduling**, to ensure the quality of services offered. Commonly employed **Fault management mechanisms** include user-level/System level check pointing and Migration of running jobs.

3.2 User Management

User management issues befit in the general Grid Architecture and Security framework employed. Administrators can further manage with fine-grained control by creating and managing **user classes** so as to grant/revoke policies or quotas collectively. Policy is a very broad term that has to be constrained in our context to include access control policies, security policies, scheduling policies and resource usage policies. Fine-grained control of user/group/community privileges can be enforced by the administrators at each of the resources. **Privilege management** covers the definition, assignment, storage, presentation, delegation and revocation of both privilege and descriptive attributes. Access policy for resources is written by policy authorities, which generally get their authority from the owner of the resource. This source of authority (SoA) definition is frequently statically configured into the Authorization Decision Framework but may also be defined in a separate Privilege Management Policy, which is under the control of the topmost authority.

3.3 Accounting and Logging

Accounting and auditing services aid in accurate billing and metering of the resources. Their benefits extend beyond managing operational costs. Accounting also links to other issues such as capacity planning, Service level management and performance management. An important requirement is to offer **Local and inter-domain accountings**, which will help in auditing and billing at the VO/Grid level. Accounting of User Policy and Resource Policy violations also help in intrusion detection and malicious breakdown attempts in the grid. Another important issue is to track the number of check pointed and restarted jobs. This gives an insight into the scalability, inter-operability and fault tolerance level of the resources in the grid.

3.4 Security

Security is at the heart of any Grid infrastructure. When jobs are run on a particular machine, the user needs assurances that the machine has not been compromised, making his proprietary application or data subject to being stolen. When a user's job executes, it may require confidential message-passing services. A user or the Grid infrastructure software may set up a long-lived service such as a specialized scheduler and require that only certain users are allowed to access the service. In each of these cases, the system should be designed to provide this required security-related functionality, and the invoker of these applications must understand how to check if these security services are available and how they can be invoked.

The most fundamental assumption in this context is that each user and principal will have a Grid-wide identity that all the other Grid principals can verify. However *some* local resource managers will require legacy local user ids for users of their resources. Access control will be enforced both by local resource managers often using legacy access control mechanisms and by Grid aware services that may want to use Grid centered access policies. In either case there must be simple and **unified framework** for users to request access rights and allocations and the stakeholders to grant them.

Authentication, Authorization, User credential delegation, Confidentiality and Integrity verification are the normal security issues that need to be addressed in any Grid infrastructure. Sites will generally make authorization decisions on an aggregate basis: on Virtual Organization (VO) membership or group membership. However, at times it will be necessary to set access rights at the granularity of a single user. Sites must reserve the right, and preserve the ability, to set authorization at this level [8]. Also, incident handling requires the ability to identify the legitimate owner of credentials presented during transactions under investigation. Apart from the normal user/group based authentication mechanisms, **Role based privileges** are also to be supported by the system. "Role" refers to the set of attributes an end entity is presenting with a particular request for obtaining or asserting a privilege. Control points must exist to allow for enforcement of authorization decisions and the inclusion of local policy decision functions. Management of these control points should not place a large maintenance demand on the resource administrator.

4 User Requirements

User requirements from a brokering and scheduling system are largely Job centered with importance on Performance and other Quality of Services offered. An equally important issue is related to the Job Description Language, which facilitates the users to formulate the job requirements. Application specific/Domain specific scheduling features and optimizations form core requirements in specialized Virtual Organizations. User level requirements also encompass some of the security concerns from grid users including confidentiality and Message integrity verification. Each of these requirements are further discussed in detail below.

4.1 Job Description Language

Job description language forms the core interface mechanism through which users in a grid specify and describe the job along with its requirements, in an unambiguous manner. The semantics and structure of such a language should be carefully designed to support all the capabilities of the brokering and scheduling system [9]. The interface should be comprehensive and extensible to include feature requests like Advance and Immediate Reservations, Array and Multi Job requests, and Job lifetime management and notifications.

The language can also follow a **Request-Response** model to be informative. The exact and minimum **resource requirements** specified by the user form the 'request'

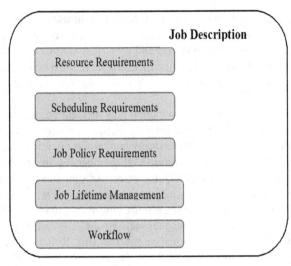

Fig. 2 Different aspects of a job description

and the feedback from the system on the actual allocations, based on the dynamic conditions of the grid form the 'responses'.

It is also desirable to have the language addressing the entire lifecycle of a job and its relation with other jobs in the system. As an extension of this, the language can also borrow the features of a **Workflow language**, which helps in specifying the intricate dependencies between the subjobs.

Description of the **scheduling requirements** fall into different categories, which include scheduling based on Job start and End times, scheduling based on the expected availability or validity of input data and scheduling based on the order of jobs in a workflow. The **lifetime management** of jobs is an important aspect of the overall management of jobs. It allows the description of the state of the job and job control directives. This comprises of the notification support for Job state changes.

4.2 Job Submission and Status Tracking:

This forms the core requirement of the Brokering cum scheduling system. This coarse requirement encompasses all the job submission related requirements including Advance Reservations and Co-allocations.

A Grid **resource reservation** framework should provide two capabilities. First, it should allow users to make reservations either in advance of when the resource is needed or at the time that the user needs it. Second, the same framework should be capable of making and manipulating a reservation regardless of the type of the underlying resource, thereby simplifying the programming when an application must work with multiple kinds of resources and multiple simultaneous reservations. Most resources cannot deal with advance reservations, however, so the reservation manager should track the reservations and do admission control for new reservation requests. The framework should also support modifying, committing, querying and canceling the previously made reservations. **Co-allocation** and Co-reservation of multiple resources should be supported through a layered, flexible architecture.

Job Types indicate the nature of the jobs running in a grid. There can be simple, serial jobs running on a single resource or parallel jobs running on a homogeneous cluster/SMP or parallel jobs spanning different heterogeneous resources [10], distributed geographically. They can be Array or Batch jobs or Multi-Jobs with different subjobs. Workflow jobs comprise of different, distinct jobs with interoven dependencies among them. Thus the job description language and hence the scheduling framework should be capable of handling submission of these job types and tracking their states.

Scheduling the jobs in a grid involves three distinct steps [11]:

a. Resource Discovery.
b. System Selection.
c. Job Execution.

Resource discovery involves selection of a set of resources to investigate in more detail in phase two, with the help of the Information infrastructure. Given a set of resources to which a user has access and the minimal set of requirements the job has, the next step in the resource discovery phase is to filter out the resources that do not meet the minimal job requirements. Given the information gathered by the previous step, a decision of which resource (or set of resources) should the system submit a job is made in the step. This can and will be done in a variety of ways. It may be the case that to make the best use of a given system, part or all of the resources will have to be reserved in advance. Job execution may involve the Preparation stage containing setup, staging, claiming a reservation, or other actions needed to prepare the resource to run the application.

Scheduling policies play a major role in achieving the performance optimizations for applications. As an extensibility feature, the system should support plugging in of new scheduling policies. Proven, common scheduling policies such as the Backfill, Fair Share, Shortest job first, FCFS and others can be supported with the infrastructure. Frameworks may also require Weighted Priority Schedule algorithms for enforcing **Real time** constraints on the applications.

4.3 Application Specific Scheduling:

Application/Domain specific scheduling algorithms are becoming widely popular as many Community oriented grids are evolving. Many research efforts are oriented in this direction to device and tune the scheduling algorithms in order to optimize the performance of critical applications/application classes.

Such algorithms can also be well tuned to specifically cater to the resource requirements of specific applications. They can also help in improving the performance by optimized selection of resources for pre-defined data storage and communication patterns.

Such a framework can also support the creation and handling of **application specific workflows**. These can be thought of as canned procedures or **Problem Solving Environments**, which transparently transform the inputs into the desired outputs. Such frameworks obviously have a great scope for optimization as their requirement and dynamic nature can be predicted in advance.

5 Comparison of the Popular Grid Brokers/Schedulers

Many popular Grid Resource Brokers and Schedulers have proven their relevance in managing grids of large scale. The following discussion tries to present a short comparison of the popular products available. Although this comparison is not exhaustive, it tries to highlight the comparison of major features available in each of these products. Three popular products namely Moab, Gridway and Condor-G have been selected for this comparison study.

Moab [12] is a commercial scheduler cum broker, from ClusterResources Inc. It is a feature abundant product ideally suited to Grid environments. It includes a separate Policy Engine and supports Advance Reservations and a variety of scheduling policies including FCFS and Backfill. A major drawback is that this product only caters to the compute resources in a grid, and thus data and network resources are not taken into consideration in making the scheduling decisions.

GridWay [13] is an Open source meta-scheduler, from the University of Madrid, Spain. It seamlessly integrates with Globus Toolkit [14], the popular Grid middleware. It also claims to support advanced adaptive scheduling features, unavailable in other products. A serious drawback of this product is the lack of fine-grained policy settings. Another issue is its trivial support for Accounting and Logging features through history, which may not be adequate in most scenarios.

Condor-G [15] is a broker with advanced Job submission interface. There are no scheduling features from Condor-G itself. A major advantage is that it can handle complex workflows with the aid of DAGMan. Condor-G also targets only compute resources, which poses as a serious drawback. Another drawback is that it does not support staging of files other than stdin, stdout, stderr and executables.

As can be seen from the above discussions, gaps exist in the popular products, giving scope for research in each of these areas. Efforts are in place to fill these lacunae and bring out the best technology in place to suit all the requirements of such a product.

6 Conclusion

The purpose of this article is to describe common patterns, which one can determine when dealing with Grid scheduling and resource management. Research efforts are on to fill out the gaps identified in many areas related to the resource management and scheduling in the grid. The list of patterns is neither exhaustive nor does it provide a normative terminology of Grid scheduling and resource management usage scenarios. But the patterns together with the use cases are the basis for defining Grid scheduling requirements and specifying the services needed to fulfill these requirements.

References

1. Grid Computing: Making the Global Infrastructure a Reality - F Berman, G Fox, AJG Hey, T Hey - 2003 – John Wiley & Sons, Inc. New York, NY, USA
2. The grid: blueprint for a new computing infrastructure - Foster, C Kesselman - 1998 - Morgan Kaufmann Publishers Inc. San Francisco, CA, USA
3. Resource Management in OGSA - GGF Common Management Model (CMM) WG - http://forge.gridforum.org/projects/cmm-wg/
4. Portable Batch System – http://www.openpbs.org
5. Platform LSF - http://www.platform.com/Products/Platform.LSF.Family/
6. LoadLeveler - http://www-03.ibm.com/systems/clusters/software/loadleveler.html
7. A Study of Meta-scheduling architectures for high throughput computing: Pull versus Push – Vincent Garonne, Andrei Tsaregorodtsev, Eddy Caron
8. Conceptual Grid Authorization Framework and Classification – GGF Authorization Frameworks and Mechanisms – WG
9. Job Submission Description Language (JSDL) Specification, Version 1.0 – http://forge.gridforum.org/projects/jsdl-wg
10. A grid-enabled MPI: message passing in heterogeneous distributed computing systems- Ian Foster, Nicholas T Karonis Conference on High Performance Networking and Computing. Proceedings of the 1998 ACM/IEEE conference on Supercomputing
11. Ten Actions When SuperScheduling – GGF Scheduling Working Group
12. Moab Grid Suite - http://www.clusterresources.com/pages/products/moab-grid-suite.php
13. Gridway – Meta-scheduling technologies for the grid – http://www.gridway.org
14. Globus Toolkit – http://www.globus.org
15. Condor-G - http://www.cs.wisc.edu/condor/condorg/

Part IV
Operation & Management

Core D-Grid Infrastructure

Thomas Fieseler and Wolfgang Gürich

Abstract D-Grid is a German implementation of a grid, granted by the German Federal Ministry of Education and Research. In this paper we present the Core DGrid which acts as a condensation nucleus to build a production grid infrastructure. The main difference compared to other international grid initiatives is the support of three middleware systems, namely LCG/gLite, Globus, and UNICORE for compute resources. Storage resources are connected via SRM/dCache and OGSA-DAI. In contrast to homogeneous communities, the partners in Core D-Grid have different missions and backgrounds (computing centers, universities, research centers), providing heterogeneous hardware from single processors to high performance supercomputing systems with different operating systems. We present methods provided by the Core D-Grid to integrate these resources and services for the infrastructure like a point of information, centralized user and VO management, resource registration, software provisioning, and policies for the implementation (firewalls, certificates, user mapping).

1 Introduction to D-Grid

In September 2005, the German Federal Ministry of Education and Research started six community grid projects and an integration project to build up a sustainable grid infrastructure in Germany. More grid projects in the same context will follow to join the common infrastructure. The initial community projects are high energy physics (HEPCG) [14], astrophysics (AstroGrid-D) [2], medicine and life sciences (Medi-GRID) [13], climate research (C3Grid) [4], engineering (InGrid) [15], and humanities (TextGrid) [19]. The first additional partner project that joined the evolving infrastructure is energy meteorology (WISENT) [22].

The community projects are heterogeneous concerning the scientific field, the structure of the community, the structure and size of data being processed, the type of grid software in use, and the experience with grid computing. Despite

T. Fieseler (✉)
Jülich Supercomputing Centre, Forschungszentrum Jülich GmbH, 52425 Jülich, Germany,
e-mail: t.fieseler@fz-juelich.de wguerich@fz-juelich.de

S.C. Lin, E. Yen (eds.), *Grid Computing*,
© Springer Science+Business Media, LLC 2009

all differences these communities are united by their common interest in grid methods for the solution of their scientific computation challenges. Some communities like high energy physics have wide experience with grid computing (HEPCG, AstroGrid-D), while others are just starting to apply the grid approach to their computational tasks (TextGrid). Some of the communities which already applied grid computing intensively have a strong affinity to use a certain middleware (HEPCG/gLite, AstroGrid-D/Globus), while communities with less experience are still open in the choice of the middleware. The requirements of the communities in the grid middleware are highly variable, e.g. in applications of the HEPCG or AstroGrid-D comparatively few but very large data transfers are needed, while applications of TextGrid tend to have many transfers of small data sets.

In order to build up a common basic grid infrastructure for these heterogenous grid communities the integration project has been started. The goal of the integration project is to build up a general, sustainable grid infrastructure, the Core D-Grid, first as a testbed and later as the productive environment for the grid communities.

In this paper, the structure of the integration project, its partners and resources, the supported middleware, and methods to integrate the resources into the Core D-Grid are presented. Services for the infrastructure like a point of information, a centralized user and VO management, a centralized resource management, software provisioning, and policies for the implementation (firewalls, certificates, user mapping) are described.

2 D-Grid Integration Project

2.1 Partners and Resources

The integration project started with seven partners who contribute their own compute and storage resources and three associated partners without a contribution of resources, but technical know-how and a strong interest in grid computing. The background and the working areas of these partner institutions are highly heterogeneous, as the resources they initially contributed: Partners are the computing centers of the national research centers and of universities; the compute resources vary from large supercomputers with several TFlops peak performance to small clusters with only a few CPUs, and have different operation systems like AIX, Solaris and various Linux flavors.

2.2 Work Packages

The D-Grid integration project (DGI) is divided into the following four work packages:

1. Basic grid software
2. Setup and operation of the D-Grid infrastructure

3. Network and security
4. Project management

2.3 Basic Grid Software

In the software section of the integration project, the basic grid middleware and further basic grid software is packaged and made available for the resource providers, grid developers, and grid users. Unlike other large grid projects as EGEE, which are mainly based on a single middleware, the requirements of the diverse D-Grid projects are too different to rely on a single grid middleware. Therefore, three middleware systems for compute resources are supported in the software stack of the integration project: LCG/gLite [18, 3], Globus (version 4) [11], and UNICORE [23] (version 5). For storage resources, SRM/dCache/[21] and OGSA-DAI [17] are supported by the integration project. Furthermore, GridSphere [20] is provided to implement portal solutions, the Grid Application Toolbox [1] is supported for application level programming.

2.4 Setup and Operation of the D-Grid Infrastructure

The second section of the integration project is the setup and operation of the Core D-Grid, which acts as a condensation nucleus to build a production grid infrastructure. The infrastructure of the Core D-Grid is described in detail in chapter "HEP Grid Computing in the UK: MOVING Towards the LHC Era".

2.5 Network and Security

In the third part, networking issues, security aspects, and firewewalls are covered. DGrid is based on the X-WiN network which is run by the Deutsche Forschungsnetz (DFN), who is coordinating this work package. Some of the partners already have 10 Gbit/s connections to other partners. The extension of the network infrastructure according to the upcoming requirements of partners and communities is coordinated in this work package. Alternative transport protocols are tested, compared to standard TCP, and optimized. Security aspects of grid middleware and firewalls are considered and advice is given to the partners in the Core D-Grid and the D-Grid community projects. Furthermore, grid security aspects like authentication and authorization are investigated in this part.

2.6 Project Management

The last section covers the leadership and coordination of all four parts of the infrastructure project and the coordination of the collaboration with the D-Grid community projects. Furthermore, dissemination and legal and organizational questions are part of this package in order to create a sustainable infrastructure for e-science in Germany.

3 Core D-Grid Infrastructure

For the operation of the Core D-Grid, different infrastructure components are required like a certificate infrastructure, a concept to install the three middlewares on one machine, a user and resource management system, resource monitoring, user support, and a point of information.

3.1 Certificates

The security of all three middleware systems is based on PKI and X.509 certificates. In Germany there are two certificate authorities for grid certificates, the Deutsche Forschungsnetz (DFN) [5] and the Forschungszentrum Karlsruhe (GridKA) [12] which have been accredited by the EUGridPMA [10]. For both certificate authorities many registration authorities have been approved. All partners of the Core DGrid and the community projects have setup registration authorities to enable an easy access of users and administrators to grid certificates. Since most of the DGrid projects are parts of international communities, foreign grid user certificates issued by any certificate authority accredited by EUGridPMA [10] and IGTF [16] are accepted.

3.2 Resources Financed by Additional Funding

The hardware which has initially been provided by the partners of the DGI was highly heterogeneous. The installation of grid middleware on less frequent platforms (e.g. Globus on AIX) and the integration of this hardware into the upcoming grid infrastructure was complicated but helpful to gain experience with different systems. At the end of 2006, the German Federal Ministry of Education and Research decided to invest additional funds for compute and storage resources located at partner sites of the Core D-Grid and the D-Grid community projects to serve as an additional incentive of the upcoming infrastructure. The additional funding was combined with the obligation to install all three middlewares for compute resources (gLite, Globus, UNICORE) in parallel on each of the new compute resources. All of the compute-nodes of these clusters (about 20 clusters have been aqcuired) must be accessible via each of the three middlewares. Furthermore, at least one of the two middlewares for storage access (SRM/dCache, OGSA-DAI) must be installed on the storage resources. Access to these additional resources must be granted to all virtual organizations (VOs) of D-Grid.

3.3 Reference Installation

The request to install the complete middleware stack of the DGI on a single resource presently is a very demanding challenge, since the different middleware systems partially have very restrictive and mutually exclusive requirements (e.g. Scientific Linux for gLite worker-nodes (WN) and even more restrictive Scientific Linux 3.0.x for the compute element (CE) on the one hand, the most up-to-date packages for Globus 4.0.x on the other hand). Since any solution to this problem is highly complicated, a reference installation, realizing the simultaneous installation of all supported middlewares systems has been set up [24]. This reference installation demonstrates how to run the different middleware systems on the same machine with access to all compute-nodes by each of the three middlewares for compute resources (see Fig. 1).

For each of the grid middleware systems (LCG/gLite, Globus, UNICORE, OGSADAI, SRM/dCache) the reference installation provides a dedicated so-called headnode for the installation of the server side of the middleware. The operation system of the head-nodes for Globus, UNICORE, and OGSA-DAI is SLES 10. The OS of the SRM/dCache head-node is Scientific Linux 4, whereas the OS of the head-node for the LCG/gLite compute element (CE) is Scientific Linux 3 (32bit) which is running on a Xen virtual machine under SLES 10. On the Globus head-node Globus Toolkit 4 is installed and the UNICORE head-node runs TSI, NJS, and UUDB. On the LCG/gLite head-node, the LCG-CE variant (production version) of

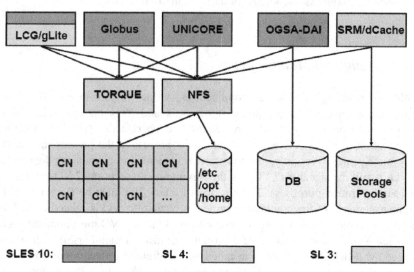

Fig. 1 Architecture of the reference installation. Jobs can be submitted via the head-nodes for LCG/gLite, Globus, and UNICORE to the TORQUE batch system which can access all compute-nodes (CN). Storage resources can be be accessed by the head-nodes for OGSA-DAI and SRM/dCache. The NFS node provides a common file system for configuration files (e.g. CA certificates), software, and home directories. The color of the nodes denotes the operating system

the compute element is used. OGSA-DAI is installed together with Globus Toolkit 4 on the OGSA-DAI head-node. The SRM/dCache head-node runs dCache 1.0.7 of the LCG distribution. Two further dedicated nodes are used for NFS which exports common directories like the certificates of the certificate authorities, the gLite user interface (UI) software, and the home directory for grid users, and a node for the server of the batch system TORQUE 2.1.6. The batch system server node is running under Scientific Linux 4. All three middleware installations for compute resources (LCG/gLite, Globus, UNICORE) connect to the same batch system. Therefore, all compute-nodes of the cluster can be access by all the middleware systems. Another special node is dedicated for interactive use and can be accessed remotely by DGrid developers and users via GSI-SSH or UNICORE-SSH. This node has the same environment (OS and configuration) as the compute-nodes and can be used for software development and testing purposes. All other nodes are compute-nodes running under Scientific Linux 4. On the compute-nodes, the client part of the batch system (TORQUE) and the gLite worker-node (WN) software are installed. To submit further jobs within a running grid job, the gLite user interface (UI) can be accessed from the compute-nodes via NFS.

Specially pre-configured packages of the middlware for the use within D-Grid are provided to ease the middleware installation and configuration for the partners. The recipients of the financial support for resources do not have to follow the exact way of the installation of the reference system. But even if the individual installations may differ according to the requirement of the local environment of the resource providers, the functionality must be the same as in the reference installation (accessby all middlewares, access for users of all D-Grid VOs).

3.4 User and VO Management

With an increasing number of communities, virtual organizations (VOs), and resources, an automated management of users and VOs on one side and of the resources on the other site are required to operate the grid infrastructure. The creation of a new VO is not an automated process in the present state of the integration project. Presently, this constraint is not a real problem, since the number of VOs is still manageable (7 VOs for the community projects and 2 VOs for testing and administration purposes). The creation of a new VO must be agreed between the managements of the community project to which the VO is related and of the integration project; one or more representatives of the new VO must nominated etc. For each VO, an own instance of a virtual organization membership registration service (VOMRS) [25] server is installed and configured on a centralized D-Grid management server. A new D-Grid user must find a VO which is appropriate for his field of research. One of the representatives of the VO in question must agree with the membership of the new member. If these requirements are fulfilled the new member can register to the VOMRS server of the VO and will obtain access to all resources of this VO.

3.5 Resource Management

In order to be integrated into the D-Grid infrastructure, each resource has to be registered at the grid resource registry service (GRRS) server, which has been developed within the D-Grid integration project (see Fig. 2). During the registration process of a resource at the GRRS server, all relevant information of the compute or storage resource and its administrators is collected and the grid server certificate of the resource is uploaded to the GRRS and stored in its database. For compute and storage resources which have several middlewares (gLite, Globus, UNICORE, SRM/dCache, OGSA-DAI) installed simultaneously, the resource has to be registered for each middleware with the grid server certificate of the head-node of the respective middleware. For the administration of the resources, a client (dgridmap) is distributed to the resource providers which must be run regularly on the resource. For resources with more than one middleware, the dgridmap client must be executed on the head-nodes for each of the middleware systems. The client contacts the GRRS server of the D-Grid resource management, authorizing itself with the grid server certificate for the respective resource (head-node). On the server side, the VOs which are allowed to access the resource are determined as entries in the GRRS database. The corresponding VOMRS servers of these VOs are queried to provide the user information (DNs of the grid user certificates, ID of the user in this VO, etc.) of the members of the VOs. The result is the user mapping for the corresponding resource in the format which is appropriate for the middleware (e.g. grid-mapfile for Globus, entries for uudb admin for UNICORE). The naming convention of the unix accounts in the user mapping is *ppvvnnnn*, where *pp* is a prefix (default *dg*) which can be changed by the administrator according to the local requirements, *vv* is a short-cut for the VO of the user entry, and *nnnn* is a number which is unique for this combination of user DN and VO. A member of a VO thus is mapped to accounts with name *ppvvnnnn* on all the resources of this VO, apart from the prefix *pp* which may vary at the provider sites.

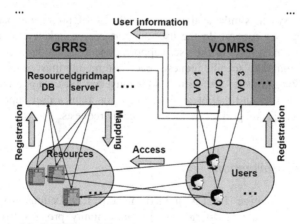

Fig. 2 Structure of the D-Grid user, VO, and resource management

In order to obtain access to the grid resources, users must register to a VO using the VOMRS server for this VO. New resources must register at the GRRS server to be integrated into the resource management. The user mapping for the resources is generated by the GRRS server which in turn obtains the information about users of the VOs from the VOMRS servers

3.6 Monitoring

On the LCG/gLite resources of the Core D-Grid infrastructure, LCG/gLite functional site tests (SFT) are performed. D-Grid users can inspect the SFT reports and find out which resources are available.

For UNICORE, the monitoring abilities of the UNICORE client can be used, i.e. D-Grid users can observe which resources are registered at the gateway and if the user has access to a resource with his certificate. Within the UNICORE client, additional information about the resources, as number of nodes, the number of CPUs per node, memory etc., and the jobs of the user can be gathered.

The Globus resources are monitored with MDS. On each Globus resource, the MDS4 software and a sensor transmitting additional information like the geographical coordinates of the site, the schedule of maintenance periods etc. have been installed. Each D-Grid resource provider is running a MDS index server for the site, collecting the MDS information of all resources of this site. The site index servers upload their information to a central D-Grid Web-MDS server, where D-Grid users can obtain the monitoring information in a hierarchical view, according to the organization levels of D-Grid. Furthermore, the resources can be displayed in a topological map.

3.7 User Support

A trouble ticket system similar as the system of the EGEE project has been installed to organize the user support. In the user support center, tickets are handled and forwarded to the next level of the user support, depending on the area of the user request. For community specific requests, each community must setup and operate an own consulting process. The partner sites must run a user support for requests concerning their site, and the integration project operates a user support for grid middleware specific and grid infrastructure specific requests.

3.8 Point of Information

The point of information (POI) is divided into different sections, a section with general information about D-Grid and the community projects [6], a section with information about the integration project [7], a user portal [9], and a provider portal [8]. The user portal is intended as a first starting point for D-Grid users. Users can find information about middleware services, i.e. installation and usage of grid middleware clients of the middleware systems that are supported within D-Grid, about the resources which can be accessed in the Core D-Grid, information how the user can get access to the resources like grid user certificates, creation of a new virtual organization, membership in an existing virtual organization, the status of the resources (Globus: WebMDS, LCG/gLite: SFT) and a link to the trouble ticket system of the user support. In the provider portal, resource providers can find the information that is needed to integrate a new resource into the Core D-Grid, as information about grid server certificates, installation and configuration of the grid middleware servers according to the reference installation, information about ports to be opened in the firewalls, integration of the compute or storage resource into the grid resource registry service (GRRS), and the integration of the resource into the D-Grid monitoring system.

4 D-Grid Integration Project 2

The first phase of the integration project ends in September of 2007. A subsequent second phase of the integration project (DGI-2) is planned with a duration three years. While the integration of new resources was the major task of the Core D-Grid during the first phase, the second phase will be more focused on the consolidation and extension of the developing infrastructure. The services of the Core D-Grid as VO and user administration, resource management (GRRS), user support, monitoring etc. will be further improved and a failsafe infrastructure will be established with redundant servers for the core services. Furthermore, accounting solutions which have been acquired within the integration project, will be integrated into the Core D-Grid infrastructure. Improved versions of policies of grid users, virtual organizations, and resource providers will be developed and published. In this phase an increasing number of new grid communities is expected to join the infrastructure and therewith a large number of new virtual organizations and resources is expected to be integrated.

Acknowledgments The D-Grid integration project is completely funded by the German Federal Ministry of Education and Research. The integration project involves a large number of colleagues who all contribute to the project and the development of the Core D-Grid infrastructure.

References

1. Allen G, Davis K et al (2003) Enabling Applications on the Grid: A GridLab Overview. International Journal of High Performance Computing Applications, 17:449–466
2. AstroGrid-D, German Astronomy Community Grid (GACG), http://www.gac-grid.de. Accessed 17 January 2008
3. Berlich R, Kunze M, and Schwarz K (2005) Grid Computing in Europe: From Research to Deployment. In: Proceedings of the 2005 Australasian workshop on Grid computing and ere-search, Newcastle, New South Wales, Australia, 44:21–27

4. Collaborative Climate Community Data and Processing Grid (C3Grid), http://www.c3grid.de. Accessed 17 January 2008
5. Deutsches Forschungsnetz (DFN), https://www.dfn.de, Deutsches Forschungsnetz – Public Key Infrastructure (DFN-PKI), https://www.pki.dfn.de. Accessed 17 January 2008
6. D-Grid Initiative, http://www.d-grid.de. Accessed 17 January 2008
7. D-Grid Integration project (DGI), http://dgi.d-grid.de. Accessed 17 January 2008
8. D-Grid Provider Portal, http://www.d-grid.de/providerportal. Accessed 17 January 2008
9. D-Grid User Portal, http://www.d-grid.de/userportal. Accessed 17 January 2008
10. European Policy Management Authority for Grid Authentication (EUGridPMA), http://www.eugridpma.org. Accessed 17 January 2008
11. Foster I (2006) Globus Toolkit Version 4: Software for Service-Oriented Systems. In: IFIP International Conference on Network and Parallel Computing, Springer-Verlag LNCS 3779, 2–13
12. Grid Computing Centre Karlsruhe (GridKa) http://grid.fzk.de. Accessed 17 January 2008
13. Grid Computing for Medicine and Life Sciences (MediGRID), http://www.medigrid.de. Accessed 17 January 2008
14. High Energy Physics Community Grid (HEPCG) documentation, http://documentation. hepcg.org. Accessed 17 January 2008
15. Innovative Grid Technology in Engineering, http://www.ingrid-info.de. Accessed 17 January 2008
16. International Grid Trust Federation (IGTF), The Grid's Policy Management Authority, http://www.gridpma.org. Accessed 17 January 2008
17. Karasavvas K, Antonioletti M et al (2005) Introduction to OGSA-DAI Services. In: Lecture Notes in Computer Science, Springer-Verlag LNCS 3458, 1–12
18. Knobloch J and Robertson L (2006) LHC Computing Grid. The LCG TDR Editorial Board. http://lcg.web.cern.ch/LCG/tdr/LCG TDR v1 04.pdf. Accessed 17 January 2008
19. Modular platform for collaborative textual editing – a community grid for the humanities (TextGrid) http://www.textgrid.de. Accessed 17 January 2008
20. Novotny J, Russell M and Wehrens O (2004) GridSphere: A Portal Framework for Building Collaborations. Concurrency & Computation-Practice & Experience 16:503–513
21. Perelmutov T, Petravick D, Corso E (2006) The Storage Resource Manager Interface Specification. http://sdm.lbl.gov/srm-wg. Accessed 17 January 2008
22. Scientific network for energy meteorology (WISENT), http://wisent.offis.de. Accessed 17 January 2008
23. Streit A, Erwin D et al (2005) UNICORE - From Project Results to Production Grids. In: Grandinetti L (ed) Grid Computing: New Frontiers of High Performance Computing, Elsevier, 357–376
24. Reference installation of the D-Grid integration project, http://www.dgrid. de/index.php?id=298, or http://www.d-grid.de/providerportal ! 'Bereitstellung von Ressourcen'! 'Grid-Middleware (Server)'!Refernz-Installation.
25. Virtual Organization Membership Registration Service (VOMRS), http://www.uscms.org/ SoftwareComputing/Grid/VO. Accessed 17 January 2008

Monitoring the Availability of Grid Services Using SAM and Gridview

Rajesh Kalmady, Digamber Sonvane, Phool Chand, Kislay Bhatt, Kumar Vaibhav, Piotr Nyczyk, and Zdenek Sekera

Abstract The Grid Middleware consists of a set of Grid Services like Computing Element (CE), Storage Element (SE), Resource Broker (RB), Replica Catalog (RC), Information System (IS), User Interface (UI) etc. The Availability and Reliability of these Grid Services is critical to the functioning of Grid Infrastructure. This paper describes Service Availability Monitoring (SAM) and GRIDVIEW, two complementary tools developed for monitoring the Availability of Grid Services and various sites in the Worldwide LHC Computing Grid (WLCG). The SAM Framework launches periodic tests at various service instances to check their status. Using these test results, Gridview's summarization module computes the Availability of individual services and the overall availability of various sites. Gridview's Visualization module displays Graphs and Reports indicating the Availability of various sites and services.

1 Introduction

The Worldwide LHC Computing Grid (WLCG) is a production data grid that provides the data storage and analysis infrastructure for petabytes of physics data that is expected to be generated when the Large Hadron Collider starts operation at CERN. The WLCG collaboration spans a large number of computing centres throughout the world that provide computing and storage resources for the grid. Some of these computing centres are also part of different grid organizations such as the EGEE, OSG and the NorduGrid.

In order to provide a reliable and available computing infrastructure to the various virtual organizations that use the grid, it is important that the health of the individual services in the grid be monitored for their proper functioning. Monitoring of grid services allows different classes of users such as site administrators, VO administrators and grid managers to keep an eye on the operational efficiencies of different grid resources. Several monitoring tools are operational in the WLCG at different levels of the grid, starting from site fabric monitors to higher level grid

R. Kalmady (✉)
Bhabha Atomic Research Centre, India, #CERN, Geneva, Switzerland

S.C. Lin, E. Yen (eds.), *Grid Computing*,
© Springer Science+Business Media, LLC 2009

monitors. In this paper, we focus on grid level service availability monitoring using two complementary tools, SAM and Gridview.

2 Introduction to SAM and Gridview

SAM (Service Availability Monitoring) framework is a centralized and uniform monitoring tool for grid services developed at CERN. It launches periodic tests at the services being monitored at various sites in order to check their status and functionality. The SAM test results are used by a wide set of monitoring tools for various purposes such as computation of availability metrics to operational purposes such as raising operator alarms on test failures.

Gridview is a grid monitoring and visualization tool developed at BARC, India under collaboration with CERN. Gridview provides a high level visualization of various performance and functional metrics in the grid such as data transfer between sites, job statistics and service availability. The raw input data to Gridview comes from various sources such as GridFTP server logs, Resource Broker (RB) logs and SAM test results.

SAM and Gridview are integrated together with tightly coupled databases and inter-dependent modules providing complementary functionality. They jointly provide the necessary infrastructure for service availability monitoring in the WLCG.

3 Service Availability Monitoring Goals

The goals of the SAM/Gridview service availability monitoring effort are:

- To provide a service level view of the operational status of the grid
- To help the operations team locate and troubleshoot the problems
- To monitor the Availability and Reliability of various services and sites in the Grid Infrastructure
- To provide a VO specific view of the service in order to enable each VO to look at the service in its own perspective

4 Service Monitoring and Visualization Architecture

The SAM/Gridview service monitoring and visualization architecture is shown in Fig. 1.

The architecture consists of the following components:

- SAM/Gridview Data Repository: This lies at the centre of the architecture and is made up of SAM and Gridview databases, tightly coupled with each other. SAM and Gridview share tables and define relations between entities in each others DBs.

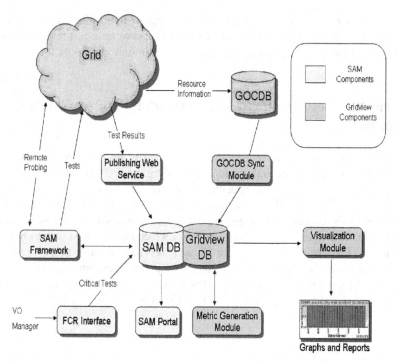

Fig. 1 SAM/Gridview Service Monitoring Architecture

- SAM Framework: The SAM framework consists of sensors which are a set of functional tests for individual grid services, a test submission module for periodic invocation of service sensors that is launching of tests and a web service client for publishing the test results to the central repository. The SAM Framework launches regular tests at grid services and publishes the results to the central repository.
- Service Discovery Mechanism: Information about resources present in the grid is taken from different sources such as the GOCDB and BDII. Gridview maintains a local synchronized replica of relevant tables in GOCDB which is used by SAM for service discovery
- Transport Mechanism: A web services based transport mechanism is used by SAM for publishing new test definitions and test results to the central repository.
- VO Policy Enforcement Mechanism: VOs can define the criticality of SAM tests using the FCR (Freedom of Choice for Resources). They can also define their own specific tests for grid services.
- Gridview's Metric Generation Module: This module computes service availability metrics per VO based on the SAM test results for the critical tests for that VO.
- Gridview's Visualization Module: This module displays the computed availability metrics in the form of graphs with multiple views and levels of details.

- Programmatic Interface: SAM provides a programmatic interface to the data repository through which sites and experiments can retrieve test results and service availability metrics for integration into local monitoring tools.

5 Grid Services Monitored and Computation of Availability Metrics

In order to compute site level availability, we classify grid services in two categories, site services and central services, depending upon the scope of the service. Site services are those that are specific to the site, whose scope is limited to the site (e.g. CE, SE). Central services are different in the sense that even though a particular site is running them, their scope is global. These services are optional for the site installation; all sites need not run their own central services such as RB and LFC but use them from some other site. The grid services currently being monitored by SAM/Gridview in WLCG/EGEE include Computing Element(CE), Storage Element(SE), Storage Resource Manager(SRM), site BDII site services and Resource Broker(RB), LHC File Catalog(LFC), gLite File Transfer Service(FTS) and BDII central services.

5.1 Service Instance, Service and Site Status

Grid services run by a site are generally comprised of multiple redundant instances such as multiple compute elements or storage elements. Each of these elements is tested individually by the SAM framework by launching periodic tests. Each VO specifies the tests which are deemed to be critical for a particular service.

The statuses of individual service instances are computed on an hourly basis by Gridview by performing a logical AND operation on the results of the latest critical SAM tests in that hour. If all critical tests have succeeded, the service instance is deemed to be UP for the whole hour, otherwise it is deemed to be DOWN. A test result is considered to be valid for a period of 24 hours after the test, after which the result is deemed to be invalid and is no longer considered for further computation. If all critical test results have expired, the service instance status is considered to be UNKNOWN and is no longer considered for further calculations.

The status of individual services (service types) such as CE and SE are computed by combining statuses of all redundant service instances in an operation akin to a logical OR. The service status is deemed to be DOWN if all its redundant instances are DOWN. If all instances are UP, the service status is computed to be UP. Otherwise, the service status is deemed to be DEGRADED.

The status of a site is computed by logically ANDing the status of the site services run by the site. The list of site services currently comprises CE, SE, SRM and sBDII. Therefore, the site is deemed to be UP or DEGRADED if all of its services are either UP or DEGRADED respectively. Otherwise the site status is set to DOWN.

5.2 Service Instance, Service and Site Availability

The availability of a service instance, service type or site is defined as the percentage of time the same was UP (or DEGRADED) in a given period of time. Consequently we have hourly, daily, weekly and monthly availability figures for each individual service instance, service type and site. The availability figures are computed from the corresponding status information.

6 Visualization

The availability calculations for all site/service instances are done by Gridview's summarization module. These derived metrics are then displayed to the user by different visualization components of SAM and Gridview. The SAM portal displays all test results and availability figures in the form of HTML tables. The Gridview visualization module also displays SAM test results along with computed status metrics for individual service instances. Moreover, the Gridview visualization module displays bar graphs for computed availability figures for individual service instances, services and sites. The different possible status values and availability figures are shown in different colours, with green indicating 'UP' or 'Available' and red indicating 'DOWN' or 'Unavailable'.

All availability metrics computed by Gridview are VO-specific; therefore the visualization module displays all graphs with respect to specified VOs, thus enabling each VO to look at a service or site in its own perspective. There is full traceability from a site's availability graphs to those of its constituent services, instances down to the SAM test results of individual services, helping a user to trace down the availability of a site and view the results of the SAM tests that contributed to the availability figure.

7 User Groups

SAM/Gridview is being used by many different user groups for different purposes. Site Administrators use it to monitor the status of the site level services run by their sites whereas VO administrators monitor the availability of all sites used by their VOs for taking decisions on where to submit jobs. The WLCG management finds SAM/Gridview useful for keeping a watch on the availabilities of all sites in the Grid and to correlate it with the agreed commitments.

8 On-going Work

Following are some of the on-going tasks in SAM/Gridview:

- Computation of service status over a continuous time scale rather in a discrete time periods of an hour as now

- Computation of service reliability metrics
- Providing Standard URL based access to Visual Components in order to enable other tools to integrate them
- Generation of Site Availability and Reliability Report for WLCG Management board

References

1. Rajesh Kalmady, Digamber Sonvane, Kislay Bhatt, Phool Chand, James Casey, Zdenek Sekera, "Gridview: A Grid Monitoring and Visualization Tool", Conference on Computing in High Energy Physics, CHEP 2006
2. The SAM Portal, https://lcg-sam.cern.ch:8443/sam/sam.py
3. SAM Document server, http://sam-docs.web.cern.ch/sam-docs/
4. Gridview Documentation site, https://twiki.cern.ch/twiki//bin/view/LCG/GridView

DEISA – Cooperative Extreme Computing Across Europe

Ralph Niederberger, Paolo Malfetti, Andreas Schott, and Achim Streit

Abstract The European DEISA[1] project is an infrastructure of infrastructures –
eleven of the leading European High Performance Computing (HPC) centers in
Europe interconnected by a 10 Gb/s high speed network – that devised an innovative
strategy to enable the cooperative operation of existing national supercomputing
infrastructures. This initiative led to the deployment and operation of a world class,
persistent, production quality, distributed tera-scale supercomputing environment
with continental scope enabling scientific discovery across a broad spectrum of sciences and technologies.

The paper describes in detail the DEISA infrastructure and high speed network
interconnect, its operation and management, as well as user support procedures. The
second part explains the used Grid middleware and Grid security models as well as
its integration into the local security policies. The third part of the paper gives a
comprehensive overview about lessons learned. The paper closes with a summary
and a vision on future DEISA project extension plans.

1 Introduction

The deployment and operation of a world class persistent, production quality,
distributed tera-scale supercomputing environment providing extreme computing
across Europe can not be handled by standard procedures of a single computing
center. Furthermore a virtual European organization requires the establishment of
virtual teams of remotely operating staff members interacting in close collaboration. DEISA is a supercomputing GRID-empowered e- Infrastructure, a European
virtual organization that, integrates national High Performance Computing (HPC)
infrastructures by means of modern grid technologies. DEISA main objective is to

---

[1]Distributed European Infrastructure for Supercomputing Applications [1] This work is partially
funded through the European DEISA and eDEISA projects under grant FP6-508830 and FP6-
031513. Within this report we do not distinguish between both projects, given the fact that eDEISA
is an extension of the former.

R. Niederberger (✉)
Research Center Jülich, Germany

S.C. Lin, E. Yen (eds.), *Grid Computing*,
© Springer Science+Business Media, LLC 2009

contribute to a significant enhancement of HPC capability and capacity in Europe for scientific and industrial communities.

The DEISA infrastructure requires the coordinated action of the different national supercomputing environments, services and staff members for both efficiency and performance of computing resources. Leading scientific users will have transparent access to this European pool of computing resources, therefore providing user support across national boundaries will be essential. The coordinated operation of the DEISA environment is tailored to enable new, ground breaking applications in computational sciences. These goals led to the DEISA Extreme Computing Initiative (DECI) started in 2005 which will be described in detail below.

2 The DEISA System and Network Infrastructure

The DEISA Consortium followed a top-bottom strategic approach for the deployment and the evolution of the infrastructure. The technologies chosen have been fully open and followed from the strategic requirements and the operational model of the DEISA virtual organization. Only some very basic strategic requirements have influenced the deployment of the current infrastructure. First of all the necessity of fast deployment of the infrastructure has been essential. Also the coexistence of the European infrastructure with the national services had to be guaranteed, which requires reliability and non-disruptive behavior and approach. A third prerequisite has been user and application transparency, hiding complex grid technologies from users and minimizing application changes, because application development should not be strongly tied to an IT infrastructure.

The current DEISA supercomputing grid architecture meets these concerns by having an inner level, dealing with the deep integration and strongly coupled operation of similar, homogeneous IBM AIX clusters, which forms a distributed European supercomputer (called "the AIX super-cluster") and an outer level made of all heterogeneous systems. Such a grid of heterogeneous supercomputers and super-clusters is tight together in a looser federation pool of supercomputing resources by means of several top-level technologies layered one on top of the other: a 10 Gbps dedicated network, a wide area network shared file system, a production quality GRID middleware able to virtualise heterogeneous resources presenting them as homogeneous and an application virtualization layer. This top-level technologies GRID-empowered eInfrastructure now includes all the leading platforms in Europe including systems from IBM (different kinds, from SP systems, to Blue Gene/L, to cluster of PowerPCs), SGI and NEC, and Cray in the next future. A third level of integration will be visible in the future when external resources (compute, storage, data generation resources as telescopes, medical devices etc.) may be loosely connected to the existing DEISA infrastructure by means of the web (and not of a dedicated network), selected GRID middleware and other virtualization tools. Currently the DEISA partners contribute a significant amount of their national supercomputing resources (approx. 10% or more) to a globally managed European resource pool.

In addition to the standard Internet connectivity that each national supercomputer centre offers, an internal network has been installed using wavelengths provided by

GEANT and the National research networks (NRNs). This network connects the partners' supercomputers offering reserved bandwidth.

The deployment of the dedicated DEISA network infrastructure has proceeded in several steps, following the evolutions of the national and European research network infrastructures and the adoption of the infrastructure by the user communities. After four core partners had verified in a proof of concept phase that the DEISA concept is sustainable, an extension to the other sites was started.

In the first phase all centres have been connected via a virtual dedicated 1 Gb/s network provided by the National Research and Education Networks (NRENs) and the multi-gigabit pan-European data communications network (GEANT2)[2]. Two years of stable operation have proven the reliability of this concept.

An intermediate phase connecting the 1 Gb/s Phase 1 network and the future star-like configuration 10 Gb/s Phase2 network has already been initiated. This Phase 2 infrastructure will operate at 10 Gb/s between all DEISA sites. The upgrade has been driven primarily by the availability of the new GEANT2 and local NREN infrastructures under construction. The Phase 2 has been the most ambitious phase, where technological requirements and application needs challenged the limits of what providers can offer to the supercomputer sites. The design of the DEISA network backbone is a so-called star network with 10 Gb/s bandwidth from DEISA sites all over Europe to a central switch located at Frankfurt/Germany. An expansion to a decentralized design with backup paths is considered for the future.

A close collaboration between the DEISA network team and staff members of the NRENs and GEANT2 as well as a close interaction with the administrators of the supercomputer systems guarantees optimum performance of the DEISA network to meet the needs of the user communities.

The IBM AIX systems are running IBM's GPFS (Global Parallel File System, [3]) as a cluster file system. IBM has incorporated wide area network functionality in GPFS, enabling the deployment of distributed global file systems. This is the basic integration technology of the AIX super-cluster currently used.

An application running on one site can access data files previously "exported" from other sites as if they were local files. Therefore, it does not matter in which site the application is executed, and applications can be moved across sites transparently to the user. Though the concept of deploying network file systems is an old one, GPFS provides high performance remote access needed for high performance computing. In 2005 the TeraGrid project [4] has shown that on their 30 Gb/s TeraGrid network in the USA, GPFS is able to achieve about 27 Gb/s network throughput when accessing remote data via GPFS. This proved that this software is capable of taking full advantage of underlying high performance networks. Therefore DEISA intended from the beginning to set up such a kind of high speed interconnect.

3 DEISA and its Grid Middleware

The strong integration of IBM AIX systems aims at providing a single system image of a distributed supercomputer. This is fully transparent to end users, which will access the super-cluster through the site in which they have a login.

The fundamental purpose of the AIX super-cluster operation is running bigger and more demanding applications than the ones that can be run today on each national cluster. One possibility of doing this would be to "grid enable" the application so that it can run on more than one platform. However, this strategy – that requires a modification of the application – does not really work for tightly coupled parallel applications. In this case, the finite signal propagation velocity induces MPI communication latencies in a wide area network that are intolerable for high performance computing.

DEISA adopts a different strategy, based on load balancing the computational workload across national borders. Huge, demanding applications are run by reorganizing the global operation in order to allocate substantial resources in one site. Therefore they run "as such" with no modification. Smaller jobs will be rerouted to other systems making room for large applications with huge amount of CPU, memory or disk resources.

DEISA global job scheduling within the "the AIX super-cluster" can be done via the Multi Cluster Loadleveler provided by IBM. This facility allows the definition of job queues, rerouting facility (jobs, not already started) and status information. Here it is possible to load balance DEISA supercomputer systems and mainly freeing huge systems by rerouting small jobs to smaller systems.

The other benefit of the AIX super-cluster comes from the possibility of transparently sharing data through GPFS. European data repositories that require frequent updates – like bio-informatics databases, for example – can be established in one site and accessed by all the others.

DEISA has a special service activity (SA3: Resource Management) to deploy and operate generic Grid Middleware needed for the operation of the DEISA supercomputing Grid infrastructure. The services provided include "basic services", which enable local or extended batch schedulers and other cluster- features to simplify user access to the DEISA infrastructure. These basic services are enhanced by advanced services which allow resource and network monitoring as well as information services and global management of the distributed resources. Examples for these services are harmonization of national job management strategies, deployment, test und update of middleware like UNICORE and Globus. Though most of these services are standard services in supercomputer environments, they have to be adapted to European distributed infrastructures. Similar adaptation activities have to be done in the batch scheduling software area.

DEISA has a "first generation" co-allocation service based on LSF Multi Cluster from Platform Computing which was extremely dependent on this particular technology provider. This new service allows a persistent integration of other future resources. eSA3 (the extension of SA3) focuses on deploying a "second generation" co-allocation service, that is vendor independent to enhance the co-allocation feature by extending the service to resources other than CPUs. Here the implementation of other types of co-allocation, as there are meta-job co- allocation or scheduled workflow co-allocation, may be promising.

User transparency is a necessity (users should not be aware of complex grid technologies) and applications transparency (minimal intrusion on applications, which, being part of the corporate wealth of research organizations, should not be strongly tied to an IT infrastructure). For this reason the UNICORE software is used as the middleware in the DEISA infrastructure to access the heterogeneous set of computing resources and managing workflow applications. Furthermore, in order to achieve interoperability with other leading Grid infrastructures in the world, new middleware is being evaluated, to decide about the best possible usage in the deployment of the infrastructure. Currently the DEISA partners are evaluating the current versions of Unicore 6, and Globus Toolkit 4 (GTK4). Only fully production quality (with RAS features) middleware will be retained and integrated into the production environment. As the specifications of OGSA and related standards are likely to evolve also middleware interoperability needs to be ensured.

Nowadays, leading scientific applications analyze or produce large amounts of data. Some of these applications also need the computational capacities offered by the DEISA Grid. With GPFS DEISA has a very efficient tool for global data management, well adapted to High Performance Computing – but this technology does not cover all the global data management requirements. First of all, not all computing systems in DEISA can be integrated into the existing Global File Systems. Moreover, because of limited space on the DEISA global file systems, large amounts of data cannot be stored for an infinitely long time, and as a consequence data can not always be directly accessible from the applications running on the DEISA facilities. Before processing data they have to be transferred to a DEISA global file system or a local scratch system. Also, at the end of an application run, output data may have to be transferred to other storage facilities e.g. mass storage facilities of DEISA partners. Therefore DEISA has deployed a second high performance file transfer service based on striped GridFTP [5], which is also capable of taking advantage of the full network bandwidth for individual transfers. Last but not least, global file systems allow different applications to share the same data, but the opposite service is also needed: an application that needs to access a distributed dataset. Therefore the DEISA global data management roadmap focuses on the complementary objective of providing high performance access to distributed data sets, by enabling database management software like OGSA-DAI [6] or grid storage software like SRB [7]. Moreover Grid based data transfers and Grid enabled data registration systems will provide DEISA users with facilities to retrieve and store data in Hierarchical Storage Management (HSM) facilities at DEISA sites and to register files independent of their physical location having global file names translated through registries and catalogues. Additionally it is planned to provide an uniform grid enabled access to specialized, in-house developed, or legacy databases by Grid enabled database access services independent of locations and formats of the databases. DEISA definitely will expand its data management capabilities in order to stay attractive for "grand challenge" applications.

The Applications and User Support Service Activity, both with the Enabling Key Applications Service Activity, is in charge of all actions that will enable or enhance the access to the DEISA supercomputing resources and their impact on computational sciences. It provides direct support to the major scientific initiatives of DEISA and helps users to run new challenging scientific applications, as there are large, demanding applications, running in parallel on several hundreds or thousands of processors in one specific site or multi-site Grid applications, running concurrently on several systems, so that each component is executed on the most appropriate platform as well as applications running at one site using data sets distributed over the whole infrastructure and multiple applications running at several sites sharing common data repositories. Additionally portals and Web interfaces used to hide complex environments from end users and to facilitate the access to a supercomputing environment to non- traditional user communities have to be supported.

To achieve these objectives, several activities have been deployed. The DEISA Common Production Environment (CPE) is running on all platforms of the infrastructure, with a very high coherency across the homogeneous super- clusters and a weaker one across heterogeneous platforms. DEISA CPE has been designed as a combination of software components (shells, compilers, libraries, tools and applications) available on each site and an interface to access these in a uniform way, despite the local differences in installation and location. CPE is automatically monitored checking its behavior continuously and identifying unexpected problems. User support also includes documentations on access and usage of the DEISA supercomputing environment as well as installing a decentralized Help Desk. Last but not least training sessions are organized to enable fast development of user skills and know-how for the efficient utilization of the DEISA infrastructure.

Enabling new challenging supercomputing applications is of key importance to advance computational sciences in Europe in the supercomputing area. The DEISA Extreme Computing Initiative (DECI) has been launched in 2005 to enhance DEISA's impact on science and technology. 29 applications have been selected on scientific excellence, innovation and relevance by a collaboration of HPC national evaluation committees and have been in operation in the 2005–2006 timeframe with an aggregated number of 9.5 Mio CPU hours. A second European Call for Extreme Computing Proposals has been closed some month ago. 23 of these projects have been selected for operation in 2006–2007 timeframe (aggregated 11.3 Mio CPU hours). 5 additional projects are in hold state and may be started as soon as computing time is available. A detailed list of the projects selected for both calls is available at "http://www.deisa.org/applications/". The main purpose of the DECI initiative is to enable a number of "grand challenge" applications in all areas of science and technology. These leading, ground breaking applications must deal with complex, demanding and innovative simulations that would not be possible without the DEISA infrastructure, and which benefit from the exceptional resources provided by the Consortium. These DEISA applications are expected to have requirements that cannot be fulfilled by the national services alone. To support these applications a special Applications Task Force, a team of leading experts in high performance and Grid computing, has been constituted. Its main task is helping users to enable the adoption of the DEISA Grid infrastructure and to enable a number of those Grand Challenge applications in all areas of science and technology. Therefore the Applications Task Force deals with all aspects of Extreme Computing projects from the European scientific community in its full complexity at all necessary levels, in order to enhance the impact on computational sciences.

Because of the application enabling activities provided by DEISA, a large number of scientific user codes, representing common applications for different scientific areas, have become available, and can be used to establish an European benchmark suite. These codes will be chosen to ensure acomprehensive coverage of major scientific areas as well as all the functionalities to be evaluated. These benchmarks will be focused on providing an efficient instrument for the acquisition of future European supercomputers. The benchmarking activity also includes the preparation of low-level tests that complement the user code tests.

4 VO and Security

The DEISA grid infrastructure forms a conglomerate of diverse security policies. Within this virtual organization users need transparent access to the DEISA Grid infrastructure with single sign-on facilities. Vice versa partners need control on usage of their resources. These facilities, commonly referred to as Authentication, Authorization and Accounting services, must be trusted by all sites to protect their local environment against unauthorized access. Because of non direct contacts between users and remote DEISA sites dispatch services, a global administration had to be developed. Within DEISA a user only needs to contact a local administrator to get a DEISA POSIX (uid/gid) account. The user information will be stored into a LDAP-services database which allows updating local information consecutively every day on all DEISA systems in a secure manner.

A secure single sign-on is realized via X.509 certificates for authentication and authorization. DEISA trusts the certificates issued by the Certificate Authorities (CAs) accredited by the EuGridPMA, one of the members of the IGTF, a worldwide federation of CAs. This guarantees uniqueness of the certificates. Matching of uids and X.509 certificates allows the deployed Grid middleware to decide which services may be accessed. Because of the availability of the LDAP-information in all locations an XML-based database has been established which holds and presents all the relevant information for accounting. Aggregated reports will be created on resource usage by individual users and projects on a monthly basis.

The security of the DEISA infrastructure depends on the trust provided by the installed middleware that operates the services and on the security services that are used by the middleware as well as by the dedicated nature of the DEISA 10 Gb/s network infrastructure. Security issues related to networking below ISO/OSI layer 5, which is transport, network, link and physical layers are very low, because of the dedicated nature of the network. Connections established or packets inserted into existing streams can be done by already known individuals residing on DEISA hosts, assuming no DEISA system has been hacked. Nevertheless an insider threat attack could be started. Because of this the CERT[2] teams of all organizations have to work closely together and have to exchange any kind of security incidences as soon

---

[2] CERT = Computer Emergency Response Team

as possible. A mutual cooperative trustfulness concerning vulnerability assessment will be indispensable. Having had no security incidence within DEISA during the whole lifetime of the DEISA project attests that this faith into each other has been justified.

5 Management and Operation

Operation and management within DEISA is done through the definition of a number of executive and working teams managing, delegating, and operating the required tasks. First of all the DEISA Executive Committee (DEC), constituted by managing staff members of all participating supercomputing centers, deals with higher level project management issues as technological strategies, scientific management, provision of computational resources, relations with other organizations and European projects etc.

The main focus of DEISA having a persistent and sustained supercomputing infrastructure required the participation of national scientific councils that establish national policies and provide funding for the national supercomputing services. The DEISA Policy committee is the board where representatives of these organizations can decide on major strategic issues e.g. strategic orientation of DEISA, models for service provisioning and global resource management.

Additional advisory committees act as external consulting boards on technology issues (ATC), scientific issues (ASC), allocation of the DEISA computational resources, external analysis of the operation and quality of service assurance (AUC).

The DEISA Infrastructure Management Committee (DIMC) is the executive extension of the DEC. It acts as a direction team for the virtual supercomputing centre and its heterogeneous Grid extensions.

Underneath these committees service activities (SAs) and joint research activities (JRAs) are responsible for the deployment and operation of the infrastructure. Beneath organizational and management structures an Operation Team, is responsible for a smooth operation of the research infrastructure.

The operation of an European wide virtual organization has to be done mainly by the involved service activities and local supercomputer persons in charge (local administrators, network and security experts). Although this works quite well in projects with a small number of participating organizations, an overall coordination team acting as link between the real organizations has to be established within greater projects. This team, coordinating local to global operations, providing guidelines for the overall virtual organization including task scheduling as maintenance outage, coordinated software upgrade, defining global security policies and advanced user administration, has turned out to be indispensable. Though all participating partners are always willing to pave the way for an advanced European wide virtual supercomputing infrastructure, nevertheless local priorities controvert these visions. At this point the operation team has to coordinate these contradictions and provide a way to overcome these congestions and advice local staff members to act accordingly.

Therefore the operation team is constituted of highly experienced system administrators of each site, who are able to coordinate the operational environments existing at each site as well as the interactions influencing the operational behavior of the infrastructure between the different SAs in DEISA. Beneath the overall operation it also acts as an emergency team, in cases where a quick reaction on problems arising in the DEISA infrastructure is needed.

All service activities have their own well defined communication and operating channels concerning their own activity. But e.g. the setup of the Global File System GPFS by service activity SA2 requires specific network settings. Most of these parameters have been exchanged directly between SA1, providing the network, and SA2, responsible for the file system. Additionally there is the need of changing configurations in the firewall, which are seen as security critical by some sites. Therefore often decisions and actions of one service activity have an influence on another service activity. Thus coordination effort between different service activities is required on a case by case basis. The Operation Team is the instance to establish this.

Though all the DEISA sites operate in principle autonomously, the actions at one site may have an influence at another site. When a site is going into maintenance, its part of the Global File System will not be available at any other site. So no jobs of users of that site may run on another site as their DEISA home and data directories are not available. This requires a dismount of the file system and a closing of the batch system for the affected users. All these actions have to be done via a cross site resource coordination, which is done by video and phone conferences, document exchange, e-mail exchange. Different mailing lists are provided for general operational issues and special maintenance information.

A trouble ticket system allows keeping track of problems until a solution has been provided. Additionally historical information concerning solved problems can be accessed.

The software component Multi Cluster - Global Parallel File System (MC-GPFS) is highly dependent on reachability of remote file systems. Though IBM has incorporated the multi cluster feature into GPFS, problems arose often from these software components because of having remote file systems connected across WANs and not only locally. Therefore the operations team maintenance mailing list has become an intrinsic component of file system management.

The RMIS (Resource Management Information System) system is used to deliver up to date and complete resource management information of the supercomputing systems. It provides information from remote sites to system administrators and end users. The functionalities needed by DEISA include a secure access to the Grid and to resources, job submission and control capability (mainly with UNICORE [8]), job rerouting capability (manual operation using relevant information), brokering capability (using relevant information), resource co-allocation capability, an advance reservation capability and an accounting capability. The information is provided based on the Ganglia monitoring tool [9] coupled to the MDS2/Globus [10] component. Ganglia provide scalable monitoring of distributed systems and large-scale clusters. It relies on a multicast-based listen/announce protocol to monitor state within clusters and uses a tree of point-to-point connections amongst representative cluster nodes to federate clusters and aggregate their state. The monitored information will be fed into the Globus Toolkit [11] 2.x information system, MDS2, which provides a standard mechanism for publishing and discovering resource status and configuration information via a uniform, flexible interface to data collected by Ganglia.

An INCA [12] system implementation provided by service activity SA4 provides an overview of and manages the DEISA common production environment (CPE) (for CPE see below). INCA is specifically designed to periodically run a collection of validation scripts, called reporters, with the purpose of collecting the version of the software installed (version reporters) and the availability and the correct operation of this software (unit reporters). The collected information is then cached on the INCA server, and can be archived to produce a historical representation of the status of the resources of a grid. The architecture of INCA is composed of a centralized server and clients, installed on each resource to be validated. Web based data consumers display the results. The installed system displays all software components used in the DEISA production environment. Software administrators and users are able to check via the "Common Production Environment" Inca status page where their application software can be run because of available compilers libraries etc.

6 Lessons Learned

The operation of an infrastructure like DEISA leads to new management problems not seen before. Managing a supercomputer system or a number of locally installed cluster system differs heavily from an European supercomputer infrastructure where staff members dealing with the same problem are thousands of miles away. There is no short cut, going to the office next door, just checking if we agree on some option settings within a software component. Within a virtual organization every small modification has to be check by all partners over and over again. Installing new software components requires checking with all participants, if any dependencies exist. Scheduling of tasks, installations, system power up and down, network infrastructure changes and others have to be agreed on. Often a task needs much more of time than estimated. Someone has to deal with those issues.

Though all these things can be handled by e-mail mostly, it is nevertheless mandatory to have regular phone or video conferences, writing minutes and checking for completion of tasks. Additionally it is often necessary to have agreed on strict rules for processing if any disagreements arise. Those dissents are mainly found among others in security policy issues, scheduling of software installation and upgrades, budget issues for needed components.

For these purposes the operation team has been established in DEISA. The planning and coordination of tasks, forwarding of information, power of decision and "managing" in general are prerequisites without which a production quality European wide infrastructure cannot be implemented. Establishing this team has simplified work extremely and it should be recommended to anyone dealing with those kinds of infrastructures not to start without adequate structures.

7 Summary

Three years of DEISA production have shown that the concept implemented in DEISA has succeeded very well. DEISA aimed at deploying a persistent basic European infrastructure for general purpose high performance computing. DEISA intends to adapt to new FP7[3] strategies. This does not preclude that organizational structures of DEISA may change because of merging with new HPC initiatives. But the general idea of DEISA will be sustained. The main next challenge will be to establish an efficient organization embracing all relevant HPC organizations in Europe. Being a central player within European HPC initiatives, DEISA intends to contribute to a global eInfrastructure for science and technology furthermore. Integrating leading supercomputing platforms with Grid technologies and reinforcing capability with shared petascale systems is needed to open the way to new research dimensions in Europe.

References

1. The DEISA Project home page, Distributed European Infrastructure for Supercomputing Applications, see http://www.deisa.org
2. GÉANT2 is the seventh generation of pan-European research and education network, see http://www.geant2.net
3. IBM's General Parallel File System, http://www-03.ibm.com/systems/clusters/software/gpfs.html
4. TeraGrid is an open scientific discovery infrastructure combining leadership class resources in the US, see http://www.teragrid.org/
5. GridFTP file transfer protocol, https://forge.gridforum.org/projects/gridftp-wg
6. Open Grid Services Architecture Data Access and Integration (OGSA-DAI) is a Globus project, see http://dev.globus.org/wiki/OGSA-DAI
7. Storage Resource Broker of SDSC, see http://www.sdsc.edu/srb/index.php/Main_Page
8. UNICORE (Uniform Interface to Computing Resources) is a ready-to-run Grid system including client and server software, see http://www.unicore.org/
9. Ganglia is a scalable distributed monitoring system for high-performance computing systems such as clusters and Grids, see http://ganglia.sourceforge.net
10. The Monitoring and Discovery Service (MDS) is the information services component of the Globus Toolkit, see http://www.globus.org/toolkit/docs/2.4/mds/
11. The Globus Toolkit, see http://www.globus.org
12. INCA - User level grid monitoring, see http://inca.sdsc.edu/

---

[3] FP7 = Seventh Research Framework Programme of the European Union (EU)

Part V
Industry & Government

Managing Parallel and Distributed Monte Carlo Simulations for Computational Finance in a Grid Environment

Ian Stokes-Ress, Francoise Baude, Viet-Dung Doan, and Mireille Bossy

Abstract Computing in financial services consists of a combination of time-critical computations completed during trading hours, such as Monte Carlo simulations for option pricing, and over-night calculations on massive data sets, such as those required for market risk measurement. To date, this has typically been done using traditional parallel or cluster computing techniques. The French National Research Agency (ANR), along with several banks and financial software companies have partnered with INRIA to explore the application of grid computing to this domain. The PicsouGrid project utilizes the ProActive Java distributed computing library to parallelize and distribute Monte Carlo option pricing simulations, concurrently utilizing 102–103 workers. PicsouGrid has been deployed on various grid systems to evaluate its scalability and performance. Issues arising from the heterogeneity and layering of grid infrastructures are addressed via an abstract process model which is applied at each layer. Timings of both the algorithms and the grid infrastructures are carefully measured to provide better insight into the behavior and utilization of computational grids for this important class of parallel simulations.

Keywords Computational grid · computational finance · grid performance

1 Introduction

The 1973 publication by Black and Scholes [1] of an analytical model for derivative financial products, namely put and call options, ushered in a new era of computational finance. The commoditization, decrease in cost, and increase in computational power of general purpose computing resources has allowed market speculators, financial services firms, economists and mathematicians to develop increasingly advanced models for asset pricing and market behavior which can be used to identify market opportunities, price products, or estimate risk. The last

I. Stokes-Ress (✉)
SBGrid, Harvard Medical School, SGM-105, 250 Longwood Ave., Boston MA 02115, USA
e-mail: ijstokes@crystal.harvard.edu

S.C. Lin, E. Yen (eds.), *Grid Computing*,
© Springer Science+Business Media, LLC 2009

several years have seen a resurgence in popularity of hedging through the use of derivative financial products. Between large investment banks which require massive computing resources for day trading and overnight risk reporting and the growing market in derivative products which require complex high-dimensional pricing simulations, the need to harness and optimally utilize any and all available computing resources is more pressing than ever. Large computing farms for batch serial execution of financial calculations are now well established within the financial services industry. The PicsouGrid project attempts to introduce grid computing concepts to the domain, to provide automated load balancing, dynamic resource acquisition, fault tolerance, parallelism, and an application framework which can be deployed on heterogeneous underlying resources. There are three target audiences for this work: large financial ser- vices firms which need to abstract their user and application interface from the underlying resources to provide a uniform, scalable, and robust computing environment; small financial services firms which need the flexibility to utilize diverse and possibly federated heterogeneous computing power; and pricing algorithm developers who want to focus on the pricing algorithm and not worry about resource management issues, or the complexity of coordinating multi-threaded, distributed, parallel programmes.

This paper reports on recent studies into the behavior of grids for the deployment of cross-site parallel applications. The ProActive Java parallel/distributed computing library [2] has been used to manage the deploy- ment and synchronization of the parallel pricing algorithms onto the French Grid5000 infrastructure [3], which provides over 3000 cores at 9 sites across the country. The key contributions of this work are empirical studies of intra- and inter-cluster heterogeneity, proposed performance metrics for parallel applications in this domain, and a layered grid process model which clarifies the stages of a grid job and provides a common syntax for timing and logging purposes.

The following section provides some background regarding the ProActive library, the Grid5000 computing environment, the previous versions of PicsouGrid, and the computational structure of Monte Carlo option pricing algorithms. The third section motivates the need for a grid process model and presents a state machine model which can recursively be applied at the various layers found in typical grid environments. The fourth section introduces a number of metrics useful in the domain of parallel grid jobs. The fifth section presents the empirical results of our study, along with observations, analysis, and conclusions. The final section summarizes our work and describes the next steps for PicsouGrid and the creation of a preferment large scale parallel Monte Carlo simulation environment for the grid.

2 Background

2.1 Project Goals

The PicsouGrid project aims to develop a framework for developing and executing parallel computational finance algorithms. As part of this work, several parallel option pricing algorithms have been developed. Options are derivative financial products which allow the buying and selling of risk related to future price variations. The option buyer has the right (but not obligation) to purchase (for a call option) or sell (for a put option) some asset in the future at a fixed price. Estimates of the option price are based on the difference between the expected market value of the underlying asset at the option exercise date and the asset price fixed by the option contract. The main challenge in this situation is modeling the future asset price, which is typically done using statistical Monte Carlo simulations and careful selection of the static and dynamic parameters which describe the market and asset. In the context of the work described here, it is sufficient to state that these Monte Carlo simulations consist of 105 to 107 independent simulations, typically taking anywhere from a few seconds to several minutes for a single asset with a fixed option exercise date (called a European option). These vanilla options can be computed in parallel, typically in blocks of 103 to 104 iterations, and then the statistics gathered to estimate option prices. Two variations on vanilla options which introduce much more computational complexity are basket options, where a set of underlying assets are considered together, and American options, where the option can be exercised at any point up to the contract expiry date. The complexity of a five asset American option compared to an otherwise equivalent single asset European option would be several orders of magnitude greater, taking hours to compute serially. In a liquid market, such delays are generally unacceptable as the market situation is continually changing. Pricing decisions generally need to be made in seconds or at most minutes to be useful to market traders, hence the need to explore alternative strategies for pricing of exotic options. Here we consider parallel pricing algorithms, with an effort to address large scale parallelisation with the goal of reducing computation time of a given exotic pricing request from hours to minutes.

Innovations over the last decade have made derivative products such as options a key part of global financial markets, partially due to computing advances which have allowed market investors to more accurately price these products. Better option pricing (that being more accurate, more advanced models, and faster results) provides a market advantage and is therefore of great interest to market traders. To date, there has been limited public discussion on the parallelisation of pricing algorithms, and even less on the computation of option prices in a grid environment. The reason for this is partially due to the trade secrets financial services firms have invested in developing their own pricing models and computing environments to give them advantages over their competitors. This work makes contributions to the domain by implementing and making publicly available various serial and parallel option pricing algorithms, a framework for developing further algorithms, and a flexible grid computing environment to perform calculations.

2.2 ProActive Java Library

PicsouGrid has been developed in Java with the ProActive [2] parallel and distributed computing library. The use of Java allows PicsouGrid to be used in a wide range of computing environments, from standard Windows desktop systems, to large

Linux clusters. ProActive implements the Active Object model to enable concurrent, asynchronous object access and guarantees of deterministic behavior. Incorporating ProActive into PicsouGrid requires minimal modification of the framework or specific algorithm implementations. ProActive requires a few constraints on the construction of Objects which will be accessed concurrently, such as empty argument constructors, limited use of self reference in method call parameters, no checked exceptions, and non-primitive, non-final return values for methods. In return, ProActive provides a generic object factory which will dynamically instantiate a "reified" version of any desired object on any available host, while providing the application with a stub which can be utilised exactly as an instance of the standard object. The reified object consists of the proxy stub, a wrapper object, a message queue, and a wrapped instance of the actual object. Only the proxy stub is on the local node. The wrapper object is started by ProActive on the remote node (either specified explicitly as a parameter to the object factory, or selected automatically by ProActive), and contains a message queue for all public method calls on the object, and finally the wrapped object itself. PicsouGrid makes heavy use of the Typed Group Communications features of ProActive [4] to enable parallel execution of Monte Carlo simulations, as well as broadcast and gather-cast features for uniform configuration and interrogation of worker object states. Through the use of ProActive it is possible to run simulations on a single machine, a desktop grid, a traditional cluster, or on a full grid environment without any additional configuration effort in the application. The ProAc- tive deployment mechanism automatically contacts and initiates services and objects on the remote nodes [5].

2.3 PicsouGrid Architecture

Previous versions of PicsouGrid have focused on fault tolerance and the use of JavaSpaces to provide a shared data object environment as the primary strategy for coordinating parallel Monte Carlo simulations across a set of workers [6]. A master-worker architectural approach was followed with three layers: master, sub-masters, and workers. The user accessed the system through the master, which in turn could be used to initiate sub-masters associated with specific groups of computing resources (typically clusters), each of which managed their own local workers. When workers failed, this would be detected via a "heartbeat" mechanism and the worker replaced from a reserve pool. When sub-masters failed they too would be replaced by the master. This architecture was developed for vanilla option pricing algorithms where each worker task consisted of a given number of iterations of the specified algorithm with a fixed set of parameters. When a worker or sub-server was lost, it was simply a matter of re-allocating the "lost" iterations to an existing or new replacement worker or sub-server to continue. "State" for any set of workers (or sub-masters) consisted exclusively of the number of iterations they had been allocated and not yet completed. With the addition of more complex algorithms for American option pricing, it is necessary to do computations in stages, and sometimes short iterative cycles where all workers must be updated with newly calculated values from the previous iteration. In this situation it is more difficult to synchronise and recover from worker failures at arbitrary points in the overall computation. The latest version of PicsouGrid shifts the focus from fault tolerance of workers and the overall infrastructure to autonomy, scalability, and efficient distribution of tasks for complex option pricing algorithms. This is achieved via a mechanism where masters and workers are merged into general simulators. A simulator has the ability either to complete any portion of the algorithmic computation itself, or similarly route it to a worker set. This model provides a greater degree of flexibility in that computations can be initiated on a given object without regard as to whether that object will complete the computation itself or draw on a local, and possibly externally inaccessible, pool of "sub"-simulators. Furthermore, any computation by a simulator is voluntary, without expectation of completion. This means a given simulator may request that its set of sub-simulators complete some stage of a computation, however it is then up to those sub-simulators to decide to do the work and return the results. The lead simulator does not expect the results for work which has been allocated, which allows for the possibility that a given sub-simulator may fail or execute the work packet very slowly. Instead, the lead simulator continues to hand out work packets until the job is complete. The asynchronous, non-blocking nature of active objects allows the fastest simulators to take more work packets and for merging of results to occur as those packets are completed, without any need for global synchronisation.

2.4 Grid5000

Grid5000 is a research-oriented grid based at 9 centres in France, and consisting of 16 clusters and over 3000 cores [3]. This research grid has a focus on parallelism and as such high performance networking is available within clusters, typically consisting of Myrinet or Infiniband interconnects. Furthermore, sites are interconnected with 10Gb/s networking, allowing for inter-site parallel computing. As a research environment, Grid5000 is on a private network and not accessible by the Internet, except through per-job port forwarding. The focus on parallelism means a specialised scheduler has been developed which can reserve blocks of nodes either on a "best effort" basis (as many nodes as possible up to a maximum), or a fixed number of nodes at a specific time and for a specific duration. In Grid5000 parlance a node is a physical host, with however many cores that host happens to have being allocated to the user job. All scheduling and reservations are done at the cluster level, with some "helper" interfaces which will concurrently launch reservations on a group of clusters, but make no effort to coordinate reservations – this is left to the user to manage manually. Finally, Grid5000 provides only a basic interface for launching parallel jobs via a user specified script which executes on a "leader" node for each cluster. The MPI-style NODEFILE variable points to a file containing the list of all nodes (by private network hostname) allocated by the cluster for the job. It is then up to this user script executing on each leader node to utilise this list of nodes to initiate the parallel computation. There is no inherent facility for cross-cluster coordination, no global file space (typically all files are synchronised to cluster- or site-local network file systems), and no automated logging facilities beyond capturing the "standard output" and "standard error" for the script executing on the leader node. While this work focuses on the infrastructure provided by Grid5000, since this was used for the results presented in Section 5, many of these characteristics are also shared with LCG [7] and OSG [8], perhaps with the key exception that they both provide grid-level scheduling. Grid scheduling allows jobs to be submitted at the grid level, and then allocated to an appropriate site and cluster based on the characteristics described in the job meta-data. While Grid5000 lacks this feature, LCG and OSG's grid level scheduling does not provide any facility for coordinated cross site reservations for distributed parallel grid computing. One special feature Grid5000 provides, and which has not been utilised in the work here, is the ability to create a custom system image which will be used by the job. This image can then be replicated to all clusters and, to a degree, a homogeneous grid operating environment can be created for the user's grid job across all reserved nodes, with Grid5000 managing the reboot and selection of system image in preparation for the job.

2.5 Parallel Monte Carlo Simulation

Monte Carlo simulations rely on a large number of independent simulations of a model which makes use of randomly generated numbers. Aggregate behaviour of the model is then determined by averaging the results, taking into consideration the variance of the independent simulations. In a parallel environment this suggests that the simulations are conducted concurrently by the available parallel processors. In a traditional homogeneous parallel environment there is an implicit assumption that these simulations all take the same amount of time, so the division of the simulations is uniform, and typically I total iterations are divided by P available processors at each stage, and each processor handles I/P iterations. Complex models proceed in stages, possibly with convergence iterations, where the results from one stage must be gathered from all processors, merged, and some updated parameters calculated and distributed back to each processor. This communication overhead can be a major bottleneck for parallel algorithm implementations, and the impact increases with the number of parallel processors.

In a grid environment it is not possible to assume the processors are uniform. In fact, during computation some processors may fail or proceed very slowly, in which case the remaining processors should be able to adjust their workload appropriately. This suggests applying a factor F to the number of processors P, such that I iterations are divided by $F \times P$. In a uniform environment, each processor would handle F packets of size $I/(F \times P)$, however in a heterogeneous environment the faster processors would acquire $> F$ packets, and the slower processors $< F$, thus providing a degree of load balancing. The selection of packet size has an impact on the waiting time for the last packet to be returned (where smaller packets are better) versus the communications overhead of many packets (where larger packets are better). Tuning this depends on many factors and is not an objective of the work presented here, but will be analysed in the future. Related to this issue of optimal packet size is the degradation in speed-up with additional processors. This is the classic problem of parallel computing, again related to the CCR: Communications-to-Computation Ratio. The goal of the work presented here is to lay a foundation for a maximum number of coordinated parallel processors to be utilised in a grid environment, without regard to the ultimate efficiency of the computation in this configuration. See Section 4 for more discussion on the experimental design used for this work and the definition we adopt for efficiency.

Some work which has been done on parallel grid deployments of computational finance algorithms have used the Longstaff-Schwartz [9], Picazo [10], and Ibanez-Zapatero [11] algorithms. In particular, [12] looks at using Longstaff-Schwartz in a grid environment, however with only a maximum of 12 processors. [13] uses MPI with no more than 8 tightly coupled identical CPUs for the Boyle quasi-Monte Carlo stochastic mesh algorithm [14, 15] uses an SGI 32-CPU SMP machine for the original Broadie-Glasserman stochastic mesh algorithm [16]. These efforts have shown the viability of parallel algorithms, with efficiencies ranging from 70–95% (depending on the number of parallel CPUs). While all of these cite market time constraints as a key issue for the parallelization of Monte Carlo-based American option pricing algorithms, none address the issues of deployment and computation on heterogeneous, distributed, dynamic, and large scalegrid infrastructures, aspects which are key goals of the PicsouGrid project.

3 Gird Process Model

The Unix process model [17], with its three primary state of READY, RUN- NING, and BLOCKED, provides a common basis for the implementation of POSIX operating system kernels, and an understanding of the behaviour of a process in a pre-emptive multi-tasking operating system. Users and developers have a clear understanding of the meaning of system time (time spent on kernel method calls), user time (time spent executing user code), and wait/block time (time spent blocking for other processes or system in- put/output). There are analogous requirements in a grid environment where users, developers, and system administrators need to understand what state and stage a "grid job" is in at any given time, and from a post-mortem perspective be able to analyse the full job life-cycle. The federated nature and automated late-allocation of disperse and heterogeneous computing resources to the execution of a grid job make it difficult to achieve this. While some effort has been made to produce a common semantic model for lifecycles and process interaction on the grid (e.g. SAGA [18] and CDDLM [19]), these have primarily focused on APIs or new SOA models for service inter- action of deployed applications, rather than a more modest goal of a logical semantic model for grid jobs, when viewed as an extension of the traditional operating system process model.

Within the context of our work on a parallel grid Monte Carlo simulation environment, it became clear that a common model was necessary in order to understand latencies and behavior within the various layers of the grid environment on which our simulations were being run. The remainder of this section defines terms related to our grid process model and presents a recursive state machine which has been used for tracking the life cycle of grid jobs. In fact, the model we have developed here is not specific to parallel Monte Carlo simulations on the grid, but is generally applicable for describing the state of a "grid process" where many sites, clusters, hosts, and "operating system processes" may concurrently be involved.

3.1 Grid Tasks and Jobs

There is no commonly agreed model for a task in a grid environment. As a result, it is difficult to discuss and design systems which manage the life- cycle of a programme executing on a grid. This is partially due to the lack of a common definition of a "grid task", and its scope. The GGF Grid Scheduling Dictionary [20] offers two short definitions which provide a starting point:

> **Job** An application or task performed on High Performance Computing resources. A Job may be composed of steps/sections as individual schedulable entities.
> **Task** A specific piece of work required to be done as part of a job or application.

Besides the ambiguity introduced by suggesting that a job is also a task, these definitions do not provide sufficient semantic clarity for distinguishing between work-flows and parallel executions. We therefore feel it is necessary to augment these terms to contain the concept of co-scheduling of resources to provide coordinated parallel access, possibly across geographically disperse resources. We propose the following definitions:

> **Basic Task** A specific piece of work required to be done as part of a job, providing the most basic computational unit of the job, and designed for serial execution on a single hardware processor. The scheduling and management of a basic task may be handled by the grid infrastructure, or delegated to a grid job.
> **Grid Job** A task or a set of tasks to be completed by a grid infrastructure, containing meta-data to facilitate the management of the task both by the user and a specific grid infrastructure.
> **Work-flow Job** A grid job containing a set of dependencies on its constituent basic tasks or other grid jobs and which is responsible for the coordinated execution and input/output management of those sub-jobs or sub-tasks.
> **Parallel Job** A grid job which requires the coordinated parallel execution and communication of a set of basic tasks.

With this set of definitions we consider a simple parallel Monte Carlo simulation to consist of a parallel job with a set of coordinated basic tasks, such that the grid infrastructure provides a set of concurrent computing resources on which the simulation can initiate the parallel computation. A more complex phased Monte Carlo simulation would consist of a work-flow job where each phase of the work-flow would consist of a parallel job, executing that phase's parallel computation as part of the larger Monte Carlo simulation. The grid infrastructure is then responsible for the appropriate selection, reservation, and allocation/binding of the grid computing resources to the simulation job (whether simple or complex), based on the requirements described within the job itself.

3.2 Recursive Layered State Machine

Figure 1 indicates the system layers typically found in a grid environment and through which a grid job will execute. For a basic grid job, this will consist of one sub-process at each layer. It is possible that the Site layer will not always be present, with Clusters being accessed directly by the grid infrastructure. The visibility of a particular Core, in contrast to the Host in which it exists, also may not be distinguishable. Some clusters may allocate resources on a "per-host" basis, with all cores available for the executing task, while others may allocate a number of tasks to a particular host up to the number of physical cores available, trusting the host operating system to correctly schedule each grid task (executing as an independent operating-system-level process) to a different core. Finally, the concept of a VM (virtual machine), whether a user-level VM such as Java or an operating system level VM such as Xen or VMWare, either may not exist within the grid environment, or may replace the concept of a core, with one VM allocated to each core within the host, and the host (or cluster) then scheduling grid tasks on a "one-per-VM" basis.

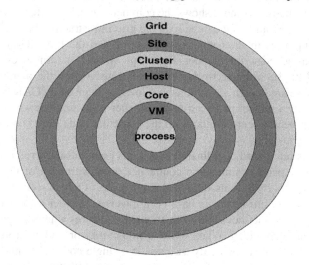

Fig. 1 Various layers through which a grid job executes

```
mygridsub-r''2007-02-05 6:05:00,-1 walltime=1, hodes=
  30es-behch1e6
```

Listing 1. Executing parallel Monte Carlo simulation on Grid5000

It should be noted that Fig. 1 only illustrates system level layers, predominantly representing the layers of physical hardware and networking. There are also the various layers of software, such as the grid framework, the local cluster management system, the operating system, and any application framework which may simultaneously be in use.

As a brief anecdotal example of this layering situation for a parallel grid job, consider the single command mygridsub -r "2007-02-05 6:05:00" -l walltime = 1, nodes = 30 es-bench1e6. This initiates the parallel execution of a Monte Carlo simulation for a simple European Option using the job launcher

```
/bin/sh -c /usr/lib/oar/oarexecuser.sh /tmp/OAR 59658
30 59658 istokes-r ees \/bin/bash ~/proc/fgrillon1.nancy.
grid5000.fr/submitN script-wrapper \~/bin/script-wrapper
fgrillon1.nancy.grid5000.fr \~/es-bench1e6
```

Listing 2. Command executed on leader node for each Grid5000 cluster

mygridsub which attempts to submit the specified job to all Grid5000 clusters at the same time. The parameter nodes = 30 requests up to 30 nodes (equivalent to hosts) from each cluster, on a best effort basis, while -r "2007-02-05 6:05:00" is the timing request for the job to start 5 February 2007 at 6:05am CET, and to run for 1hour (walltime = 1). The parameter esbench1e6 is a script file which performs the actual simulation.

Once the Grid5000 infrastructure fulfils its reservation request, the es-bench1e6 script is initiated on one of the worker nodes on each cluster which has agreed to provide resources. Listing 2 shows the command which is actually executed on this leader node. From this it can be seen the grid infrastructure has added another layer of wrapping with the oarexecuser.sh script, and the PicsouGrid application framework has added script-wrapper. The script-wrapper, in turn, is responsible for accessing all the subordinate worker nodes allocated within the particular cluster (the list of these are known via a file whose location is given by OAR NODEFILE, which is used by a sub-script spread-task), and then spawning one worker simulator per physical processor core available on the particular node (host) (via yet another sub-script all-cpus).

Only at this point (and coordinating when this point has occurred is non-trivial) can the primary parallel simulation commence, now with each of the distributed worker nodes properly initialised. In total, eight levels of nested software scripts and six levels of system infrastructure have been traversed in order to get from a single grid submit node to the thousands of distributed grid cores where the parallel compute job is finally executed. When working in a cluster or grid environment many of the aspects which can be easily assumed in a single node environment must be made explicit, and the staging of execution is managed with possible time delays for synchronization and queuing, and on completion it is necessary to properly "tidy-up" to return the collective results. Taking these various factors into consideration, a five stage model is proposed which is applied at each layer of the grid infrastructure. The stages, in order, are defined as follows:

CREATE prepares a definition of the process to be executed at this layer.

BIND associates the definition, possibly based on constraints within the definition, with a particular system at this layer.

```
http://www.example.com/grid/jobs/Job1000/SITE/
    BIND.ACTIVE
http://www.example.com/grid/jobs/Job2030/CLUSTER/HOST/
    JVM [1]/PREPARE.ACTIVE
http://www.example.com/grid/jobs/Job2030/CLUSTER/HOST/
    JVM [2]/EXECUTE. DONE
http://www.example.com/grid/jobs/Job2030/CLUSTER/HOST/
    JVM [3]/EXECUTE.ACTIVE
http://www.example.com/grid/jobs/Job2750/SITE/HOST/
    CORE [1]/EXECUTE.ACTIVE
```

Listing 3. Examples of unified grid job states as URLs

PREPARE stages and data required for execution to the local system which the definition has been bound to and does any pre-execution configuration of the system.

EXECUTE runs the programme found in the definition. This may require recursing to lower layers (and subsequently starting from that layer's CRE- ATE stage). In a parallel context, it is at this stage where the transition from serial to parallel execution takes place, possibly multiple times for the completion of this stage's execution.

CLEAR cleans the system and post-processes any results for their return to the caller (e.g. next higher layer).

The grid infrastructure handles the transition from one stage to the next. To accommodate the pipelined and possibly suspended life-cycle of a grid job it is not possible to consider each stage as being an atomic operation. Rather, it is more practical to add entry and exit states to each stage. In this manner, three states are possible for each stage: READY, which is the entry state; ACTIVE, which represents the stage being actively processed; and DONE, when the stage has been completed and transition to the next stage is possible. A grid job starts in the CREATE.READY state, which can be seen as a "blank" grid job. Once the system or user has completed their definition of the actions for that layer (done by entering CREATE.ACTIVE), the grid job finishes in the CREATE.DONE state. At some later point, the grid infrastructure is able to bind the job to a resource, and later still prepare the bound node(s) for execution. When the node(s) are ready the grid job can execute, and finally, once the execution is complete, the grid job can be cleared.

We have developed this model to be applied recursively at the various layers shown in Fig. 1. The layering also includes the software systems, and is arbitrary to a particular grid environment. For example, a grid job could be in the state "CLUS-

TER/BIND.READY", indicating that a cluster- level job description has been prepared, and now the grid job (or this portion of it) is waiting for the cluster layer of the grid infrastructure to make a binding decision to submit the job to a particular queue. The queue, in turn, would have to allocate the job to a particular host, and so on. In the case of distributed asynchronous parallelism, where different parts of the computation may be in different states, layers can be enumerated such as "CORE [1]/EXECUTE.READY" and "CORE [2]/EXECUTE.DONE".

The context for a particular state when there are parallel processes as part of the same grid job is based on the enumerated state of the higher level layers, noting that recursion to lower layers only happens when a particular layer is in the EXECUTE.ACTIVE state. In this way, a notation using the prepended chain of higher layers and commencing with the grid job identifier is possible. In a URL context, some examples of this are shown in Listing3.

This example shows generic layer labels, as taken from Fig. 1, how-ever these can also be replaced by a specific label. For example, the state label http://www.example.com/grid/jobs/Job2030/sophia.inria.fr/helios/helios22/cpu0/jvm-15542/PREPARE.ACTIVE would tell us that part of grid job 2030 is executing at the sophia.inria.fr site, on the helios cluster, on the helios22 node, running on cpu0, and the Java JVM with process ID15542. Of course if job 2030 is a parallel job, other parts of this job may be in other states on other sites and hosts.

While this model has been developed with the intention to incorporate it into a larger grid workload management system, the current model is only used for logging, time stamping, a monitoring. In many cases (e.g. Grid5000 and EGEE) we do not have access to the internals of the grid infrastructure and either do not have

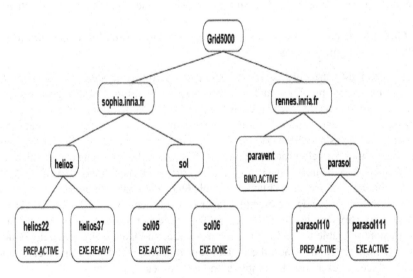

Fig. 2 A simple example of a parallel grid job state snapshot on Grid5000. Nodes without an explicit state are implicitly in the state EXE.ACTIVE, which is the only valid state for entering into a lower layer

visibility of some of the state transitions or are only able to identify state transitions and time stamps during post-processing of grid job logs made available once the job is complete.

This model has allowed us to gather behaviour and performance details for a consistent comparison between three key aspects of any parallel grid application: the grid infrastructure impact; the parallelization framework; and the core application code. It is the basis for all the monitoring and timing information which is provided in the results presented in Section 5. We finish this overview with Fig. 2 which is a simplified grid network snapshot showing the state of various entities contributing to a fictitious small parallel computation. It shows two sites, each with two clusters. Three of the clusters have started executing the grid job on their worker nodes, and those six workers are in different states, while one cluster is making binding decisions regarding which workers to execute on.

4 Grid Efficiency Metrics

This work has focused on establishing a foundation for coupled parallel simulation on the grid, and as such does not focus on parallel speed-up per se. To simplify the experiments presented here and to highlight the issues introduced by the grid infrastructure and parallel computing environment we have only executed the first stage of the parallel computation, and removed the syncrhonisation at the end of the Monte Carlo simulations. In this way, the experimental jobs appear to be embarrassingly parallel. The work presented here focuses on the capabilities and characteristics of the underlying grid infrastructure to provide for such application-level parallelism. In this environment, we define four metrics relevant to our problem domain

Time window unit-job through put this metric counts the number of "unit jobs" executed by the grid infrastructure in a fixed time window. Typically the time window is taken from the start of the earliest computation to the end of the last computation, although this can be "time shifted" to align each cluster start-time as $t = 0$. A "unit job" is some standard job unit which is representative of the application and clearly defined. This would always take the same amount of time for serial execution. This metric measures the capacity and bulk efficiency of the grid infrastructure for a particular grid task. If the number of grid nodes (processors/cores) is somehow fixed, this gives a comparative performance measure of the grid.

Speed-up efficiency limit with some reference system serial calculation time for a unit job, the speed-up efficiency is defined as the time taken for the reference system to process N unit-jobs divided by the total occupancy time at a particular grid layer required to compute the same N unit-jobs. The metric assumes zero communication time for parallel jobs. For example, a cluster containing 40 cores is occupied for 70 seconds, and in this time completes 200 unit jobs. The reference system serial calculation time for a unit job is 1.2 seconds. The speed-up efficiency limit for the given cluster is $(200 \times 1.2)/(40 \times 70) = 240/280 = 85.7\%$. Of course it is possible that the unit-job computation time for a given system is better than that of the reference system, in which case the speed-up efficiency limit may be $> 100\%$. This metric is in contrast to the common definition of speed-up which simply calculates the parallel compute time for a homogeneous cluster of N systems compared to the serial compute time on a single processor from the same system. In this case the speed-up limit would always be N and the speed-up efficiency limit 1. Equation 1 defines this metric, where $n_{unitJob}$ is the total number of unit jobs completed by the grid system, n_{procs} is the number of processors contributing to the total computation time, and ti represents the wall time of the occupancy of that layer of the grid. For instance, efficiency at the level of each core would be calcualted by summing the core occupancy times for each processor, while the host efficiency would be the total time the particular host for that processor was in use during the calculation of the unit job (even if the particular processor was finished), and the cluster-level efficiency would take the occupancy time of the full cluster for each unit-job, regardless of whether the host or processor occupancy time was much shorter.

$$\frac{n_{unitJob} \times t_{ref}}{\sum_{i=1}^{n_{procs}} t_i} \tag{1}$$

Weighted speed-up efficiency limit when there is some knowledge of the relative performance of each processor within the grid, the weighted speed-up efficiency can be calculated, which takes into account the best performance which can be expected from each contributing processor. Equation 2 defines this, where wi is the weighting factor and is proportional to the relative performance of the processor (higher values mean higher performance). We do not make use of this metric here as no common benchmarks were available at the time the experiments were run. It is planned to build a profile of every node and utilise this in performance prediction and a priori load partitioning.

$$\frac{n_{unitJob} \times t_{ref}}{\sum_{i=1}^{n_{procs}} t_i / w_i} \tag{2}$$

Occupancy efficiency this measures what fraction of the total time available for computation was actually used by the application, measured at the various layers within the grid. This is defined by Eq. 3, where $n_{comp}U_{nits}$ indicate the number of computational units (*e.g.* hosts, cores, VMs, threads, processes) available at that layer. The figures found in Section 5 show *node eff* and *sim eff* which are the node and simulator occupancy efficiency respectively. Values less than 100% indicate that wastage has occurred and the application had a reservation for a computational unit which it did not utilise. Figure 3 shows an example of a realistic 'optimal' occupancy efficiency for parallel Monte Carlo simulations in a grid environment with a score of 92.7% over a 90 second time window.

$$\frac{\sum_{i=1}^{n_{compUnits}} t_i}{n_{compUnits} \times t_{reservation}} \tag{3}$$

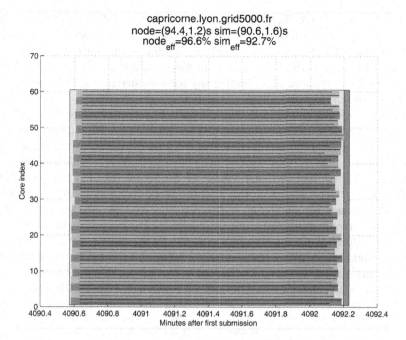

Fig. 3 Realistic optimal parallel Monte Carlo simulation, with 92.7% occupancy efficiency

5 Parallel Experiments on the Grid

The starting point for discussing parallel Monte Carlo simulation on the grid is to understand an ideal situation. Ideally all available computing resources would be used at 100% of capacity for the duration of their reservation performing exclusively Monte Carlo simulations. The time to merge results would be zero, and there would be no communications overhead, latencies, or blocking due to synchronisation or bottle necks. This is the classic definition of "linear speed-up", modified for a grid environment by adjusting expected "optimal" results according to the relative power of each individual resource (i.e. weighting results according to some benchmark). In reality, as discussed in Section 4, there are many parameters which have an impact on the actual performance of a parallel Monte Carlo simulation. As the fol- lowing results will show, predictable coordinated access to resources within a single cluster can be difficult, and synchronisation of resources between clusters or sites even harder. Due to this observation, the work here focused on identifying the issues which lead to poor resource synchronisation, and to facilitate evaluation of resource capability. In order to do this, the following results eliminate coordinated simulation and merging of results, and only initiate independent partial Monte Carlo simulations. All the following experiments were performed in early March 2007 on Grid5000, using all available sites, clusters, and nodes. The figure headings show the statistics for the time spent in the states NODE.EXECUTE.ACTIVE and

SIMULA-TOR.EXECUTE.ACTIVE in the form node = (M, S)s and sim = (M, S)s where M is the mean time in seconds and S is the standard deviation. nodeef f is the node occupancy efficiency, and simeff the simulator occupancy efficiency, as defined in Equation 3. The "simulator" is the part of the application where the Monte Carlo simulation is executed, excluding any software startup (i.e. JVM initiation), configuration, and tear-down time.

Figure 3 shows an almost ideal situation where 60 cores running on 30 hosts from the same cluster all start processing within a second of each other, run their allocated simulations for the same duration (around 90 seconds, shown by the black "life line"), and complete in a time window of a few seconds. This provides a simulation efficiency of 92.7%, and we take this to be our "cluster-internal" efficiency standard.

By contrast, some clusters showed node (host) and core start and finish windows of several minutes, as seen in Fig. 4. This particular example consists of 240 dual-CPU nodes, representing 480 cores. A simulation efficiency of only 43.1% was achieved, indicating that the resources were idle for the majority of the reservation time (the time outside of the black lifelines). Furthermore, the majority of this idle time was in the finishing window, where only a few inexplicably slow nodes delayed completion of the computation on the node block within the cluster. The space prior

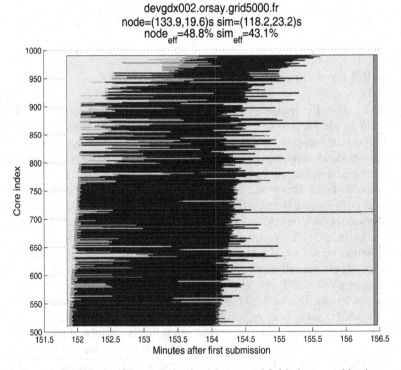

Fig. 4 Cluster exhibiting significant variation in node start and finish times, resulting in an occupancy efficiency of < 50%.stage) – again, wasted computing time when the job held a reservation for the node and core, but failed to utilise it

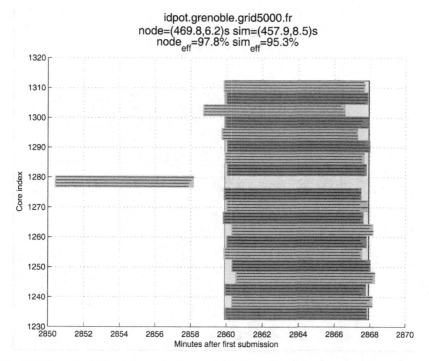

Fig. 5 NTP configuration problems leading to clock skew of seconds to several minutes on certain nodes

to the start of the simulator life-line is due to grid infrastructure delays in launching the node- or core-level process (i.e. due to delays in the CLUSTER.PREPARE

Another common issue across many sites within Grid5000 was the clock- skew due to poorly configured NTP services, or miss configured time-zones (i.e. certain nodes believing they are in a different time zone and therefore reporting a time-stamp exactly one hour different from their cluster neighbours). This can be seen in Fig. 5. Many parallel and distributed computing libraries rely heavily on well-synchronised timestamps, not to mention network services such as NFS. The effect of this clock-skew is unpredictable but certainly undesirable, not to mention the difficulty it introduces when attempting to take timestamps and track performance, as these activities typically must be done locally due to the complexity of trying to centralize all logging within a large distributed parallel computing system.

Figure 6 shows a situation where a supposedly uniform cluster of dual- core dual-CPU 2.2 GHz AMD Opteron nodes had a dramatic variance in the completion time, both on the inter-node (between hosts), and intra- node (different cores within the same host) completion time. This led to an average computation completion time of 99 seconds, with a standard deviation of 25 seconds, and resulted in only a 64.6% computation efficiency. Approximately two thirds of the nodes completed their simulations in 82 seconds; however the remaining third took around 133 seconds. If this sort of behaviour was very rare it could be ignored, however this study

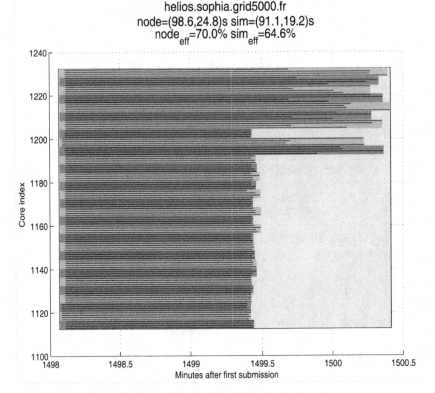

Fig. 6 Dedicated cluster of uniform nodes showing wide variation in performance

suggests that it occurs with sufficient frequency to be a major concern for communicating parallel computations, and even for embarrassingly parallel computations where the division of the workload may be done based on inaccurate static measures for the relative performance of a node.

Finally, we return to the question of coordinated cross-cluster (and cross-site) parallel computing. Besides inherent technical issues present when attempting regular communications across long network segments, it is difficult to satisfy on demand requests for grid-wide multi-node reservations.

There is the initial challenge of immediate availability, and then the subsequent challenge of promptly completing and confirming the distributed node reservations and the requisite site, node, or cluster preparation (pre-execution configuration). Figure 7 shows an example of such a situation for a 1270-core multi-cluster job, where a request for approximately 80% of the reported available nodes from each cluster was made at a fixed point in time, and most clusters took over an hour before this request could be fulfilled. One cluster took two and a half days (not shown in figure due to effect on time scale). This is not a surprising result given the nature of Grid5000 and the style of computations which are done on it, namely experimental

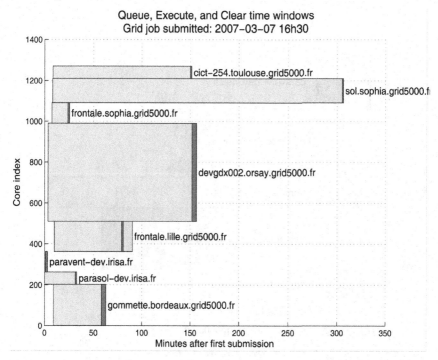

Fig. 7 Light grey boxes indicate queuing or clearing time, dark grey boxes indi- cate execution time. This graph illustrates the difficulty in coordinated cross-site on-demand parallel computing

(therefore usually less than one hour) parallel and distributed computing. At any given time it is expected that the clusters will be full with jobs which require blocks of nodes, and for the queue to contain multi-node jobs as well, therefore newly submitted jobs would expect to wait at least several hours to both make it to the front of the queue and for the requisite block of nodes to be available. While Grid5000 provides simultaneous submission of jobs, it does not coordinate reservations and queues, so the individual clusters became available at different times. Using normalised cluster start-times, all the unit-job computations took place in a 274.2 second time window, for a total execute stage time block of 1270 cores $\times$ 274.2 seconds = 348234 core $\cdot$ seconds = 96.7 core $\cdot$ hours. Compared with a reference unit-job execution time of 67.3 seconds, the speed-up efficiency limit, as given in Equation 1, is (1270 cores $\times$ 67.3 seconds)/96.7 core $\cdot$ hours = 25.5%.

A more realistic multi-cluster parallel grid job uses explicit cluster and node reservation. Figure 8 shows the results of a multi-cluster reservation for a large block of nodes per cluster at a fixed time of 6:05 AM CET (5:05UTC), approximately 18 hours after the reservation was made. It was manually confirmed in advance that the requested resources should be available on all clusters, and a reduction in the number of nodes was made to provide for a margin of unexpectedly failed nodes. The 5 minute offset from the hour was to provide the grid and cluster infrastructures

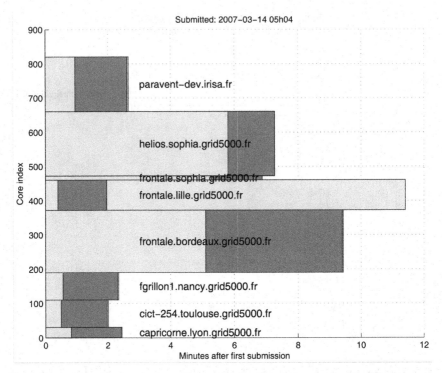

Fig. 8 Even with reservations for cross-site synchronized parallel computing it is difficult to coordinate resource acquisition. Light grey boxes show waiting time, dark boxes show execution time

with time to clean and restart the nodes after previous reservations ending at 6 AM were completed. In fact, this result does not include clusters which completely failed to respect the reservation or failed to initiate the job, and also three clusters with abnormal behaviour: two where the leader node failed to initiate the task on the workers, and one where the task commenced three hours late. It can be seen that only five clusters, consisting of approximately half of the 800 cores, were able to start the computation within a minute of the reservation. This poses serious problems for coordinated, pre-scheduled, pre- planned multi-cluster parallel computations, since it suggests it is difficult to have disparate clusters available during the same time window. The Lille cluster shows grey box for waiting time after execution, due to problems with synchronising data from worker nodes back to leader node and user home directory. Other nodes also have this stage, but it takes < 1s so is not visibile at this scale (*see paravent-dev.inisa.fr*).

6 Conclusions and Perspectives

These studies have quantitatively revealed the difficulties with executing coordinated cross-cluster and cross-site parallel computational tasks. The layered state machine model from Section 3.2 for grid jobs has facilitated detailed tracking of state transitions through the various layers of the grid, and been a part of identifying mis-configured clusters and nodes. The metrics defined in Section 4 provide measures which suggest a 90–95% occupancy efficiency at the cluster level is reasonable if the clusters are correctly configured and operating normally. Regarding parallel computing at the cluster level, it is clear that heterogeneity is rampant, even when a cluster claims it is composed of identical machines. Latencies in binding grid tasks to particular nodes, and initiation of tasks on a particular core can introduce delays of several seconds to minutes. This presents two major challenges for parallel computing on the grid: i) synchronisation of the task start time; and ii) partitioning of the computational load. While static measures of relative performance on a cluster or node level are valuable, it is clear that these cannot always be trusted, hence it is reasonable to imagine the need for dynamic, application-layer determination of node performance prior to the initiation of parallel computations. Ideally this responsibility would be taken by the grid infrastructure (and by implication the cluster owner), however the federated and unreliable nature of grids suggests the user or application needs to manage this for the present. At the level of cross-cluster parallel computing the key challenges are coordinated reservation and start-up. The work here has not yet investigated what granularity of computations are practical, however the start-up delays and unreliable fulfillment of reservations suggest that "contributory best-effort" Monte Carlo simulators may be approprirate, where simulators enter and exit a simulator pool in a dynamic peer-to-peer fashion, and are acquired by a simulation manager and assigned to particular compuations "on demand", rather than with a simulation manager expecting a set of simulators based on a prior reservation.

The future work for PicsouGrid is to implement and deploy American option pricing algorithms which factor in the heterogeneous and dynamically varying state of available grid resources, to evaluate the degree of parallelism which can be achieved, and at what cost, and to discover the performance impacts of real cross-cluster communicating parallel computations in a grid environment. It will also be important to evaluate PicsouGrid on other grid infrastructures such as EGEE, who over the last year have put specific effort into the parallel computing capabilities of gLite and the grid middleware [21, 22]. Once a foundation for parallel computing on the grid has been established, the operational requirements for on-demand option pricing will need to be evaluated. This will comprise a combination of response time performance of American option pricing algorithms, through- put of a larger multi-user pricing application deployed on the grid, and the dynamicity and fault-tolerance of the application in the presence of changing grid resources.

References

1. F. Black and M. Scholes, "The pricing of options and corporate liabilities," Journal of Political Economy, vol. 81(3), pp. 637–654, 1973.
2. D. Caromel, C. Delb'e, A. di Costanzo, and M. Leyton, "ProActive: an integrated platform for programming and running applications on grids and P2P systems," Computational Methods in Science and Technology, vol. 12, no. 1, pp. 69–77, 2006.

3. R. Bolze, F. Cappello, E. Caron, M. Dayd, F. Desprez, E. Jeannot, Y. Jgou, S. Lantri, J. Leduc,
    N. Melab, G. Mornet, R. Namyst, P. Primet, B. Quetier, O. Richard, E.-G. Talbi, and T. Ira,
    "Grid'5000: a large scale and highly reconfigurable experimental grid testbed.," Inter- national
    Journal of High Performance Computing Applications, vol. 20, pp. 481–494, Nov. 2006.
4. L. Baduel, F. Baude, and D. Caromel, "Asynchronous typed object groups for grid program-
    ming," International Journal of Parallel Programming, vol. 35, no. 6, pp. 573–614, 2007.
5. F. Baude, D. Caromel, A. di Costanzo, C. Delb'e, and M. Leyton, "To- wards deployment
    contracts in large scale clusters & desktop grids," in Int. Worshop on Large-Scale, volatile
    Desktop Grids, in conjunction with the IEEE IPDPS conference, (Denver, Colorado, USA),
    Apr. 2007. Invited paper.
6. S. Bezzine, V. Galtier, S. Vialle, F. Baude, M. Bossy, V. Doan, and L. Henrio, "A Fault Tolerant
    and Multi-Paradigm Grid Architecture for Time Constrained Problems. Application to Option
    Pricing in Fi- nance.," Proceedings of the Second IEEE International Conference on e-Science
    and Grid Computing, 2006.
7. CERN, "The LHC Computing Grid Pro ject." http://lcg.web.cern.ch/LCG/.
8. "The Open Science Grid." http://www.opensciencegrid.org/.
9. F. Longstaff and E. Schwartz, "Valuing American options by simulation: a simple least-squares
    approach," Review of Financial Studies, 2001.
10. Jorge A. Picazo, Monte Carlo and Quasi-Monte Carlo Methods 2000:: Proceedings of a
    Conference Held at Hong Kong Baptist University, Hong Kong SAR, China, November
    27-December 1, 2000, ch.Amer- ican Option Pricing: A Classification-Monte Carlo (CMC)
    Approach, pp. 422–433. Springer, 2002.
11. A. Ibanez and F. Zapatero, "Monte Carlo Valuation of American Options through Computation
    of the Optimal Exercise Frontier," Journal of Financial and Quantitative Analysis, vol.39, no.
    2, pp. 239–273, 2004.
12. I. Toke, "Monte Carlo Valuation of Multidimensional American Options Through Grid Com-
    puting," LECTURE NOTES IN COMPUTER SCI- ENCE, vol. 3743, p. 462, 2006.
13. J. Wan, K. Lai, A. Kolkiewicz, and K. Tan, "A parallel quasi-Monte Carlo approach to pricing
    multidimensional American options," International Journal of High Performance Computing
    and Networking, vol. 4, no. 5, pp. 321–330, 2006.
14. P. Boyle, A. Kolkiewicz, and K. Tan, "An improved simulation method for pricing high-
    dimensional American derivatives," Mathematics and Computers in Simulation, vol. 62, no.
    3–6, pp. 315–322, 2003.
15. A. Avramidis and Y. Zinchenko and T. Coleman and A. Verma, " Efficiency improvements for
    pricing American options with a stochastic mesh: Parallel implementation," Financial Engi-
    neering News, Decem- ber 2000.
16. M. Broadie and P. Glasserman, "Pricing American-style securities using simulation," Journal
    of Economic Dynamics and Control, vol. 21, no. 8, pp. 1323–1352, 1997.
17. W. Stevens et al., Advanced programming in the UNIX environment. Addison-Wesley, 1992.
18. S. Jha and A. Merzky, "GFD-I.71: A Requirements Analysis for a Simple API for Grid
    Applications," tech. rep., Open Grid Forum, May 2006. Simple API for Grid Applications
    Research Group.
19. D. Bell, T. Ko jo, P. Goldsack, S. Loughran, D. Milo jicic, S. Schaefer, J. Tatemura, and P.
    Toft, "Configuration Description, Deployment, and Lifecycle Management," November 2003.
20. M. Roehrig, W. Ziegler, and P. Wieder, "GFD-I.11: Grid Scheduling Dictionary of Terms
    and Keywords," tech. rep., Global Grid Forum, November 2002. Grid Scheduling Dictionary
    Working Group.
21. Richard de Jong and Matthijs Koot, "Preparing the Worldwide LHC Computing Grid for MPI
    applications," tech. rep.,CERN, June 2006.
22. "Grid Ireland MPI Technical Computing Group." http://www.grid.ie/mpi/wiki

Index